EFFECTIVE SOCIAL WORK WITH CHILDREN, YOUNG PEOPLE AND FAMILIES

SAGE has been part of the global academic community since 1965, supporting high quality research and learning that transforms society and our understanding of individuals, groups and cultures. SAGE is the independent, innovative, natural home for authors, editors and societies who share our commitment and passion for the social sciences.

Find out more at: **www.sagepublications.com**

EFFECTIVE SOCIAL WORK WITH CHILDREN, YOUNG PEOPLE AND FAMILIES

Putting Systems Theory into Practice

Steven Walker

Los Angeles | London | New Delhi
Singapore | Washington DC

Los Angeles | London | New Delhi
Singapore | Washington DC

SAGE Publications Ltd
1 Oliver's Yard
55 City Road
London EC1Y 1SP

SAGE Publications Inc.
2455 Teller Road
Thousand Oaks, California 91320

SAGE Publications India Pvt Ltd
B 1/I 1 Mohan Cooperative Industrial Area
Mathura Road
New Delhi 110 044

SAGE Publications Asia-Pacific Pte Ltd
3 Church Street
#10-04 Samsung Hub
Singapore 049483

Editor: Sarah Gibson
Assistant editor: Emma Milman
Production editor: Katie Forsythe
Copyeditor: Audrey Scriven
Proofreader: Kate Wood
Marketing manager: Tamara Navaratnam
Cover design: Lisa Harper
Typeset by: C&M Digitals (P) Ltd.
Printed in India at Replika Press Pvt Ltd

© Steven Walker 2012

First published 2012

Library of Congress Control Number: 2011944780

British Library Cataloguing in Publication data

A catalogue record for this book is available from the British Library

ISBN 978-1-4462-5224-6
ISBN 978-1-4462-5225-3 (pbk)

To Anna and Evie

CONTENTS

ACKNOWLEDGEMENTS

I first met Eileen Munro when I did postgraduate study in social work and social policy at the London School of Economics and Political Science nearly thirty years ago. This followed voluntary work with the Family Welfare Association in Hackney, East London. Eileen was among a group of inspiring, dedicated and knowledgeable people with expertise and skills in every aspect of social work. Today Professor Munro is one of the country's leading child protection experts and rightly was selected to review child protection for the coalition government that came to power in 2010.

Others who have had an impact on me subsequently include: every client I have worked with; every student I have learned from; and every colleague I have worked with or been motivated by as a practitioner or academic. The following people especially require my gratitude: Joy Nield, Hugh Jenkins, Rose Rachman, Shula Ramon, Bob Holman, Lena Dominelli, Peter Leonard, Steve Herington, Jane Dutton, Annie Turner, Barry Mason, Damian McCann, Andrew Maynard, Maire Maisch, Ann Jackson-Fowler and Judy Hicks. There are many others I could mention and while space does not permit their inclusion here their absence does not imply a lesser importance to me: they will know who they are. I am also indebted to Sage and Sarah Gibson for their confidence and support and the practical help offered by Katie Forsythe and the copyeditor and proofreader. Any omissions in terms of copyright or acknowledgement are regretted and will be rectified upon notification.

The strength and love I derive from Isobel and Rose ensure they are my bedrock and secure base, as well as the source of much support and inspiration. There is a symmetry about my beginnings in social work in Hackney more than three decades ago and the contemporary inner city borough as the crucible for the ideas and practices informing the Munro Report and its current impact on social work practice. The circle feels complete. Hindus and Buddhists have a word for this, *Karma*, which refers to actions/deeds that cause a cycle of cause and effect, or in Tibetan parlance, this means a continuous pursuit or flow of life. The cover image for this book is a *Mandala*, which is the Sanskrit word for a circle, and a variety of images can be found to symbolise this. The Celtic circle is also a variation on the theme of an unending circular link which is highly symbolic of systems theory.

ABOUT THE AUTHOR

Steven Walker has worked in social work for thirty years, starting as a volunteer with the Family Welfare Association in Hackney, East London. His work has included all aspects of social work with children, young people and families: adoption and fostering; family support; child protection and safeguarding; residential child care; youth justice; therapeutic work; domestic violence and forced marriage. He is a senior social work academic, consultant and expert witness, with eight published books, and has recently conducted research into the mental health effects on young people suffering from cyber-bullying.

INTRODUCTION

It is reported that Nelson Mandela once said 'There can be no keener revelation of a society's soul than the way in which it treats its children' (Bakan, 2011). Bakan understands the importance of keeping children in mind in this thoughtful and compassionate text which echoes key themes throughout the following pages. The changing context of children and young people's services involving the planned structural, organisational and funding changes heralded in the Munro Report, together with an austere economic environment, highlights the need for every social work practitioner to develop the capacity to undertake unified assessments and interventions in a wide variety of settings – with individuals, families and groups –where there are child protection/safeguarding concerns. Central to this prospect are a reduction in long-criticised bureaucratic procedures, the notorious Integrated Children's System, and the release of social workers to allow them to spend more time with families using a systems theory framework. However, it is noteworthy that the present government has not ring-fenced any extra funding or produced an outcomes timetable or any definitive measure of how the Munro proposals are to be measured and evaluated. This book has not been written as a dry theoretical text: it uses systems theory lightly to inform relatively simple practice changes that can make a difference to the safety and well-being of children and young people.

The different ways children's services will develop will increase the requirement for staff to understand their particular role and responsibilities and how to enhance working together with others within new organisational systems. Such activity needs to be understood in the context of statutory duties, agency requirements and the needs and wishes of service users, specifically those of children and young people, and firmly underpinned by anti-racist and anti-discriminatory practice.

'Child protection' and 'safeguarding children' are used synonymously throughout social work and other agencies concerned with children's welfare. These terms appear interchangeably in social work texts, yet they will mean different things to different people while official government policy guidance can add to any confusion about the distinction between the two. They indicate a shift that was meant to take place after the Laming inquiry into the death of Victoria Climbie, from a focus on investigative procedures designed to 'prove' abuse or harm which would lead to a child being placed on the Child Protection Register, and a care plan focused on their eventual removal from the register. The term 'safeguarding children' began to substitute 'child protection' as a signal that the focus for social work and other agencies would shift towards early intervention, the development of preventive resources and better working together/collaborative practice, especially communication between agencies. However, as Parton (2011) argues the recently elected government has shifted the emphasis back toward child protection, implying a policy of increased surveillance of vulnerable families and targeted interventions based on assumptions drawn from dubious risk assessment factors. Both of the above terms will feature in this text to acknowledge their currency and historical use among a variety of agency staff.

Recent estimates from reputable researchers, including those from the Institute of Fiscal Studies (Jin, 2011), indicate that current government policies will push an extra 300,000 children below the poverty line, while England and Wales still imprison more 14 year olds than any other European Country (Home Office, 2010). Thus the social policy context, which is a crucial aspect of systems theory and practice, is challenging practitioners to think differently.

In Britain at least one child dies each week as a result of adult cruelty. It has been estimated that about 5000 minors are involved in prostitution in Britain at any one time. In 2010 there were about 384,200 children in need in England. Of these 69,100 were looked after in state care while the rest were in families or living independently (DfES, 2010). By the end of the same year there were 21 per cent of children in Britain living in poverty, increasing their risk of neglect (DWP, 2011). One quarter of all rape victims are children. Seventy-five per cent of sexually abused children do not tell anyone at the time. Each year about 30,000 children are on child protection registers. Recorded offences of gross indecency with a child more than doubled between 1985–2010, but convictions against perpetrators actually fell from 42 per cent to 19 per cent. Fewer than one in fifty sexual offences results in a conviction, plus there is still a major shortfall in the supervision and treatment of sexual offenders thus reducing the opportunity to reduce re-offending rates.

This statistics sample conveys the scale of the problem facing those who care about children's welfare and want to safeguard them. Individual and family-level factors have historically dominated the analysis and locus of child protection legislation, policy and practice. With the publication of the Munro Report (2011a) there is now an opportunity to ensure that the community-level factors inherent in child abuse and neglect are fully considered. There is now a more intensive focus on integrated work in safeguarding children and young people, and a reminder if one was needed to maintain every child at the centre of all activities. This means reinforcing the conclusions drawn from evidence that demonstrates that child abuse is *everybody's business*. And this does not just mean every professional working with children but the *whole community system* within which children and young people live, work, play and are educated.

The police always remind us that they cannot stop crime without the help of the community and it is the same with safeguarding children. An African proverb states that it takes a whole village to raise a child, while ancient Maori custom expects whole communities to get involved when a family has a problem. This is not a manifesto against professionalism but an illustration of a neglected area in modern welfare organisation which has lost sight of the fundamentals in our computerised, technocratic and bureaucracy-driven culture. Our task is to find innovative ways to engage communities and other systems in safeguarding children by encouraging and enhancing people's protective instincts that are currently dulled by stress, anxiety, oppression, discrimination, and social exclusion. Or, as Lord Laming put it: *'Safeguarding children and child protection are too seldom considered to be everybody's business'* (Laming Report, 2003).

This book is divided into three parts: the practice implications of theoretical and philosophical foundations; the dilemmas and challenges in applying systems theory in practice; and creating the difference that makes a difference. A systems concept is that *'the whole is greater than the sum of its parts'*, which neatly describes the book and its tripartite layout. The chapters have been organised into these separate parts in order to help the reader navigate their way to specific areas of interest and to provide a linked, thematic process through which will flow practical pragmatic advice, guidance, reflective activities and case studies. Difference, connectedness, interactivity, circular causality, uncertainty, constant change, reflective practice and skilled supervision are some of the central tenets of systems thinking. This book will equip social workers, students, managers and trainers with the knowledge base, cognitive skills and alternative perspective necessary to understand and harness systems theory in making effective assessments, care plans and interventions. It will enable them to explore a crucial practice resource in work with children and families and learn how the contribution of participatory practice can enrich this experience. The chapters offer practical guidance for different interventions and approaches based on systems theory and assist social workers in considering creative ways in which these might be used in working in partnership with individuals, families, groups and the community.

'Collaborative working' and 'partnership working' are terms that are used frequently in the practice guidance and professional literature, but without a great deal of reflection about their theoretical base, what they mean, or how to realise them in practice. Reflective practice is easier said than done but is now more than ever a critical facet of modern social work that is constrained by cutbacks, shortages and time pressures. Reflective practice is another fundamental aspect of the Munro recommendations and this book illustrates throughout how it should be a core skill for all staff, as well as fundamental to the learning requirements for trainee/ student social workers and experienced practitioners. It will challenge the orthodoxy for compartmentalising practice processes that lead to narrow, resource-driven procedures and conflicts between agencies by revealing more efficient working practices through a systems lens. The core interdisciplinary systems methods and models of child and young person practice skills shared by staff in human services will be highlighted, explored and critiqued using up-to-date evidence and knowledge. The aim will be to produce a rich, informative resource that can be valued by a range of practitioners requiring a synthesis of systems theory and social work practice in an accessible, understandable, pragmatic and practice-focused text: it hopes to offer social workers practical resources to draw upon and also enhance a progressive perspective that will deliver empowering, child-focused practice. There is a need to provide social workers with an accessible, practice-oriented book to help guide their work in the developing context of multi-disciplinary team working, joint budget arrangements, care management and integrated services.

This book is primarily aimed at social workers, but because of the nature of the Munro concept this will be of great value to an interdisciplinary audience including health, education and youth work practitioners. It will offer a valuable resource for those employed in statutory, voluntary or independent organisations offering support to children, young people and their families in the context of the imperatives of Every Child Matters (2003), The Children Act (2004), The National Service Framework (2004), Children's Trusts, new Working Together guidance (2010), the Social Work Reform Board (2010), the new Capabilities Framework (2011) and the Munro Report (2011), in addition to government policy drivers requiring the integration of children's services and the expansion of providers in the third/charitable sector. It will also be particularly relevant to students undertaking foundation degrees in social care, the early years and social work degrees, as well as social work practitioners who are embarking on social work post-qualifying studies or training.

TERMINOLOGY

The terminology in this book has been kept as accessible as possible within the confines of the editorial guidelines and the intended audience. It is necessary however to explain how certain terms have been used in order to at least offer the reader sufficient context to understand their use. Principally there is still confusion and a lack of clarity about the terms 'safeguarding children' and 'child protection' as mentioned previously. Therefore both terms will appear throughout the text due to their continued use in legislative and practice guidance from government and employing organisations in health, social care and education contexts. This will ensure that the wide interprofessional readership feels included. 'Culture' is used in places where it is specifically defined but elsewhere it is used in the sense of the organisation of experience shared by members of a community, including their standards for perceiving, predicting, judging and acting. 'Black' is used in the contemporary accepted sense of meaning that group of people who by virtue of their non-white skin colour are treated in a discriminatory way and who experience racism at a personal and institutional level every day of their lives. 'Race' as a term is declining in use due to its origins in meaningless anthropological classifications by early imperialists seeking to legitimise their exploitation of indigenous land and wealth. It is a social construction but one that is still found in statutes, policy material and common parlance.

'Therapy' is used in the generic sense here to mean counselling, psychotherapy or systems practice that seeks to attend to the complex intra-familial and obscure web of connections within and between communities. 'Ethnicity' is subject to much definitional debate in the literature, but for clarity and brevity the term is used throughout this text to mean the orientation it provides to individuals by delineating norms, values, interactional modalities, rituals, meanings and collective events (Sluzki, 1979). 'Family' is also a term around which there is some debate as it is both a descriptor and a socially prescribed term loaded with symbolism. In this book the term is used to embrace the widest ethnic and cultural interpretation possible, one that includes same sex partnerships, single parents, step families, kinship groups, heterosexual partnerships and marriage, extended family groupings and friendship groups or community living arrangements.

ENGLAND, SCOTLAND, WALES AND NORTHERN IRELAND

Within Britain there is huge diversity in the legislative and governmental guidance for safeguarding children and young people. This text has been generally based on English law for reasons of space and the avoidance of confusion. The Scottish system operates under its own legal system and system of guidance, while in Northern Ireland the health and social services boards make up a very different organisational context for child protection work. The devolved national assemblies in Scotland and Wales further add to this diversity. However, the book's contents have been adapted and designed to provide significant learning opportunities for practitioners in all the constituent countries of the United Kingdom and indeed other countries who are endeavouring to develop new ideas to tackle child abuse and provide appropriate family support: they will hopefully find much of value here.

PART I

THE PRACTICE IMPLICATIONS OF THEORETICAL AND PHILOSOPHICAL FOUNDATIONS

1

SYSTEMS THEORY

INTRODUCTION

One of the earliest references to social work and systems theory goes as far back as the mid-1970s (Forder, 1976). At that time the theory was being articulated most notably in works seeking to provide social workers with a unitary model of practice (see Goldstein, 1973; Pincus and Minahan, 1974), one that could offer a holistic framework within which to place social work practice. Social work as a new profession was evolving and experimenting with ideas from psychology, sociology and social policy to try to find an identity and set of skills based on solid theories: as a result there was a lot of effort expended into creating a professional identity, value base and intellectual framework that could explain what social work was. This debate has continued ever since, mediated through changes in society, economic upheavals, population trends and legal and educational developments. Because society is in constant flux it is inevitable that social work should be unsettled, and theoretically promiscuous. This is not a problem but a reflection of how social work must evolve in order to respond to new challenges and constant changes.

Forder (1976) considered the philosophical implications of systems theory, concluding that it offered more than the prevailing reductionist psychological theories that were concerned with behaviour and stimuli and that it could develop sociological theories that would place human behaviour in the context of a desire for equilibrium and maintenance of the social and economic status quo. It was argued that systems theory could happily incorporate the concept of free will as well as self-determination and fit into Marxist-inspired conflict theory. Goldstein (1973) observed that the process of social work using a unitary model could be cyclical rather than having a linear start and finish. Together with Pincus and Minahan (1974) the concept of a contract between social worker and client, and what they termed 'target systems' for activity, was incorporated to emphasise the interactivity of the whole. A kaleidoscope provides a useful metaphor for understanding this abstraction: when this is twisted (i.e., an action is implemented) the whole pattern being observed changes its shape and colour from that of the original and does so *ad infinitum*.

Modern systems theory, and its link with family therapy and the systemic ideas that have developed from it, is generally credited with emerging in the 1950s as a result of a number of developments in the fields of psychology, communication theory and psychiatry. At a broader level it is also important to acknowledge here the socio-economic context of a post-Second World War economic expansion, population growth and the significance of cultural changes affecting people's attitudes to sex, marriage, leisure and intimate relationships. Thus in developed industrialised countries the fifties were a time of rapid sociological change and economic growth when new ideas were more easily articulated and received (Walker, 2005). As a result there was a broad cultural change and a focus on scientific ideas that looked for improvements in the way psychological problems were addressed, moving from mainly medical and pharmacological treatments towards adopting in the 1960s what we now refer to as 'talking therapies'.

One of the important factors that stimulated the embryonic ideas that were to grow into a new form of social work was the need to build upon the traditional psychoanalytic model of individual therapy. This individual psychodynamic model was constructed on the basis of theories of the unconscious, psycho-sexual development and defence mechanisms that offered elegant explanations for internal conflicts leading to anxiety, depression and more serious problems resulting in interpersonal difficulties (Yelloly, 1980). New research that demonstrated effectiveness when groups of people were brought together to talk about their problems began to influence practice. Two key figures stand out from this time as being influential in moving forward the ideas that were to crystallise in systemic practice. Ludwig von Bertalanffy (1968) was a German biologist who devised a general systems theory that could be used to explain how an organism worked: this could be achieved by studying the transactional processes happening between different parts. He understood that the whole was greater than the sum of its parts and that using this theory we could observe patterns and the way relationships were organised in any living system.

Gregory Bateson (1973) and others in the USA took this concept of a general systems theory and combined it with the new science of cybernetics: they then applied it to social systems such as the family. Cybernetics had introduced the idea of information processing and the role of feedback mechanisms in regulating mechanical systems. Bateson utilised this notion to argue that families were systems involving rules of communication and the regulatory function of feedback that influenced patterns of behaviour within them. In the UK, Ronald Laing (1969) challenged the orthodoxy in psychiatric practice by arguing that schizophrenia was a product of family dysfunction, while John Bowlby (1969) moved from treating individuals to treating families where an individual was displaying mental health problems.

An idea thus began to take root that individual experiences within families were continually being shaped and influenced by the evolving interaction patterns of communication. Bowlby is more generally recognised as a key figure in the development of attachment theory, yet he was among the first of this new generation to recognise the limitations of individual work and began to work with families rather than individuals. Individuals were not therefore determined by early traumatic experiences or distorted developmental transitions, as the prevailing therapeutic orthodoxy argued (Freud, 1973; Segal, 1975; Yelloly, 1980). Systemic thinking conceptualised that individual personality and identity could change along with changes in family dynamics. From this common root theory (systems theory) a number of models and methods of practice evolved and this has continued through to the present day (Walker and Akister, 2004).

SYSTEMS THEORY

Thinking of families as living systems with all the dynamics that this implies was quite revolutionary in its time as it challenged the prevailing orthodoxies which perceived emotional and psychological problems in individual terms:

> Family therapy ... looks at problems within the systems of relationships in which they occur, and aims to promote change by intervening in the broader system rather than in the individual alone. (Burnham, 1984: 2)

It enabled professionals to think about how the dynamics are constantly altering as each family member deals with life both inside and outside the family. This also introduced ideas about family boundaries and the permeability of these. It moved the thinking away from linear causality and introduced the idea of circular causality, except where direct child abuse is being perpetrated by a powerful individual exercising bullying, intimidating and financial and psychological power. Crude interpretations of family therapy ideas saw this as absolving perpetrators of responsibility, particularly where a 'no blame' culture was employed in family work. Other critiques rightly pointed to some of the different methods and schools of family therapy practice as being manipulative and even combative (Howe, 1989). However, as we shall see later family therapy, just like systems theory, is constantly evolving, learning from its mistakes and adapting to new circumstances. The important theoretical concept we must grasp here is that change impacts and reverberates around the system in ways that are often unpredictable, for example in child protection interventions or family support measures. These systemic ideas were readily embraced by social workers as helping them to understand how the pieces of each family puzzle would fit together. So what do we mean by these unpredictable results of change?

The activity that follows aims to illustrate the interconnectedness of families, groups, organisations and interprofessional relationships, whereby one action can invoke another reaction in these systems.

A mother, father and their two children (boys aged 9 and 4) live together. The parents are having difficulty with the elder boy's behaviour. Family work is undertaken which results in clearer rules for both boys' behaviour and the father spending more time with the elder boy. The elder boy's behaviour improves and everyone is happy until they notice that the younger boy's behaviour has deteriorated.

ACTIVITY

Commentary

What has happened here? It would appear that the improvement in one problem area has led to another problem developing. This is not uncommon when working with families and using systems theory can help us to consider and anticipate some of the possible dynamics of change. The impact of change on all parts of the system needs to be considered. In social work practice when a child is removed from a family it is not unusual to find that another child takes on the role of the child who has been removed and that the problems begin again. In other words dealing directly, or only, with the problem presented can lead to another issue developing and the use of systems theory can help prevent this 'symptom replacement'.

The key points which we need to think about and incorporate into our practice are:

- The parts of the family are interrelated.
- One part of the family cannot be understood in isolation from the rest of the system.
- Family functioning cannot be fully understood by simply understanding each of the parts separately.
- A family's structure and organisation are important factors that determine the behaviour of family members.

In all areas of practice there will be times when there can be a preoccupation with one or two family members and the others will be marginalised. In the above family the younger child's needs were not given enough priority when designing the intervention that was targeted on attempting to improve the elder child's behaviour. This can easily happen and even with experienced practitioners and so it is useful to revisit the interrelatedness of the family members.

These four points make the case for considering families systemically. In relation to social work practice the second and third are of particular note. It is still not uncommon in social work to try to piece together a family's story by accessing or understanding *separate parts* of that family. The notion that this does not enable an understanding of the whole, if true, throws into question much of social work practice where family members are not seen together and indeed some may not be involved at all. So if we cannot understand, let's say, a child in isolation from their family (bullet point 2), and if we cannot understand the family by simply interviewing members separately (bullet point 3), then the task of convening the family members relevant to the system under consideration needs to be undertaken.

It is easy to state this and even if it is apparently true many professionals working in the human services will feel more comfortable interviewing people individually and believe that this enables people to speak more freely. The problem with this viewpoint is that in doing so they are not communicating with the relevant family members and as that family's worker/therapist they will become the sole holder of all the information available as well as the person who decides what is sufficiently relevant for other family members to know. This is a very powerful position to occupy and non-compatible with ideas of working in partnership with users and carers. In addition, as individuals we will each have our own slant, bias, preferences or interpretation of the facts and it is more effective to share these in a family meeting using a relevant system that can also provide a reality check (Walker and Akister, 2004).

A family's structure and organisation (bullet point 4) will determine to some degree what is possible within that particular family. There is no 'normal' family structure. The question therefore must be 'Does this structure work for this family?' And further, does it allow for the healthy growth of family members? This is where issues such as the permeability of boundaries can be explored. Each system will have a boundary and each system will also contain subsystems and be located within suprasystems. In family terms there will subsystems within every family which will have their own boundaries. Examples of possible subsystems are those of parental, marital or sibling. There can also be grandparent subsystems and the existence of a suitable hierarchy between the various generations is important here. The suprasystems to which the family may belong concern the extended family, community and other ecological groupings. If a family's boundaries are relatively impervious they may be isolated from their community and might also be enmeshed in their relationships within that family. If on the other hand a family's boundaries are too permeable, the individuals in that family may be disengaged from one another and over-involved with the wider community. This enmeshment and disengagement were first described by Minuchin (1974).

Recent inspections and joint reviews following the death of Peter Connelly (DH, 2010a) have illustrated the need for social workers to rediscover their core skills of assessment, so that decision making and care planning are based on a sound analysis and understanding of each client's unique personality, history and circumstances. Munro confirms that a systems perspective offers the most holistic tool for undertaking informed assessment work that takes into full account the wider environmental factors combined with the inter-personal relationship patterns influencing family experience. Government guidance is recognising the importance of a therapeutic dimension to contemporary practice. It has long been established that social workers' own therapeutic skills need to be seen as a resource that must be used and offered in assessment work (DH, 2000a). This has been repeated since by Munro as recently as 2011.

Community care reforms, child care fiascos and mental health panics have fuelled the drive towards a managerialist culture in social work reducing the professional autonomy of social workers. Munro evidenced this and underlined the critical importance of freeing up social workers to spend more time in direct contact with families, rather than repeatedly filling in paperwork and tickboxing narrow procedures and timescales. The evidence from social work practitioners is of a strong demand for the practical and theoretical resources to equip them to deal with modern family life and rediscover the value of interpersonal relationship skills (BASW, 2003). The Department of Health has long conceded that assessment processes have become de-skilling for social workers (DH, 2000b), while others have shown how assessment frameworks are impeding therapeutic communication between social workers and service users (Crisp et al., 2007).

SYSTEMS THEORY AND INTERVENTION PRACTICES

Three broad schools of family therapy can be identified within the systems literature: structural, strategic and systemic. These will be elaborated on along with various others in Chapter 3, but briefly described in this context. First, the characteristics of structural family therapy stem from the technique of observing the interactive patterns in a family. Once this baseline behaviour can be understood as contributing to the problem a structural approach would seek to highlight these, interrupt them when they are happening, and then have the family to re-enact them in ways that will lead to different outcomes. The attraction for practitioners of this way of using family therapy techniques is that it aspires to provide families with problem solving practical solutions while also maintaining a strict structural hierarchy between children and parents/carers. In direct family work therefore the task is to enable families to try out a variety of ways of doing things: for example, by coaching a parent on how to maintain a boundary or limit the behaviour of their child.

Second, the strategic family therapy approach, in contrast to the structural approach, does not have a normative concept of the family that should exist according to set hierarchies and sub-systems of parents/children, etc. Rather, the focus for strategic family therapists will concentrate on the day-to-day interactions which have resulted in problems and the cognitive thinking that is being applied to solve them. The perceptions that people have about these problems will invariably influence how they try to tackle them. In this way a culturally relevant approach will focus on the perceptions within the family system rather than seek to impose one. Attempted solutions and behavioural responses that actually maintain the problem require challenging and shifting, with alternatives being promoted by the worker (Walker and Akister, 2004).

Third, the development of the Milan Systemic Model began in Italy in the 1970s where a group of psychiatrists were experimenting with treating individuals who had been diagnosed as schizophrenic in a radically different way to the orthodox methods then employed. This is an example of a challenge to the prevailing culture within Anglo-American practices that was mounted by a team that had been influenced in their thinking by their particular cultural context. They reported better outcomes when they worked with an entire family rather than the individual patient. The central theoretical idea informing this approach is that the symptomatic behaviour of a family individual is part of a transactional pattern that is peculiar to the family system in which it occurs. Therefore the way to change the symptom is to change the rules of the family (Walker and Akister, 2004).

The goal of this work is to discover the current systemic rules and cultural myths which sustain the present dysfunctional patterns of relating and to then use the assumed resistance of the family towards outside help as a provocation to change. This change is achieved by clarifying the ambiguity in relationships that occur at a nodal point in the family's evolution. Milan Systemic therapists do not work to a normative blueprint of how an ideal family should function (Burnham, 1984).

Furthermore this approach emphasises the significance of the underlying cultural beliefs held by family members about the problem which affected an individual's behaviour. It avoids being perceived as blaming the non-symptomatic members of the family by working on the basis that the actions of various family members are the best they can do (Dallos and Draper, 2000).

FAMILY LIFECYCLE AND TRANSITIONAL CHALLENGES

Why is the family lifecycle so important? It identifies the tasks that family members have to deal with at the particular stages of life they occupy. Each stage will have different developmental tasks for members. Being a couple requires quite different adaptations to being a couple with a baby, while the needs and tasks faced by a family with young children are very different from those for a family with older children in the process of leaving home and so on. By looking at the family lifecycle we can access a window into the developmental needs of individuals within a family. If these are not being met then family members are likely to experience problems (Dryden, 1988; Brown and Christensen, 1999).

Much has been written about family development, particularly the family lifecycle, but for reasons of space only a brief summary is included here. Essentially the family lifecycle tends to be thought of as a series of stages, each with its own developmental task. The stage of the lifecycle which a family has reached will have relevance to our understanding why family members are experiencing difficulties at that particular point in time. It has been widely proposed that families may experience problems at various transition points in the lifecycle (see Carter and McGoldrick, 1999, for a full description of these stages). It is thus vital to be aware of the main transitions and some of the disruptions to these that can occur. A key factor in this view is that many families function well, or at least do not perceive themselves as having problems for long periods of time. Therefore there must be something specific that triggers family difficulties: it does this by creating circumstances which produce a level of stress that the family will be unable to negotiate. Many family workers believe that moving from one stage of the lifecycle to another can produce such stress (Hoffman, 1981; Madanes, 1981). Examples of this include adjusting to the arrival of another child or coping with a child entering adolescence. Each of these stages will demand alterations to family routines and there will also be an emotional process involved in such transitions.

The main stages of a modern culturally-relevant lifecycle which have been identified are shown in Table 1.1. Within these stages are many substages and it is perhaps noteworthy that families do not proceed neatly through all these stages. We might expect adolescents to be leaving home around the time that grandparents are requiring more care, a stage when families thus have some spare capacity to deal with this. However, grandparents can often become ill when children are still dependent and as a result there will be a conflict of interest as well as a heavy workload to negotiate. Similarly, as a family enters the stage of being a family with adolescents another baby may arrive, this event thereby necessitating that the family needs to negotiate two developmental stages at the same time.

Increasingly there are families where divorce and/or remarriage have taken place and this also adds a different set of issues to the lifecycle stages that have to be negotiated as well. These may involve the loss of a natural parent and/or gaining a step-child/parent/grandparent. These can also involve negotiations between different family systems. Such extensive family arrangements will inevitably result in complex family lifecycle stages. Often a new couple will want to have children together as well as care for the children they already have. This increases the possibility of being a

Table 1.1 Culturally inclusive life cycle

Life cycle stage of transition	Emotional process	Changes in family status
1. Between families: the unattached young adult	Individuation requires coming to terms with ethnicity	Differentiation of self from family – not necessarily separation
2. The young couple	Definition of sex roles. Commitment to couple as separate partners or as merged identity	Cultural attitudes can influence female recruited into male line; separate from families of origin; or social norms conformity
3. Transition to parenthood	Observing birth rituals with/without partner, home/hospital. Accepting new members into system	Making space in relationship; parenting responsibilities; extended family involvement
4. Families with adolescents	Tension and flexibility in boundaries contending with separation and different political/religious values/social norms	Parent/child struggle to accept independence/moving in and out of system. Gender issues over different levels of freedom for males/females
5. Launching children and moving on	Accepting different versions of exits from and entries to family system	Cultural context such as established majority, or stage or immigration/migration. Expectations of success, financial support, loyalties. Inclusion of in-laws and dealing with disability/parent death
6. The expanding family in later life	Accepting the changes in generational roles, issues of dependency switch, forms of child care: individual or group	Maintaining own/couple functioning. Supporting older generation. Managing multiple losses – parents, spouse, siblings, peers

Adapted from Kemps, 1997

family with young children as well as older children who may need to live elsewhere for all or part of the time: such arrangements can require complex adaptations.

There are numerous possibilities concerning the lifecycle which will need social workers' consideration and awareness and which may be key to the presenting problem. In the example of the arrival of a new baby in a family with adolescents, it will often be expected that the adolescent is old enough to understand a baby's intense physical demands. This may indeed be the case at one level, but almost invariably the adolescent will experience mixed emotions on the arrival of this new child and may find the decrease in parental attention difficult to cope with. In families presenting at this stage issues such as these must be appraised.

Changes in lifecycle stages can be difficult for many reasons including, for example, anxiety about letting go in adolescence and adjusting to altered responsibilities with new arrivals in the family. In the intensity of dealing with a whole family interview we may lose sight of lifecycle issues which can often offer simple explanations which will make sense to a family. Prior to the first meeting the social worker should consider the lifecycle stage a family has reached. They should also consider what the lifecycle issues and transitions appear to be for that family and be prepared to confirm or moderate these during their assessment of the presenting problems and family functioning. Sometimes the lifecycle transition can be key to the whole child protection process, so it must be recognised here as a highly useful feature in any preparation for making an initial assessment of a family.

KEY ELEMENTS IN SYSTEMS-BASED WORK

SUPERVISION

Family therapy possesses a rare openness in relation to exposing practice to wider scrutiny. Apart from the use of video recordings as a way of analysing the complex family patterns of interaction that are impossible to track during an interview, they can also be used as a training tool. Family therapy sessions are usually supervised live: this will involve at least one other person observing the session who will offer feedback and suggestions during the work or at a planned mid-point break. The person/s observing may be behind a screen or present in the room and thus will be able to gain a different perspective to that of the worker involved with the family. In this way they can spot important aspects that may benefit from a supportive suggestion. This notion has been developed to include the use of reflecting teams, whereby the individual(s) behind the screen/mirror will join the family and the worker in front of it to openly discuss their perceptions. Individual-oriented therapists or counsellors who have usually undergone intense personal analysis are also expected to open their practice to scrutiny and supervision, whether in public or private practice. In addition convergence is occurring nowadays whereby family therapists are coming under pressure to demonstrate a degree of personal therapeutic experience before qualifying as registered therapists.

CONTEXT OF PROBLEMS

This is more than anything perhaps the most defining characteristic of social work practice. It means that whatever the problem being presented to you as a practitioner using systems theory is you will automatically begin to ask a series of questions that will be linked to the context of the presenting problem. This relates not just to the family context but also to the wider professional, public, socio-economic and cultural context of the problem. In other words, it is an ecological approach in that it posits not just that individuals are inter-linked within families but also that families are inter-linked in communities that are in turn inter-linked with classes, ethnic groups and cultures. It is a way to start the reframing process and look at the problem from a different angle so that the concept of blame begins to be eroded and replaced with the concept of understanding the patterns that have created and are maintaining the current problem. For example, one question can prove very helpful here: at some point ask each member of a family 'If this problem were to disappear what problem would be left that would concern you?' This illustrates a different way of working when compared with approaches that can unwittingly reinforce families' dependence on a particular problem. Understanding the overall context of a problem can offer another way of tackling it, rather than seeking to change an individual or indeed trying to change an entire family.

CIRCULARITY/PATTERNS

These are characteristic of systems-based work. It is a foundational assumption of systems theory that problematic behaviour is conceived of as forming part of a reflexive, circular motion of events and behaviours without a beginning or end. Being able to spot this circular process and articulate it in a meaningful way with an individual or family offers a positive way forward. This releases the social worker and the family so they are able to think beyond linear causality and blaming or scapegoating behaviour. The important distinction when using this conceptual framework is where abusive adults use grooming behaviour and their power to abuse children and young people. In these child protection cases, and in domestic violence situations, the motivation and responsibility will need to be firmly located with the perpetrator who may need to be removed physically from the family system. The circular understanding of problems offers an elegant explanatory tool to uncover the reasons for the symptoms and other dysfunctional behaviour. Within a family any action by one member will affect all other members and the family as a whole. Each member's response will in turn prompt other responses that will affect all members, whose further reactions will then provoke yet more responses. Such a reverberating effect will in turn affect the first person in a continuous series of chains of influence (Goldenberg and Goldenberg, 2004).

It is vital not to take theoretical concepts to a level of abstraction where they cease to be useful. It is easy to be seduced by the technocratic skills and mechanisms of systems-based working at the expense of missing individual human responses in families or individual members as well as yourself to what emerges during your work in safeguarding children and young people. You may be an efficient social worker in terms of technical ability, but you may also be experienced by the family/ individual as cold, distanced, and emotionally unavailable. One way of guarding against this is to do some preparation before embarking on the work by reflecting on your individual experiences within your own family system. This includes early childhood memories which you may want to prompt with the use of photographs or familiar objects and places.

This practical activity will immediately enable you to visualise the concept of systems and connectedness that will not just be restricted to your own family system. The experiential nature of this activity should arouse strong feelings and give you a greater insight into the impact of your work with vulnerable families.

- Try constructing your own family geneogram using the symbols and example in Figure 1.1.

ACTIVITY

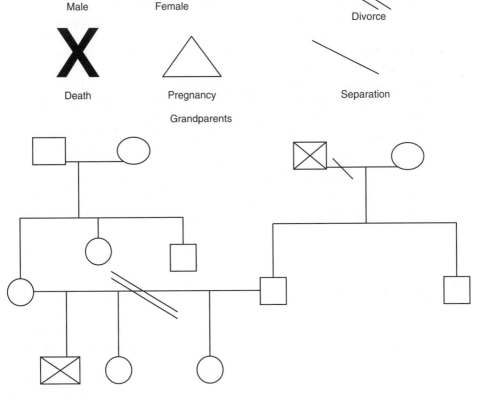

Figure 1.1 Geneogram symbols and illustration of three-generational family

- Draw connections between other family members you feel close to or distanced from.
- Think about the family history and culture going back several generations, writing pen pictures of grandparent relationships and characteristics/behaviours/mannerisms.
- By recalling those poignant stories or significant events that affected you and your family, you can begin to appreciate the impact of your own interventions with families and individuals.

Commentary

This exercise should help you maintain contact with the real feelings and experiences generated when working at a therapeutic level with client families or individuals. Some people can find this exercise too distressing or uncomfortable while others will find it enlightening and empowering. You may find it helpful to conduct the exercise jointly with a trusted colleague or friend, or even a family member. Be prepared for a powerful experience and try to anticipate the need to talk it through with someone afterwards: this could be a team leader or counsellor, or a friend who is good at listening in a non-judgemental way. Knowing yourself is a pre-requisite for modern social work practice and this is very much the case when working with families where you are engaging with individuals at a deeper level. Understanding your own family culture and heritage and the events and issues that have shaped all the individuals within it can offer you some personal insights into the meaning of culture and the deep feelings of identity it evokes.

Thinking about your own community and where you come from, as well as the idea of what it feels like to expose the past and explore its impact on the present, is a powerful experience. A thorough knowledge of your family process can help you to avoid over-identifying with a similar family or persecuting a different family. An awareness of your own feelings of vulnerability and sensitive family issues can also prepare you for negotiating these in a more sympathetic and thoughtful way with families and the individuals you work with. A sophisticated understanding of culture will enable you to consider the multifarious nature of the term 'culture' and how it can protect you against assuming a knowledge and understanding of similar people when in fact you are very different.

DECISION MAKING

Social work, with children and families, will involve critical decisions about whether or not children should remain in their parents' care. The knowledge on which such decisions are based is drawn from theories of child development, parenting capacity and family functioning. Social work practice in this field has been criticised for failing children when tragedies occur. Sadly it is inevitable that such tragedies will continue to happen. However, it is also clear from inquiries into child deaths that social work practice can be improved: see, for example, the inquiries into the deaths of Maria Colwell (DHSS, 1974a) and Peter Connelly (Department of Health, 2010). Whether the approach taken by an inquiry promotes changes that lead to better outcomes for children is unclear. The inquiry into Maria Colwell's death confined itself to procedural conclusions, investigating the way in which care had or had not been provided and the coordination of services. Unfortunately, the focus of that inquiry and of subsequent reforms was on the existing system and how to improve it. Nowhere did the inquiry suggest that children's interests could be better served by interventions directed towards the systemic context on which those children are dependent. Minuchin stated:

> Looking at the Maria Colwell case from the point of view of a family therapist, I see a group of good people, including dedicated servants of social and legal services, who couldn't respond to Maria because they thought in fragmented ways. Their cognitive models imposed a kind of acoustical screen so that Maria's cries were absorbed and blunted. If I am right, then the reforms introduced to improve those legal and social service systems will only help to retain incorrect points of view. (1984: 144)

The Munro Report has now energised a new generation of officials and government ministers and provided a solid evidence base from which they can draw conclusions and implement changes in child protection. It has taken twenty years for systems ideas to become integrated into policy relating to working with children and families. The government proposed a framework to try to improve social work practice through more structured approaches to family assessment (Department of Health, 2000b; Bentovim and Bingley-Miller, 2002). Improving both family assessments and workers' understanding of attachment relationships was key to this initiative.

Most individuals will have significant others with whom they will relate. Skills in working with two or more people are vital to all those involved in the caring professions. An intervention with one person will affect their significant others and we need to be cognisant of this. As social workers we are required to work with people in their family and community or ecological contexts. The skills of working with two or more people are best described and developed in the introductory texts in social work and family therapy literature (see for example Barker, 1998; Dallos and Draper, 2000; Trevithick, 2005; Okitikpi and Aymer, 2008; O'Loughlin and O'Loughlin, 2008). Once these have been incorporated into our decision-making processes they can be utilised in many and varied situations. The skills demanded by systems theory are readily transferable and relevant to all age groups.

The popularity of systems theory and the practice of family therapy arose from its apparent effectiveness in enabling rapid change for families experiencing problems. One of the reasons for this appears to be the active inclusion of all family members in the change process (Gorell Barnes, 1998), thereby avoiding situations where people feel excluded from what is happening to those they are close to or they are resentful of change. The experience of feeling excluded can occur in many settings.

However, it is not easy to get families together and many workers do not feel comfortable dealing with the complexities of working with the family system where child abuse is suspected: obviously this is contra-indicated where a family member is actively abusing another. For all professionals working in the human professions some of these skills will prove essential since it is the people who live together and relate together who are in the best position to alter the circumstances for each other and to promote positive change. The reason that people come to need interventions is that they have encountered difficulty in dealing with a particular set of circumstances and need assistance to move on and re-establish their family system using the strengths that exist within that family. Thus systems theory is quite consistent with the strengths approach to social work practice, as it seeks to focus on what a family can do well rather than on what they are failing to do.

There are many excellent introductory texts on family therapy (for example Barker, 1998; Dallos and Draper, 2000). Rather than try to repeat what has already been written, the core concepts and considerations for working with a family have been described above and then linked to social work and systems practice. All family therapy is predicated on working with each family as a system and therefore we have looked briefly at the key components of systems theory as these are relevant to social work. The importance of convening and engaging with a family and their lifecycle issues and multicultural aspects is crucial to setting up work with that family. How the process begins and work is done even before seeing a family is critical to the potential success of any decision and subsequent intervention. People do not seek the help of professionals lightly, nor do they take kindly to unwanted intrusions in their lives. Because of this our preparation for working with a family is crucial but also easily rushed in our busy professional practice. Time spent in preparation will be repaid in our reaching the best available decision: it also stands a better chance of sustaining change or safeguarding children and young people in the long term.

MULTICULTURAL SYSTEMS

McGoldrick, Pearce and Giordano (1982) were among the first to draw attention to culture and ethnicity as crucial influences on the interactional style and structure of families. They also highlighted the importance of giving attention to ethnic groups within what is typically referred to as the majority culture. In order to train multiculturally sensitive therapists, an understanding of one's own ethnic and cultural background will enable us to have a context within which to understand the culture of others (as the previous exercise sought to achieve). We need to appreciate that within the majority culture there is no homogeneous group (Preli and Bernard, 1993; Muncie et al., 1997). Social workers must be aware of the subtleties of their own ethnic and cultural make-up since multicultural practice applies to both majority and minority cultures: the point here being that we cannot make assumptions about the internal structure of a family from their known cul-ture, as defined by crude stereotypes or lazy generalisations, since there will always be individual interpretations in any culture or religion and we need to take the time to reflect upon and understand these. This does not mean devouring texts that seek to define ethnic minority characteristics or religious customs, rather it requires us to shed stereotypes, challenge orthodox assumptions and open our imagination to any possibility. Or as Einstein eloquently put it: 'knowledge with-out imagination is useless'.

Pursuing these cultural ideas further, Berg and Jaya (1993) looked at Asian-American families. They explored the concept of family uniqueness and started from the understanding that Asian-American families are like all other families, like some other families, and like no other families. They believed that cultural sensitivity can be learned and looked at some culturally important values for this group. What follows here are, however, some generalisations for the sake of brevity, but we must always remember that each family is unique and requires an individual approach. The need for careful, reflective assessment and high quality supervision before any intervention is made is vital.

FAMILY CULTURE A

There is a long tradition in Asian culture of solving problems through mediation rather than using head-on confrontations. Berg and Jaya suggest social workers are in a good position to mediate within a family's conflict because of their position of authority, knowledge of family relationships and use of techniques that can enhance face-saving with Asian families.

> In this situation meeting with family members separately is suggested since airing their difficulties together at the outset may be too confrontative. This is in contrast to the suggestion above of the importance of beginning family work with whole families. It highlights how every family situation needs an individual appraisal by the social workers on receiving referrals to assess whether standard procedures, whatever those are in a particular agency, are appropriate for the particular family referred. The task of convening and engaging with that family will therefore vary, though it will remain the case that simply understanding the various parts of the family will not enable an understanding of the whole family and the individual contact will need to prepare family members for a family meeting.

Berg and Jaya also give a salutary example of how the different cultures will approach the same problem, using the example of behaviour control.

FAMILY CULTURE B

American and British children who misbehave are often 'grounded'. Their punishment is to be forced to be with their family and it seems that one of the results of grounding is that children will fight their way out of the family (a process that Americans call emancipation). With Asian children, being excluded from the family is extremely rare and is viewed as a severe punishment. Thus if children misbehave they are threatened with banishment from the family and told to get out. These children will have to fight to stay in the family and the expectation will be that they will remain within the family and will also bring their spouses to join it.

> The point here is that neither approach is better or worse, simply that they are different and need to be understood before we try to intervene. An intervention based on the wrong premise for 'grounding' would otherwise totally fail and as social workers we would be perplexed by this if we have assumed majority culture norms. Indeed with any family these expectations should be checked thoroughly.

The systems model of a careful, systematic assessment of how a family organises itself in relation to the necessary tasks of family life is particularly appropriate for understanding the uniqueness of any family. It enables social workers to spend a number of sessions with each family, in a structured way exploring their interaction patterns before embarking on ideas and strategies aimed at encouraging change. It is also a model which focuses on our role as facilitators, working in partnership with a family and enabling or empowering family members rather than instructing or directing them.

Messent (1992), working with Bangladeshi families in East London, also points to the appropriateness of systems theory with Asian families because of the importance of interconnections between different family members while also urging caution with the techniques used. Later in this book a variety of methods and techniques are described, however in this context Messent advises that structural techniques would be appropriate but unbalancing the family should be avoided as this approach may prove too confrontative.

Is it necessary or even desirable for social workers to come from the same religious or cultural background? Various difficulties can arise in a situation of workers having the same culture, particularly where this is not the majority culture and issues around integrating with the majority culture arise. There may be some benefit to having the same cultural/religious identity, but there may also be dis-benefits: Toledano (1996) has written of an issue that may arise when the family and the therapist do come from the same religion or culture (in this case Judaism) and when the culture is a minority one in society.

Commentary

'How can staff use their own experience and knowledge of their shared culture without imposing it on the family? ... A position of "not knowing" is helpful when the therapist operates almost as a curious anthropologist studying an unfamiliar culture. It is however problematic when the worker is known to share the client's culture' (Toledano, 1996: 293). This is helpful as it emphasises the difference within groups and the difficulties that can arise when the assumption is of shared values and the expectation is that the social worker will support these. It is not necessary to have the answers to a cultural or religious dilemma within a family, however it is necessary to facilitate the process of the family in coming to a resolution of the dilemma. An awareness and preparedness by the social worker to question both their own and the family's position with respect to cultural and religious issues is essential. But it cannot be stressed strongly enough the need for an appreciation of uniqueness within any grouping.

Recent research and theoretical constructs are creating a context where systems ideas can be understood and put into action (Chapter 9 examines some of these in more detail). Ferguson (2008), for example, has examined the nature of social work from the perspective of movement and mobilities. He argued that social work is at all times 'on the move', yet theory and analyses of policy and practice largely depict it as static, solid, and sedentarist. This draws on the new mobilities paradigm (Sheller and Urry, 2003) through which a concern with flows and movements of people, objects, information, practices, speed and rhythm, along with complexity, fluid images and liquid metaphors, is moving to the centre of social theory. This is consistent with a systems perspective of constant change (for example, as seen in the Buddhist belief that you cannot put your foot in the same river twice). An understanding of the liquid, mobile character of social work means producing accounts that are much closer to what its practices are; acknowledging how and where they are performed and experienced by service users and professionals; and recognising the opportunities and risks inherent to them.

2

A CHANGING WORKING ENVIRONMENT

INTRODUCTION

The government is predicting a fundamental change to the child protection system by the time the Munro reforms are implemented over the next two years. Already they have committed themselves to the establishment of a Chief Social Worker whose remit will be to provide a permanent presence in government. This will chime with the establishment of another reform: the appointment in each local authority of a Principal Child and Family Social Worker. They offer the chance to provide a focus for Child Protection which has recently been eclipsed by Education. Social workers, whether they are newly qualified, in training, very experienced, or in education and teaching roles, will be familiar with the policy and practice changes that have appeared regularly over the past forty years.

These usually stem from enquiries and recommendations that are the result of unusual, rare and disturbing cases involving the death of a vulnerable person and especially that of a child or young person. Changes also arise from the regular pattern of economic strengths and weaknesses that prompt a re-organisation and reduction in welfare provision as politicians and civil servants seek to make adjustments to spending in order to satisfy the financial markets in a global system that regularly experiences capital flow problems. In addition to the Munro proposals, the latest social work policy and guidance has been issued by the Social Work Reform Board (2010) which has developed an overarching standards framework – the Professional Capabilities Framework for Social Workers in England – which will support and inform the national career structure. The main elements and proposed capabilities are as follows.

PROFESSIONALISM

Identify and behave as a professional social worker, committed to professional development.
    Social workers are members of an internationally recognised profession, a title that is protected under UK law. They must demonstrate their professional commitment by taking responsibility for their conduct, practice and learning, with support through supervision. As representatives of the social work profession they must safeguard its reputation and be accountable to the professional regulator.

VALUES AND ETHICS

Apply social work ethical principles and values to guide professional practice.
    Social workers have an obligation to conduct themselves ethically and to engage in ethical decision making, including through their partnership with people who use their services. Social workers must be knowledgeable about the value base of their profession, as well as its ethical standards and relevant law.

DIVERSITY

Recognise diversity and apply anti-discriminatory and anti-oppressive principles in practice.
    Social workers need to understand that diversity characterises and shapes human experience and is critical to the formation of identity. Diversity is multi-dimensional and includes race, disability, class, economic status, age, sexuality, gender and transgender, faith and belief. Social workers must appreciate that, as a consequence of difference, a person's life experience may include oppression, marginalisation and alienation, as well as privilege, power and acclaim, and should be able to challenge appropriately.

RIGHTS, JUSTICE AND ECONOMIC WELLBEING

Advance human rights and promote social justice and economic wellbeing.
    Social workers should recognise the fundamental principles of human rights and equality and that these are protected under national and international law, conventions and policies. They must ensure these principles underpin their practice. Social workers must also understand the importance of using and contributing to case law and applying these rights within their own practice. They need to recognise the effects of oppression, discrimination and poverty.

KNOWLEDGE

Apply knowledge of social sciences, law and social work practice theory.
   Social workers are required to understand psychological, social, cultural, spiritual
and physical influences on people; human development throughout the lifespan; and
the legal framework for practice. They must apply this knowledge in their work with
individuals, families and communities. They must also know and use theories and
methods of social work practice.

CRITICAL REFLECTION AND ANALYSIS

Apply critical reflection and analysis to inform and provide a rationale for profes-
sional decision making.
   Social workers have to be knowledgeable about and able to apply the principles of
critical thinking and reasoned discernment. They must identify, distinguish, evaluate
and integrate multiple sources of knowledge and evidence. These will include practice
evidence, their own practice experience and service user and carer experience,
together with research-based, organisational, policy and legal knowledge. They will
need to utilise critical thinking that is augmented by creativity and curiosity.

INTERVENTION AND SKILLS

Use judgement and authority to intervene with individuals, families and communities
to promote independence, provide support and prevent harm, neglect and abuse.
   Social workers are required to engage with individuals, families, groups and
communities when working alongside people in order to assess and intervene.
They must enable effective relationships and be effective communicators, using
the appropriate skills. Exercising their professional judgement, they must employ a
range of interventions: promoting independence; providing support and protection;
taking preventative action; and ensuring safety whilst balancing rights and risks.
They must also understand and take account of the differentials in power and be
able to use their authority appropriately. They are required to evaluate their own
practice and the outcomes for those they work with.

CONTEXTS AND ORGANISATIONS

Engage with, inform, and adapt to changing contexts that shape practice. Operate
effectively within own organisational frameworks and contribute to the development
of services and organisations. Operate effectively within multi-agency and inter-
professional settings.
   Social workers must be informed about and pro-actively responsive to the
challenges and opportunities that come with changing social contexts and constructs.
They need to fulfil this responsibility in accordance with their professional values

and ethics, both as individual professionals and as members of the organisation in which they work. They must collaborate, inform and be informed by their work with others, both inter-professionally and with communities.

PROFESSIONAL LEADERSHIP

Take responsibility for the professional learning and development of others through supervision, mentoring, assessing, research, teaching, leadership and management.
The social work profession evolves through the contribution of its members in activities such as practice research, supervision, assessment of practice, teaching and management. An individual's contribution will gain influence when this is undertaken as part of a learning, practice-focused organisation. This learning may be facilitated by a wide range of people, including social work colleagues, service users and carers, volunteers, foster carers and other professionals.

Running through this framework are a number of cross-cutting themes which are so fundamental to social work that they will eventually be embedded within several or all of the capabilities, including:

- Partnership working with service users and carers.
- Communication skills.
- A knowledge and application of the law.
- Use of evidence and research.

Figure 2.1 illustrates this diagrammatically and uses a systems style conceptual map showing interconnectedness and evolutionary ideas.

Further detailed guidance is available in the following documentation from the Department for Education (DfE, 2011):

- *An overarching professional standards framework* – this sets out a proposed framework showing expectations of social workers at every point in their career. This framework will be used to inform the design and implementation of education and training and the national career structure for social workers.
- *Standards for employers and a supervision framework* – taken together these set out the proposed employer responsibilities for the work conditions social workers require for safe and effective social work practice.
- *Principles for a continuing professional development framework* – these principles should underpin a framework of continuous learning for social workers in order for them to develop specialist knowledge and improve their practice.
- *Proposed requirements for social work education* – these proposals should enable student social workers to receive high quality preparation in their degrees that will give them the right skills and knowledge to join the profession.
- *Proposals for effective partnership working* – these proposals show how partnerships between employers and higher education institutions can provide better practice placements for degree students, as well as continuing professional development for social workers.

Proposed Professional Capabilities Framework for Social Workers

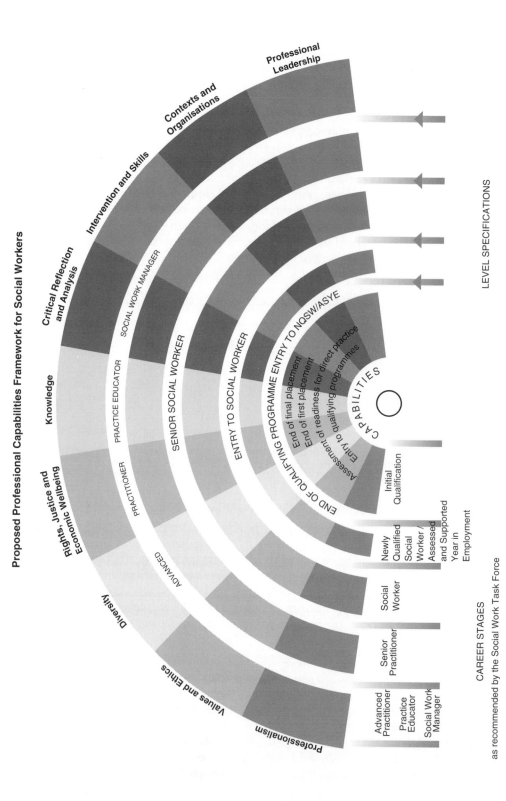

Figure 2.1 Available at: www.education.gov.uk/swrb/a0074240/professional-standards-for-social-workers-in-england

There is likely to be some confusion as training courses adjust their content and social work providers realign their operational guidance to reflect the new working environment and try to distinguish between the sets of principles listed above and older occupational standards (Topss, 2004; Skills for Care/Children's Workforce Development Council, 2010). A certain amount of frustration among social workers is likely to surface as yet again more guidance is produced, thereby following a pattern that stretches back forty years, when to some experienced people the fundamentals of social work practice remain pretty much the same. As always, it will be *how any new guidance is interpreted* and translated into practice by those in the frontline of child protection that will prove critical. Especially important here will be whether the guidance helps or hinders the aspirations voiced within the Munro proposals for more time to be spent in working directly with children and families.

FROM THE GENERAL SOCIAL CARE COUNCIL (GSCC) TO THE HEALTH AND CARE PROFESSIONS COUNCIL

The GSCC was set up in 2001 further to the Care Standards Act 2000, which was enacted partly in response to criticisms in the late 1990s of social services in Britain, in particular the high-profile case of Victoria Climbié, who was abused and eventually killed by her relatives in north London while of concern to local social services and other agencies. The GSCC inherited the mantle of the Central Council for Education and Training in Social Work (CCETSW), a previous body which had responsibility solely for managing and funding social work education. The GSCC was given a broader remit to take a lead not only in education but also in the strategic development and promotion of the whole social care sector in Britain.

The work of the General Social Care Council (GSCC) currently regulates the social work profession and social work education in England. It aims to protect the public by requiring high standards of education, conduct and practice from all social workers: they work with some of the most vulnerable people in society, so it is vital that only those who are properly trained and committed to high standards practise social work.

The GSCC maintains a compulsory register of social workers as well as issuing and enforcing the codes of practice for the profession. These codes set out the standards of professional conduct and practice required by social workers as they go about their daily work. They are intended to ensure that employers, colleagues, service users, carers and members of the public know what standards they can expect from registered social workers.

The Health Professions Council (HPC) is a statutory regulator of 210,000 health professionals from 15 professions in the United Kingdom. It was set up in 2003 under the National Health Service Reform and Health Care Professions Act 2002, to replace the Council for Professions Supplementary to Medicine (CPSM). The HPC's main purpose is to protect the public. It does this by setting and maintaining standards of proficiency and conduct for the professions it regulates. Its key functions include approving the education and training programmes which health professionals must complete before they can register with the Council and maintaining and publishing a register of those health care providers who meet pre-determined professional requirements and standards of practice.

The Health and Social Care Bill (DH, 2011) includes plans to rename the HPC the Health and Care Professions Council (HCPC) in order to reflect the transfer of social workers from the General Social Care Council, which is to be abolished in 2012. It has also been reported that it is being accorded new powers to set up voluntary registers for unregulated professions or related professions, including students seeking to enter a regulated or unregulated profession or related occupation.

The work of the HPC and other health professions regulators in the UK (e.g., the General Medical Council, Nursing and Midwifery Council, General Dental Council, etc.) is overseen by the Council for Healthcare Regulatory Excellence (CHRE). Instances of professional misconduct, namely if an individual provider is found to not meet Council standards, can lead to dismissal.

STAGES OF THE SAFEGUARDING PROCESS

It is still possible to discern and identify the stages a safeguarding case may pass through regardless of the organisational structure. Many cases do not move beyond the investigation and initial assessment stage while fewer still will reach the stage of legal proceedings. At each of these stages the system asks whether a person has suffered, or is likely to suffer, significant harm. If the answer is yes, the case proceeds to the next stage. If it is no, that person drops out of the system. At the same time, if that person is considered to be in extreme danger, at any stage of the process, a Legal Order may be requested (usually by social workers from a magistrate's court) that can remove the person for a short period of time to a safer environment. The series of stages within any safeguarding system is as follows:

- Observation and recognition.
- Referral.
- Investigation and the initial assessment.
- Conference.
- Assessment and the review conference.
- Observation and recognition.

The government has already moved to discard the distinction between initial and core assessments in response to Munro and her critique of artificial timescales. The Laming inquiry (2003) discovered several occasions when Victoria Climbié should have been included in the protection system but was effectively excluded by the practitioners who dealt with her. Dingwall et al. (1995) have also argued that there are certain belief systems that prevent practitioners from recognising the signs of abuse. The most influential of these is *the rule of optimism* which leads to a belief on the part of an individual practitioner that child abuse would not happen in their class, patient list or caseload. A second factor that might hold a practitioner back from acting on a suspicion of significant harm is called *cultural relativism*. This is where the practitioner suspects that something is wrong, but this is excused as normal in that culture, family or community (Murphy, 2004).

In Victoria Climbié's case, the poor relationship between Victoria and her great aunt was reframed as normal in West African families. At some time a threshold will be crossed when the practitioner will begin to suspect abuse and further evidence may then lead to a subsequent referral. Often it will be difficult for the practitioner to judge if that threshold has actually been passed, in which case it would be advisable for the staff member to get help both from within their own agency and from the outside system. Paradoxically, practitioners who have had their awareness of child abuse increased by study or training can express fears that they will employ a *rule of pessimism* and see abuse in every child that they work with (Murphy, 2004).

REFERRAL

The referral stage is often the first stage of inter-agency co-operation and communication and can set the scene for the interactions that subsequently occur. Referrals can be made to social services, the NSPCC or the police. When a referral is made a conflict of expectations can sometimes arise. The referrer will often come from a non-social work agency, or can sometimes be a family member or from the public. Making such a referral is an unusual, often stressful, event during which they will require reassurance and time to discuss their concerns. The duty social worker, however, will need to elicit the maximum amount of hard information about the case in order to judge whether it is an appropriate referral or not. Systems thinking can help that social worker place the referral within a wider inter-linked context of different agencies, previous contacts and any on-going work.

THE INVESTIGATION AND INITIAL ASSESSMENT

The first task of the investigation will be to access as much information as possible about that particular person and their family. Social services databases and records should always be checked. Access to education, health, probation and police information will also be requested. Any specialist mental health involvement needs to be highlighted and investigated to ascertain the background and explanations for parental disturbed behaviour. In Britain, police checks can reveal if any member of a household has been convicted of serious crimes against children (i.e., Schedule 1 offences). If it becomes known that a family has had regular contact with any other agency relevant information from their databases would also be sought.

Most agencies will have safeguards against the disclosure of confidential information to third parties which will militate against an holistic systems approach. However, the needs of a child, via the child protection procedures, will supersede these safeguards, and relevant information will usually be forthcoming, however reluctantly. In practice, the test of relevancy and the breaking of confidentiality for some practitioner groups is still an area of some difficulty (Kearney et al., 2000).

The risk of sabotaging sensitive therapeutic work addressing a child's emotional wellbeing must be balanced with the necessity of obtaining reliable evidence that can be put before a court. Gathering all of this information can take a substantial amount of time. There can also be a considerable time delay between a referral and the actual investigative interview. This delay can increase the anxiety for the child concerned as well as the referrer (Murphy, 2004).

Following this information-gathering, the investigating social worker will interview a number of people and will sometimes do this jointly with the police: the referrer; the child; the child's parents or carers; the alleged abuser; the child's brothers and sisters; and any other person with relevant information to disclose. Police work to an evidence-gathering procedure and will be unfamiliar with circular causality or open-ended questions. Preparing in advance can enable both strategies to complement each other. Although the interviews with relevant adults may be quite direct and detailed, the interviewers will be conscious of the need to form a close working relationship or partnership with the adults who care for the child concerned. When interviewing children, great emphasis is now placed on not leading, suggesting or influencing a child's story in any way (Home Office/DH, 2001).

In British child protection systems, a medical examination will commonly occur in cases of physical and sexual abuse, and sometimes in the cases of neglect, organised and professional abuse. A child will always have the right to refuse to be medically examined, and the parent, in some circumstances, will also have the right to refuse on their behalf. In practice however this refusal seldom occurs. There are three reasons for this investigative medical examination:

- To inform other agencies about the likelihood of abuse having occurred.
- To gather forensic evidence for use in legal proceedings.
- To assess the immediate medical needs of the child or adult.

There can be significant differences between the medical examinations involved in physical and in sexual abuse. In physical abuse, the medical will frequently be undertaken by a hospital paediatrician. Signs of physical trauma can last for some considerable time, but as far as forensic evidence is concerned the medical examination needs to occur as soon as possible after the abusive event. In child sexual abuse the examination will usually be done by a police surgeon. Forensic evidence in child sexual abuse needs to be gathered as soon as possible, often within 72 hours of the last occasion of abuse.

These investigative medical examinations have been criticised in the past for having been too intrusive (thereby re-abusing the child) and for being too inconclusive (thereby not giving the system any clear message on which to work). However, experienced practitioners can make the medical examination a non-intrusive, positive experience for the child concerned (Murphy, 2004), although they can also tend to focus on physical forensic matters and neglect the associated mental health and emotional issues.

The following activity aims to encourage the development of skills that are vital in communicating across professional boundaries, including the capacity to negotiate and compromise.

Discuss a recent safeguarding assessment with a colleague/supervisor and reflect back on how well you did this. In retrospect, and using the Munro principles, consider what you would have done differently.

- Identify three areas for improvement and the means for doing so.

Commentary

The definition of significant harm is not precise but this can mean the term can be adapted to different circumstances. It is the harm which has to be significant and not the act that caused it. Thus a sustained series of privations, while not individually harmful as in the case of neglect over time, could amount to significant harm as far as a person's development was concerned. Not all harm will be significant, nor will significant harm in one context necessarily be significant in another.

One definition of this is: 'A compilation of significant events, both acute and long-standing, which interrupt, change or damage the child's physical, social and psychological development. Long-term physical or emotional abuse can cause impairment to such an extent that it constitutes significant harm. For each child it is necessary to consider the harm they have suffered in the context of the family's strengths and support' (DH, 2002).

Ultimately it is a matter for the court to determine whether the harm is significant for the particular child in question (Butler and Roberts, 1997). The problem is that mental health and emotional wellbeing are difficult concepts for the criminal justice system to comprehend and measure, especially in cases of neglect where no sexual or physical abuse has been detected. This is where extra expertise and knowledge from the professional system can significantly benefit a client by helping the court understand what psychological impact has occurred.

The Munro principles together with systems ideas can help you broaden your perspective and observe the interactivity of all the significant people in the whole system that exists in and around the child, thus broadening and deepening your evaluation of the evidence gained. Systems theory also permits hypothesising rather than the definitive conclusions demanded by an inflexible bureaucratic process/procedure. This can pose a difficult dilemma if you become aware that a system and the individuals within it cannot tolerate uncertainty.

THE CHILDREN ACT 1989

The Children Act Report (DfES, 2002) discovered that '30% of updated child protection plans were unsatisfactory ... However all agencies accepted that they have a fundamental responsibility to ensure that children are safeguarded, and in most cases this was backed up with a firm commitment by senior managers to ensure that their agencies did so'. The DH (2003e) developed a straightforward document, *What To Do If You Are Worried A Child Is Being Abused*, which progressed the child-care practitioner through a number of flowcharts highlighting the appropriate approach to take if they suspected abuse was occurring and how they could work alongside other professionals. Yet the Munro Report highlights the limitations, redundancy and dangers of too much paper-filling and not enough direct work.

The Children Act aimed to consolidate a number of child-care reforms and provide a response to the evidence of failure in children's services that had been mounting throughout the 1980s (DHSS, 1983). The Act provided the legislative foundation on which subsequent policy guidance has been built to inform planning and intervention in safeguarding children and young people. There is a specific legal requirement under the Act that different authorities and agencies must work together to provide family support services with better liaison and a corporate approach.

The revised working together guidance (DfE, 2011) is a key element of the government's programme for transforming the management and delivery of children's social services. This is part of the evolution of other government guidance on protecting children from harm – *Working Together to Safeguard Children* (DH 1999a), augmented with the *Every Child Matters* (DfES, 2003b) programme of reforms aimed at developing more effective child protection work and the Children Act 2004. The duties under the terms of the Children Act 1989 are straightforward and these are still underpinned by the following principles:

- The welfare of the child is paramount.
- Children should be brought up and cared for within their own families wherever possible.
- Children should be safe and protected by effective interventions if at risk.
- Courts should avoid delays and only make an order if this is better than not making an order.
- Children should be kept informed about what happens to them and involved in decisions made about them.
- Parents should continue to have parental responsibility for their children even when those children are no longer living with them.

Section 17 places a duty on local authorities to safeguard, promote the welfare of, and provide services for, children in need. The definition of 'in need' has three elements:

- the child is unlikely to achieve or maintain, or to have the opportunity of achieving or maintaining, a reasonable standard of health or development without the provision for the child of services by a local authority, or;
- the child's health or development is likely to be significantly impaired, or further impaired, without provision for the child of such services, or;
- the child is disabled.

The Act further defines disability to include children suffering from a mental disorder of any kind. In relation to the first two parts of the definition, health or development is defined to cover children's physical, intellectual, emotional, social or behavioural development and physical or mental health. These concepts are open to an interpretation of what is meant by a 'reasonable standard of health and development', as well as the predictive implications for children having the 'opportunity' of achieving or maintaining this. However, it is reasonable to include the following groups of children within this part of the definition of those in need and to argue the case for preventive support where there is a risk of children developing problems (Ryan, 1999):

- Children living in poverty.
- Homeless children.
- Children suffering the effects of racism.
- Young carers.
- Children separated from parent/s.
- Young offenders.
- Refugee and asylum seekers.

Some children from these groups may be truanting from school, getting involved in criminal activities, or experiencing behaviour problems at school and/or home. Agency responses will tend to address the presenting problem and an intervention to address this rather than looking at the underlying causes. Assessing the needs of individual children and families therefore is often cursory, deficit-oriented and static. It should be more positive and enabling, building on strengths and being undertaken alongside family support measures. Mental health and emotional well-being needs should also be fully explored. In this regard the 30 children who have died in custody since 1990 because of self-inflicted harm are testimony to the vulnerability of this group of young people, while countless others regularly self-harm or fail in their suicide attempts. In 2010 there were nearly 3,000 young people aged 10–17 years in custody where the institutions involved admitted systemic failings in their care (Shaw and Coles, 2007).

Care orders can be made in respect of children under *Section 17*. These will result in children being placed in the care of the local authority which then assumes parental responsibility for those children. Parents will still retain parental responsibility for their children but this will be shared with the local authority. The grounds for a care order are:

- the child concerned is suffering significant harm, or is likely to suffer significant harm; and the harm or likelihood of harm is attributable to:
- the care given to the child, or likely to be given if the order were not made, not being what it would be reasonable to expect a parent to give to that child, or;
- the child is beyond parental control.

Section 26 provides for a *complaints procedure* through which children and young people can appeal against decisions reached by social workers. There are informal and formal stages to the procedure, with an expectation that an independent person will be included at the formal stages. When these procedures have been exhausted a judicial review can be applied for within three months of the decision being appealed against. The three grounds for succeeding with a judicial review are:

- *Ultra vires*: the social services department did not have the power to make the decision.
- *Unfair*: the decision was reached in a procedurally unfair manner, or by an abuse of power.
- *Unreasonable*: all relevant matters were not considered, the law was not properly applied, or there was insufficient consultation.

Section 27 requires local education authorities and other organisations to *assist in functions* derived from *Section 17*.

Section 31 enables staff to apply for a *care order or supervision order* if the child is suffering, or is likely to suffer, significant harm, or the likelihood of harm is attributable to the care being given to the child not being what would be expected from a reasonable parent. The court decision will be based on the balance of probability, which means a parent can still lose care of their child even though in a preceding criminal court they were found not guilty because the standard of proof had been beyond reasonable doubt.

Section 43 enables staff to apply for a *child assessment order* from a court following a parental lack of co-operation in a child protection assessment. Workers in situations like this, and in full care proceedings, will have a crucial role in balancing the need to protect children with the future consequences on them and their families of oppressive investigations and interventions.

Section 44 enables staff to apply for an *emergency protection order* where they need to investigate suspected child abuse and access to the child is being refused. The order allows for the immediate removal of a child to a place of safety for eight days.

Section 46 permits the police to *remove and detain* a child for 72 hours without reference to a court where they have reasonable cause to believe that child would otherwise be likely to suffer significant harm.

Section 47 gives the local authority a *duty to investigate* where they suspect a child is suffering or is likely to suffer significant harm. Guidance suggests the purpose of such an investigation is to establish facts, decide if there are grounds for concern, identify any risk, and decide on protective action.

There is a very extensive body of government policy and practice guidance in relation to assessment in child protection. Research on assessment in child and family work affirms that mental health and emotional wellbeing apply specifically to child care and child protection. However, it is also clear that the over-emphasis on risk control which followed the Children Act 1989 and various child protection failures in these complex situations missed the systems nature of the problem. Evidence now concludes that child protection has a de-skilling effect on staff who were previously only expecting to respond to families in crisis, and occasions where children were at risk of significant harm (Social Services Inspectorate, 1998; Thompson, 2005).

Munro discovered that social workers felt the policy emphasis was on reacting to child protection and looked-after children cases to the exclusion of support for other families of children in need. Therefore too narrow a focus on danger can lead to the neglect of the bigger picture, whereas a strategy of risk management which takes the wider context into account is more likely to address need effectively. Alternatively the policy emphasis will swing towards more early intervention that is designed to prevent abusive situations developing.

Practice has tended to focus on the assessment of risk rather than need (of which risk is only a part). As long ago as 1996 a national commission of inquiry into the prevention of child abuse recognised the need for a more holistic approach. It included in its definition of child abuse not only direct and acute forms (such as violence) but also indirect forms such as poor housing, family health and poverty (DH, 1996). Nonetheless the narrow view has persisted and frequently led to a failure to provide supportive services to children and families in need, such that:

- Over half the estimated 160,000 children subject to child protection enquiries each year receive no further services;
- While interagency work is often relatively good at the early stages of child protection enquiries, its effectiveness tends to decline once child protection plans have been made;
- The discussions at child protection conferences tend to focus too heavily on decisions about registration and removal, rather than concentrating on plans to protect the child and support the family.

The following case example examines the skills derived from systems theory that could be used when developing a safeguarding children plan and reviewing its progress. Imagine that as a practitioner you have inherited the case from a colleague who has moved job leaving a risky situation in which a mother is finding it difficult to trust anyone.

Case Example

Ms B is a depressed young Muslim woman with three children under five years of age exhibiting disturbed behaviour and a 10 year old at primary school with poor attendance. The family are refugees and have experienced severe trauma in recent years. Her partner, who is ten years her senior, has been involved with drug and alcohol abuse and is also suspected of abusing her. She is terrified that her children will be removed because she is unable to care for them properly or protect them from her partner's violence. Ms B is hostile towards social workers, health visitors and teachers who have expressed concerns about the welfare of all four children. She feels persecuted, does not want any involvement, and resents any interference in her life.

The following activity provides the opportunity to problem solve, work collaboratively, and consider the different nature and culture of all systems.

- Together with a colleague consider the case illustration and map out an action plan, including alternatives and the reasons for them.

Commentary

Whilst the main focus of intervention must be on the care and safety of the children, practitioners will also need to use systems theory and practice skills to engage Ms B by addressing her own needs for safety and protection. She is aware that her partner will harm her if she asks him to leave so she is stuck in an impossible situation. If he stays the practitioner will allege she is failing to protect the children; if she tries to make her partner leave she will endanger herself as well as the children. If staff acknowledge this dilemma in an uncritical way, without blaming Ms B or by pretending that there is a simple solution, then they will be more likely to begin the process of gaining her confidence and working collaboratively rather than coercively.

The systems context of her culture and religion are important factors in seeking to understand the complexities of her situation. A social worker will need to be open and direct about this without giving the false impression of knowing how she feels or by signalling their discomfort or embarrassment at such sensitive matters. Consideration should also be given here to employing an interpreter or translator even though she may be able to make herself understood, as this will signal a respectful approach and provide a cultural connection that will be emotionally supportive.

Engaging Ms B in a conversation about her experiences as a wife and mother in Serbia, and comparing her life with how it is now, will open up a rich seam of information which simultaneously can serve a therapeutic purpose. Getting Ms B to list her worries and concerns about the children will enable her to demonstrate that she is a capable mother and help a social worker appreciate the emotional aspects of her experiences. Locating this information within the context of family and environmental systems will be crucial. Attempts to engage her partner will need to be made, but not at the risk of inflaming the situation or putting both her and the children at greater risk.

The child protection plan summary could look something like this:

- Younger children to attend nursery daily.
- Ms B to play with the younger children once a day.
- Ms B to attend domestic violence survivors group.
- Ms B to take 10 year old to school.
- Partner to attend anger management course.
- Partner to attend drug counselling.
- Family network to visit Ms B weekly.

You can then help her consider how to tackle her worries in small, practical ways before addressing the major issue of her complex relationship with her partner. The review needs to examine every element of the plan; check whether these are happening; clarify which agency is responsible for each element, what impact the intervention is having on each child's development, and whether additional needs have emerged or alternative interventions need to be considered. The review should also check whether the plan is addressing and meeting each individual child's developmental needs, mental health and emotional wellbeing, as well as their collective needs as a sibling group.

In addition it must examine the parenting capacity of Ms B on her own and conjointly with her partner. The wider family context should be explored here to see what pattern of relationships exist with a view to encouraging increased supportive contact. If no immediate family exist then a wider definition of 'family' could identify religious, spiritual or social support networks in their unique ecological system. In a safer environment the children's behaviour may regress and deteriorate, so it is important to distinguish these temporary healing experiences from sustained developmental problems due to continued abuse.

Ms B may not be able to manage every aspect of the plan because it feels overwhelming. For example, the survivors group may be poorly organised by unskilled people who cannot meet her particular needs. She might also be the only Muslim and a target for racist abuse within the group. Thought needs to be given to finding the right group for her particular needs rather than just locating the first available resource. However, she may be succeeding in getting the older child to school and she must be genuinely congratulated for this.

By establishing a solid platform for her to feel supported, empowered and capable of defining her children's needs she will be more likely to feel strong enough to deal with her violent partner. A systems perspective can help illuminate patterns of interaction and the impact of changes in one part of the system on the rest. If the situation were to become more risky then the practitioner would need to confront Ms B with the likely consequences of inaction on her part. However, this will need to be done alongside Ms B and offering maximum support from all the agencies involved in a co-ordinated package. An effective review and closure will more likely happen if a collaborative relationship with Ms B has developed which will enable her to seek further help in the future if this is required.

THE CHILDREN ACT 2004

The Children Act 2004 provides a legislative backbone for the wider strategy for improving children's lives and their emotional wellbeing. The Act covers the universal services which every child can access as well as more targeted services for those with additional needs. It defines children and young people to mean those aged 0–19, but also includes those who are:

- Over 19 and receiving services as care leavers under *Sections 23c* to *24d* of the Children Act 1989;
- Over 19 but under 25 with learning difficulties within the meaning of *Section 13* of the Learning and Skills Act 2000 and receiving services under that Act.

The overall aim here is to encourage the integrated planning, commissioning and delivery of services as well as improved multi-disciplinary working, thereby removing duplications, increasing accountability, and improving the co-ordination of individual and joint inspections in local authorities. The legislation is enabling rather than pre-scriptive and provides local authorities with a considerable amount of flexibility in the way they implement its provisions. The Act forms part of a mosaic of developments for safeguarding children and young people's welfare that have radically changed the shape of provision and created a new organisational context for their protection.

Section 10 came into force in April 2005 and placed a duty on *local authorities and relevant partners to co-operate in order to improve the wellbeing of children* in their area. Wellbeing covers the following: physical and mental health; emotional wellbeing; protection from harm and neglect; education, training and recreation; the contribution made to society; and general wellbeing. However these terms are not well-defined and neither is the linkage between the separate elements: this could lead to very different perceptions on the part of the various agency staff who can be involved with the same child. The notion of co-operation includes working together to understand the needs of local children; agreeing the contribution each agency should make to meet those needs; the effective sharing of information about individual children at a strategic level to support multi-agency working; and the commissioning and delivery of services.

Schools and GPs have only recently been included in the specific list of 'relevant partners' in the Act that are mandated to co-operate. This had caused serious concerns among child-care organisations who fear the current government's drive to increase the autonomy of schools will undermine the coherence and collaboration that are explicit in safeguarding policy. The National Youth Agency was also disappointed that youth work was ignored in this legislation, despite evidence of youth workers' effectiveness in safeguarding young people and managing their mental health and emotional wellbeing. The coalition government believes that other guidance implicitly expects all agencies to co-operate in safeguarding children and young people.

Sections 11 and *28* of the Act introduced *a general duty of care on services to safeguard and promote the welfare of children.* This applies to the Children's Services Authority; schools; the district council; the Strategic Health Authority; the Primary Care Trust; the NHS or Foundation Trust; the Police Authority; the Probation Board; the Youth Offending Team; prison governors; and Connexions. The duty to co-operate is meant to lead to integrated services via Children's Trusts; the National Outcomes for Children and Young People; the Common Assessment Tool; information sharing databases; and Safeguarding Children Boards.

Safeguarding means the prevention of and protection from maltreatment. Promoting welfare means ensuring children and young people have opportunities to achieve physical and mental health, as well as their physical, emotional, intellectual, social and behavioural development. However, the current guidance on *Section 11* fails to establish a clear line of accountability between Children's Trusts and Safeguarding Children Boards or to make explicit how the two bodies must relate to each other on child protection matters.

Section 12 provides for *the creation of a database to facilitate a new identification, referral and tracking system*. This was one of the key practical measures to emerge following the 2003 Laming Report and is an information system designed to enable all staff concerned about any child or young person to access a database in order to ascertain who else might be involved and contact them if necessary. However, the aim of encouraging better inter-agency communication has been at the cost of reducing the much-valued confidentiality desired by young people who are in contact with sexual health, HIV and mental health services. There was no guarantee this information system would actually deliver better inter-agency communication and a real prospect of placing some young people at greater risk of harm if they had been deterred from seeking help because of fears that their confidential details would be exposed.

The original system was designed to contain only the child's name, address, gender, date of birth, and a unique identifying number, plus the name and contact details of any person with parental responsibility or day-to-day care of the child, the education provider and primary care provider. A flag would indicate that a professional working with a child had a cause for concern. The nature of that concern would not be described on the system. This has attracted criticism because there have been no published threshold criteria for *what constitutes reasons for concern*. This has resulted in a variety of definitions from staff in different agencies and defensive practice whereby minor concerns are flagged to ensure legal cover, thereby causing unnecessary work. The guidance suggests that concerns need to be flagged when:

- a practitioner feels that others need to know about the important information that cannot appear on the database;
- this information may affect the types of services made available to the child or young person;
- the practitioner has completed an initial assessment under the Common Assessment Framework and wants to discuss their findings.

Security for this database has been questioned because of fears that a lack of staff training combined with the sheer numbers of staff able to use the system will invariably lead to a breach of security. In addition users need to ensure compliance with the Data Protection Act 1998 and the Human Rights Act 1998, where a client's rights will sometimes conflict with child protection procedures. Children and young people, when consulted about this, accept that information should be shared between agencies if it will help them gain access to the services they need, but they wish to be consulted, know with whom that information is being shared, and be reassured that it is accurate, will be used properly, and kept safe. In practice social workers have criticised the Integrated Children's System and its accompanying bureaucracy for tying them up for hours in front of computer screens. Munro equally reserved some of her more strident criticism for this particular system.

Sections 13 **to** *16* provided for the establishment of *local Safeguarding Children Boards* which replaced the previous Area Child Protection Committees (ACPCs). Their responsibilities include the following:

- Developing local procedures.
- Auditing and evaluating how well local services work together.
- Putting in place objectives and performance indicators for child protection.
- Developing effective working relationships.
- Ensuring agreement on the thresholds for intervention.
- Encouraging evidence-based practice.
- Undertaking Part Eight reviews when a child has died or been seriously harmed.
- Overseeing inter-agency training.
- Raising awareness within the community.

With Safeguarding Children Boards put on a statutory footing their expanded role was meant to cover the monitoring of practice, training and service development, however the evidence suggests that in too many examples this has not been the case. The majority of the membership were drawn from a diverse range of agencies, but the quality of their individual contributions has been variable (Murphy, 2004).

Sections 17 **and** *26* introduced *a new Children and Young People's Plan (CYPP),* which from April 2006 was the strategic, overarching plan replacing the Behaviour Support Plan; the Children's Services Plan; the Early Years Development and Childcare Plan; the Education Development Plan; the ACPC Business Plan; and the Teenage Pregnancy Strategy and Youth Services Plan. The CYPP set out the improvements that local authorities intended to make to meet the five outcomes for children and young people identified in *Every Child Matters* (DfES, 2003b):

- *Enjoying and achieving*: this means getting the most out of life and developing broad skills for adulthood; attending school and achieving national educational standards; achieving personal social development; and enjoying recreation.
- *Staying safe*: this means being protected from harm and neglect and growing up able to look after themselves; being safe from maltreatment, neglect, violence, sexual exploitation, bullying and discrimination; being protected from crime and anti-social behaviour; learning and developing independent living skills.
- *Being healthy*: this means enjoying good physical and mental health and living a healthy lifestyle; being emotionally and sexually healthy; and choosing not to take illegal drugs.
- *Making a positive contribution*: this means to the community and to society and not engaging in anti-social or offending behaviour; making decisions and supporting community development and enjoying positive relationships; choosing not to bully or discriminate, develop self confidence and manage challenges.
- *Economic wellbeing*: this means overcoming socio-economic disadvantages to achieve their full potential; engaging in further education or training and preparing for employment, family life and independent living; having access to decent homes, transport and sustainable incomes.

THE NATIONAL SERVICE FRAMEWORK FOR CHILDREN, YOUNG PEOPLE AND MIDWIFERY SERVICES 2004

The National Service Framework for Children, Young People and Midwifery Services (NSF) was designed as a 10 year programme intended to stimulate long-term and sustained improvements in children's health. It aimed to ensure fair, high quality and integrated health and social care, from pre-birth right through to adulthood. Overall, the NSF set the national standards for children's health and social care for the first time, which promoted high quality, women and child-centred services and personalised care that would meet the needs of parents, children and their families. The standards required services to:

- *give* children, young people and their parents increased information, power and choice over the support and treatment they receive and involve them in planning their care and services;
- *introduce* a new child health promotion programme designed to promote the health and wellbeing of children from pre-birth to adulthood;
- *promote* physical health, mental health and emotional wellbeing by encouraging children and their families to develop healthy lifestyles;
- *focus* on making an early intervention, based on a timely and comprehensive assessment of a child and their family's needs;
- *improve* the access to services for all children according to their needs, particularly by co-locating services and developing managed local children's clinical networks for children who are ill or injured;
- *tackle* health inequalities, addressing the particular needs of communities as well as children and their families who are likely to achieve poor outcomes;
- *promote* and safeguard the welfare of children and ensure all staff are suitably trained and aware of the action to take if they have concerns about a child's welfare;
- *ensure* that pregnant women receive high quality care throughout their pregnancy, have a normal childbirth wherever possible, are involved in decisions about what is best for them and their babies, and have choices about how and where they give birth.

Standard five of the NSF stated that 'all agencies work to prevent children suffering harm and to promote their welfare, provide them with the services they require to address their identified needs, and safeguard children who are being, or who are likely to be, harmed' (DH, 2004: 48). The responsibility for contributing to this new multi-agency integrated framework rested with the following:

- *Primary Care Trusts* which were responsible for improving the health of their whole population (and are currently being abolished and replaced by GP consortia).
- *Strategic Health Authorities* which were the performance managers.
- *NHS Trusts* which were required to designate a named doctor and nurse to take a professional lead on safeguarding children.

- *Ambulance Trusts, NHS Direct and NHS walk-in centres* who needed to have similar arrangements in place.
- *Local Authorities* which had to ensure there was a designated professional for safeguarding children in *Social Services, Housing* and *Education Departments.*

These original parameters have since been overtaken by a new coalition government review which emphasises that GP groups can assume the functions of the PCTs. Safeguarding and promoting the welfare of children must now be prioritised by all agencies, working in partnership to plan and provide co-ordinated and comprehensive services. Agency roles and responsibilities should be clarified to ensure that harmed children are identified and assessed as soon as possible by appropriately trained staff with suitable premises and equipment. Under the NSF an up-to-date profile of the local population must be compiled to facilitate a needs assessment and provide the integrated services to meet that need.

The following activity will enable you to familiarise yourself with the latest practice guidance which strongly emphasises the need for better interprofessional working.

ACTIVITY

- Obtain a copy of your agency safeguarding children procedures and the revised Working Together practice guidelines.
- Examine these carefully and make sure you know how, and to whom, you should refer cases involving child protection: then consider where the Munro principles could be used to make this more effective.

HUMAN RIGHTS ACT 1998

The Human Rights Act (United Nations, 1998) came into force in 2000 and incorporated into English law most of the provisions of the European Convention on Human Rights. The Act applies to all authorities undertaking functions of a public nature, including all care providers in the public sector. It supports the protection and improvement of the health and welfare of children and young people throughout the United Kingdom. In terms of safeguarding children both the Act and the UN Convention on the Rights of the Child provide a powerful resource for social workers who are seeking to realise the potential of the Munro Report's vision of child-centred practice.

Article 3 concerns the *freedom from torture and inhuman or degrading treatment.* Children and young people who have been subjected to restraint, seclusion, or detention in public care as a result of alarming behaviour could use this part of the Act to raise complaints.

Article 5 concerns the *right to liberty*, and together with *Article 6* concerning the *right to a fair hearing*, are important to children and young people detained under a section of the Mental Health Act 1983, the Children Act 1989, or within the youth justice system. Workers involved in such work must ensure that such detentions are based on sound opinion, in accordance with clearly laid out legal procedures that are accessible to the individual, and that this only lasts for as long as the mental health problem persists. In the context of youth justice work, particular attention needs to be given to the quality and tone of pre-sentence reports which can prove stigmatising. The formulaic structure of these pre-sentence reports might not enable an assessing social worker, working under deadline pressures, to provide an accurate picture of a young person.

Article 8 guarantees the *right to privacy and family life*. Refugees and asylum-seeking families can become entangled in complex legal procedures relating to citizenship and entitlement. This provision can then be invoked when UK authorities are considering whether a person should be deported or may remain in this country. Compassionate grounds can be used for children affected by the proposed deportation of a parent or in cases where a parent is not admitted. Workers attuned to the attachment relationships of often small children can use this knowledge to support *Article 8* proceedings. In such circumstances the maintenance of the family unit will be paramount.

Staff involved in care proceedings or adoption work will have to consider very carefully whether such plans are in the best interests of the child, but also whether they are consistent with the child's rights under the Convention. For example, the Convention emphasises that care orders should be a temporary measure and that children should be reunited with their families as soon as possible where this is appropriate. In the case of a parent with a mental health problem detained in a psychiatric hospital, the Convention could be employed by their children to facilitate regular visits if these have been denied.

Article 10 concerns *basic rights to freedom of expression* and in the context of children's welfare is a crucial safeguard for ensuring that practitioners work actively to enable children and young people to express their opinions about service provision. Practitioners have an opportunity within this specific provision to articulate and put into practice their value principles of partnership and children's rights.

Article 14 states that *all children have an equal claim to the rights set out in the Convention* 'irrespective of the child's or his or her parent's or legal guardian's race, colour, sex, language, religion, political or other opinion, national, ethnic or social origin, property, disability, birth or other status'. This provision could be used to argue for equality of service provision and non-prejudicial diagnosis or treatment. Workers need to ensure they are employing anti-racist and non-discriminatory practice, as well as facilitating children and young people to:

- access information about their rights;
- contact mental health services;
- access advocates and children's rights organisations;
- create children's service user groups.

However, in a damning 2004 report by the Children's Rights Alliance for England it was revealed that the UK government had only made progress in 17 of the 78 recommendations made by the UN Committee on the Rights of the Child in 2002 that were designed to make UK law, policy and practice compatible with the UN Convention on the Rights of the Child.

3

CONTEMPORARY
SYSTEMS METHODS
AND MODELS

INTRODUCTION

Working with families, whatever the focus of the social work assessment or intervention is, probably forms the bedrock of modern practice whether this takes place in elderly care, community care, child protection, or mental health care. It is little wonder then that systems theory and the practice of family therapy or family support has always had an enormous attraction for social workers who want to help and support individuals and families in thoughtful and effective ways that have a sound evidence base. Despite contemporary service provision being systematically defined in narrow case/care management terms, there are many opportunities inside and outside the statutory social services for using some of the skills and techniques associated with systems theory to aid assessment and intervention practice (Walker, 2005). The Munro Report has set the scene for a renaissance in interpersonal skills in social work, child-centred practice and an environment for creativity to flourish.

The added bonus here is that individuals, couples and families have consistently reported their satisfaction with the approach (Carr, 2000). Nevertheless, many social work staff feel ambivalent or at least apprehensive about using therapeutic techniques, especially as there are institutional constraints and organisational barriers that serve to magnify their personal reservations. At best this is because social workers do not wish to do any harm, or because they fear unleashing psychological forces within families that they will feel responsible for. These are understandable concerns that need to be put in perspective against the reliable evidence and testimony coming from those practitioners and service users who can confirm positive experiences.

The full range of practice models and methods employed by social work staff can be subject to the same doubts, yet these do not seem to prevent social workers from using task-centred or crisis intervention techniques. Some workers feel they should be fully qualified family therapists or at least in training before trying to use systems theory and skills. Yet social workers do not have to be fully qualified psychotherapists to use psychodynamic skills, or psychologists in order to utilise cognitive-behavioural methods which are part of everyday practice for many. It is also the case that seemingly functional/administrative procedures without any *ostensible* therapeutic intent can stimulate unexpected behaviours or emotional reactions in service users that are consistent with a therapeutic effect (Walker, 2005).

In the same way, social workers can quite properly use the skills and techniques of family therapy as part of their broad repertoire of applied theories that they can bring to bear on the challenges presented to them by service users in safeguarding children. As we shall see the advantages outweigh the disadvantages, particularly as the model for family therapy was envisaged as a short-term intervention in contrast to the traditional long-term individual casework relationship identified in earlier social work practice. Even small pieces of work can make a big difference and the most intractable of situations can be transformed by the application of systems theory. Indeed this application may not need to be within the family, instead it can be directed at the wider professional system where a bigger problem may reside that is negatively impacting on service users. For example, a child's behaviour that is putting them at risk of physical abuse in the home may have its root cause in school bullying, so by only focusing on the individual child/parent a systems approach enables you to consider a wider perspective and locus for that problem. Intervening with the school/teacher may be all that is required, thus saving everyone concerned a great deal of wasted time and energy.

The following activity is a practical one to enable you to visualise just how complex social work can be because of the number of different organisations/systems involved in that work. It demonstrates vividly the need for improved interprofessional communication.

- Using your increasing knowledge of systems theory, consider the number of systems in which you function both professionally and personally. It may help to draw a map of some kind here.
- Now re-arrange that map into a series of concentric circles (see an example of this in Figure 3.1). Now place the most powerful individual/system and the weakest/most vulnerable in whichever circle fits with your understanding of the situation.
- What impact does this perspective have on you and how might it change your practice?

(Cont'd)

ACTIVITY

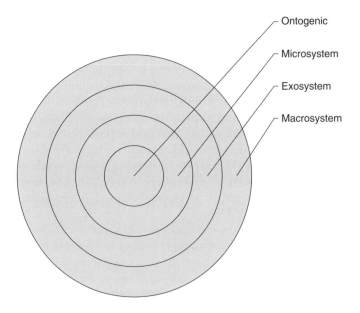

Ontogenic

Microsystem

Exosystem

Macrosystem

Figure 3.1

METHODS, MODELS AND PRACTICE

Some of the important developments in systems theory, and some of the more popular and accessible methods and models of practice including family therapy, will now be assessed and in doing so will challenge the notion that social workers do not have the time, training, or appropriate context to employ them. Systems interventions can be aimed at individuals, couples, families, teams or organisations. Although family therapy or systemic therapy is the prevailing and more common form of intervention, the principles underlying its practice can be universally applied throughout social work. You may be working in a team/unit where family therapists are practising, so your understanding of their skills and methods will be very valuable, or you may need to undertake joint work with a qualified family/systemic therapist. There are challenges in using systems theory in certain statutory settings, especially where the bureaucratic structures require families to acquire labels such as 'in need' or conform to child protection terminology. These professional systems do not lend themselves to empowering therapeutic working methods, even though they have the potential for being experienced as more helpful and more cost-effective in the long term.

And just as you would explain the aims and intentions of your work using any other method of intervention, so it is the same for employing a systems approach. If you are trying to work in partnership and offer a degree of choice in the way you can help, there is probably some advantage in being able to explain the rationale behind your practice approaches. Naturally, for those who are reluctant and resentful clients, this may feel like a false exercise. But if you persevere and have a preference about this way of working, then the process of an open and honest discussion can create the framework for engaging service users as well as signal a respectful attitude (Walker and Akister, 2004).

INTERVENING AT THE STRUCTURAL LEVEL

Structural family therapy and the conceptual thinking around it represent a therapy of action. The tool of this therapy is to modify the present, not to explore and interpret the past. Since the past will have been instrumental in the creation of a team's, individual's or family's present organisation and functioning, it will be manifest in the present and available to change via interventions that can alter that present (Minuchin, 1974). A structural worker engages with the family or another system and then sets out to transform it. The main focus of this approach is the family/team/organisational structure, with the underlying assumption that the problematic behaviour is related to a fault with the functional normative structure. Structural family therapists believe that by changing the family structure they can change the position of family members and therefore alter their subjective experiences.

The process of the model is that changes to the structure of the system will create the possibility for further changes. The notion that the system is organised around the support, regulation, nurturance and socialisation of its members means that the worker needs to repair or modify the system's functioning so that it can better perform these tasks. Once a change has been introduced the family or team will therefore preserve that change by using their own self-regulating mechanisms. Changes in the multiple interactions between system members will then lead to the possibility of change in the experience of the individual.

The characteristics of structural family therapy stem from the classic systemic technique of observing the interactive patterns in a family. Once this baseline of behaviour can be understood as contributing to the problem a structural approach would seek to highlight these, interrupt them when they are happening, and then enable the family to re-enact these in various ways that can lead to different outcomes. The attraction to social workers of this way of practising systems techniques is that it aspires to provide families, teams or individuals with problem solving practical solutions. In a family session therefore the task will be to enable that family to try out different ways of doing things, for example by coaching a parent on how to maintain a boundary or limit a child's behaviour.

Social workers who are attracted to behavioural approaches to their practice will find certain similarities with structural work in that the learning is practical, thereby

enabling family members to observe their own changes. Below are listed some of the
key features (Gorell Barnes, 1998):

- *Intensity:* this creates a very focused experience of an emotionally charged interaction
  rather than skipping over uncomfortable feelings.
- *Persistence:* this concentrates on these long enough to make a difference to the problem
  patterns that have been brought to your attention.
- *Homework:* this takes home tasks which will transfer what has been learnt to the home
  context. These will assist in maintaining the momentum for change.
- *Confirmation:* this sees the positive connotations of behaviour and emphasises that people's competence is necessary in order to challenge negative, fixed ideas.
- *Enactment:* this involves requesting a family to move from description to actually showing the problem live in the session. It also encourages people to talk directly to each other
  rather than through the medium of the social worker.
- *Changing space:* this literally involves moving people around in the session. It is especially
  powerful when a child is being caught in the crossfire between fighting parents or used
  as a go-between. Asking the parents to sit down and face each other can be a simple
  action yet it can prove to be incredibly transformational.
- *Creating boundaries:* these can be applicable in situations where age-appropriateness and
  enmeshment are issues. For example, where there is poor individuation it helps family
  members to separate themselves. It can also be of value where parents are experiencing
  small children as tyrannical and out of control, or where adolescents are finding independence difficult.

STRATEGIC PRACTICE

One of the guiding principles in strategic systems practice is that problems apparently
residing in one individual are frequently associated with the difficulties resulting from a
system's need to change and reorganise at transitional stages. These can occur at various
times, such as the birth of a baby or when a young person is considering leaving home
(Dallos and Draper, 2000). This can be particularly the case with older adolescents who
present with mental health problems or a history of school refusal. Doing so can indicate a family dynamic whereby that young person becomes symptomatic in order to
help their parents avoid conflicts in their relationship. Thus the attention is focused on
the young person rather than the parents. Or it could relate to a team or organisation
experiencing changes due to a loss of staff, a re-organisation, or budget-driven service
changes. This can particularly be the case in social work where change and transitional
processes are constants due to legislative and other impositions.

   One of the central premises of the strategic approach is that people are essentially
strategic in the way that we are involved in predicting how others may feel, think, and
act. Some writers characterise this as being indicative of a constant power struggle
in which system members are trying to influence each other and define themselves
(Haley, 1976). Furthermore this struggle is not contained within families but also
occurs when a family seeks help. In social work practice various family members will
seek to influence a social worker in order to try to gain sympathy or have that person

agree with their particular perception of the problem. This will often be mirrored in the professional system where attempts at persuasion and the building of alliances will be acted out. Recalling your own experiences of team meetings, case conferences or multi-agency events can swiftly reveal evidence for these processes.

The implication here for social work practice is that you can use this approach starting from the basis that parents, for example, will seek to enlist you for their side in struggling with an unruly adolescent. Or a team manager may try to recruit you for a proposal for change in order to build support within a decision making meeting. Child protection chairs can also be detected in trying to influence decisions. Colluding with this will only distance you from the adolescent, other team members, or conference participants as well as diminish your effectiveness in resolving the various problems that can exist between people. The strategic approach explicitly recognises the dilemmas presented by families who seek help, or team leaders, or chairpersons, but all the time want to remain in control. These beliefs and premises highlight the role played by attempted solutions to problems which will either make matters worse or result in a denial of the seriousness of the problem (Walker and Akister, 2004).

The strategic approach, in contrast to the structural approach, does not have a normative concept of the family or system that should exist according to set hierarchies and sub-systems of parents/children, etc. Rather the focus with strategic workers is on the day-to-day interactions which have resulted in the problems and the cognitive thinking that is being applied in order to solve these. The perceptions that people have about these problems will invariably influence how they try to tackle them. Attempted solutions and behavioural responses that are actually maintaining a problem will require challenging and shifting with various alternatives promoted by the worker. What follows are some of the key features of strategic family therapy (Dallos and Draper, 2000):

- *Staged approach*: a detailed exploration of the difficulties to be resolved is translated into an action plan that has been designed to disrupt embedded problematic sequences. Assessment and a reappraisal of the outcomes of intervention can be used to revise or continue tasks.
- *Directive tasks:* these will usually consist of the homework that family members will be asked to carry out between family sessions. They are most effective when every family member is involved in such tasks. The aim is to alter the problematic sequences of family interactions. The important point here is that the task must be reasonable and must also fit with the family's repertoire of achievable limits.
- *Paradoxical tasks*: this is where the family will be asked to do the opposite of what the therapist intends to happen. They will be employed when families find it impossible to carry out directive tasks. The aim will be to encourage symptomatic behaviour, in other words to try to unblock a cycle of failure and poor motivation and hopelessness. An example of this would be when a family reports constant bickering and loud arguments, describing family life as conflictual and uncaring. By suggesting that the family has one huge argument at a regular time each evening presents them with a double bind. If they do this then they are demonstrating that they can control their behaviour and are therefore not helpless: if they do not do so because it feels stilted and manufactured then they are learning not to argue. Either way change will have occurred.

SYSTEMIC FAMILY THERAPY

The development of this model began in Italy in the 1970s when a group of psychiatrists were experimenting with treating individuals diagnosed as schizophrenic in a radically different way to the orthodox methods then employed. They reported better outcomes when they worked with the whole family rather than the individual patient. The central theoretical idea informing this approach is that the symptomatic behaviour of a family individual is part of a transactional pattern that is peculiar to the family system in which it occurs. Therefore the way to change the symptom is to change the rules of the family.

The goal of this therapy is to discover the current systemic rules and traditional myths which are sustaining the present dysfunctional patterns of relating, and to use the assumed resistance of the family towards outside help as a provocation to change. That change is achieved by clarifying the ambiguity in relationships that occur at a nodal point in the family's evolution. Systemic therapists do not work to a normative blueprint of how an ideal family should function (Burnham, 1984). Furthermore this approach emphasises the importance of the underlying beliefs held by family members about the problem which affected a person's behaviour. It avoids being perceived as blaming the non-symptomatic members of the family by working on the basis that the actions of various family members are the best they can do (Dallos and Draper, 2000). These are some of the key features:

- *Positive connotation:* this technique is used as an extension of the strategic paradoxical task by reflecting back to the family a positive reason for all their actions. This is supported by providing a rationale for why they behave as they do and maintains the therapist in a non-judgemental stance. It places the family members on an equal footing, thus avoiding scapegoating.
- *Hypothesising:* this is a way of bringing together all the available information prior to the family session and collating it into a coherent whole which is fully circular and systemic. In other words, it attempts to explain why the family are having a problem. This unproved supposition is tentative and used as the basis for guiding the family session. The task for the therapist is to confirm or disprove the hypothesis and create a new one if necessary.
- *Circular questioning:* this unique style of questioning is both elegant and simple. It requires the therapist to ask questions of one member about the relationship between two other family members. The family will not be used to communicating in this way and will be placed in a position of having to speak freely about ideas they would normally keep to themselves. Differences in perception and distinctions in behaviour can be explored and discussed according to the interviewer's curiosity and hypothesis.
- *Neutrality:* once again this is another distinguishing feature of systemic family therapy practice. It involves the therapist siding with everyone and showing no allegiance or favouritism towards any individual family member. Although the therapist may feel distinctly biased towards, say, a victim of child abuse or domestic violence, the neutrality refers to behaviour during the interview and not a moral injunction. The aim is to maximise

the family's engagement and not to collude with blaming behaviour which will undermine the desired change.

- *The intervention*: at the end of a family session a prescription or intervention will be delivered to all those present and mailed to any absent members. This can consist of a paradoxical injunction, a simple task, or a complex ritual designed to interrupt dysfunctional behavioural patterns (Campbell and Draper, 1985).
- *Team working*: this is not exclusive to systemic family therapy but it is a particular characteristic of this method where the concept of live supervision during a family session is considered essential. The use of one-way screens, videos and audio-tapes is to enable several people to bring their collective experience and knowledge to bear on the presented problems. This helps to guard against the individual therapist being drawn into subtle alliances or missing important information during lively sessions. You can adapt this in your social work context by having a colleague join you in some work and act as an observer for the process.

BRIEF SOLUTION-FOCUSED WORK

As the title suggests this approach is primarily aimed at a short-term period of work, with the emphasis on encouraging families or systems to recognise their own competencies. The mantra of practitioners using this way of working is '*focus on solutions not problems*'. For example, a family or parents will often discuss a child or a parent in sweeping generalisations when explaining their problems: 'He's always getting into trouble with teachers', or 'She never does as she is told'. These are recognisable complaints and express an over-emphasis on the negative rather than the reality, as if the parents are trying to convince you of their case for help and their desperation. Or equally a team leader, colleague, meeting chair, or line manager may try similar tactics by identifying what they see as a problem. Solution-focused workers can urn this idea around and carefully enable the complainants to recall an exception to this general rule about a troublesome child, person or event (de Shazer, 1982; Berg, 1991).

Once the system has recognised that exceptions can occur and a person can behave/do as they have been asked, the focus of the approach will be to emphasise these exceptions and help the family to make more of them happen. This requires patience and hard work in order to excavate every element surrounding these exceptions, thereby allowing a family or team to prepare for them, recognise them, sustain them, and reproduce them. These are then translated into clear, recognisable goals that can be specifically described so that everyone involved can perceive them. Goal setting can often be difficult especially with parents/families with poor self-esteem, lacking in confidence, and feeling disempowered. Teams of social workers can develop a self-reinforcing negative identity, low levels of morale and cynicism. To help overcome this difficulty the 'miracle question' will be designed to help systems identify specific behaviours and actions that can indicate change, rather than talking abstractly about wanting to 'be happy again', 'like a normal family', 'to behave more professionally as a team', 'to be more effective in assessing child protection'.

The miracle question entails asking the family/team to imagine that while they were all asleep a miracle happened and the problem was solved. When they awoke they were not aware a miracle had happened. They then have to describe what would be different that would show them a miracle had occurred. In describing this difference they are encouraged to make concrete the conditions for change and by doing so they are in fact illustrating the goals they desire. The practitioner's job is to work collaboratively with the family or team's *own definition of change* and help them devise ways of achieving it. Overall the brief solution-focused approach can be summarised in terms of three rules (Dallos and Draper, 2000):

- *If it ain't broke don't fix it*: even the most chronic of problems will show periods where the troublesome patterns or symptoms are absent or reduced. The therapist needs to have a broad and tolerant view of what is not broke (i.e., what competencies are present). These can then be built upon so that the therapy does not become bogged down in attempting to build a utopian family.
- *Once you know what works do more of it*: once these exceptions and competencies have been discovered families are then encouraged to do more of these. This can lead to a self-reinforcing cycle of success which will start to replace one of failure, incompetence and desperation.
- *If it doesn't work don't do it again, do something different*: families can often become involved in cycles where they cannot see any alternative but will continue to act in the ways they always have, or will even do more of the same. In searching for the exception they can be helped to notice an alternative pattern that happens occasionally but with more positive consequences. This is then built upon until it replaces the previous more common negative pattern.

The following activity will help you recognise areas where you feel confident and those where there are gaps in your knowledge. Some insights into where your own preferences lay and where there are areas of ambivalence may be revealed.

ACTIVITY

- Examine closely what are for you the core elements of each method and model, then discuss these with a colleague.
- What do you feel are the key differences and which approach appeals to you and why?

CONTEMPORARY DEVELOPMENTS

CONVERGENT PRACTICE

This is characterised as a narrowing of the gap with some traditional psychodynamic theories that have informed individual therapeutic work. This represents an interesting development in the sense that the development of family therapy has come full circle and returned to the original theoretical base it sprang from. Several contributors have discussed the previously unspoken notion of a combined or integrated family therapy practice that reflects and incorporates elements of psychodynamic therapy (Pocock, 1997; Larner, 2000; Donovan, 2003). This development demonstrates that systems theory is still a flexible, evolving paradigm within which approaches and techniques have remained fixed in some ways and changed in many others. This should suit social workers who whilst interested in particular approaches to their work are nevertheless agile enough to incorporate ideas and skills that can best help clients at particular times. Given the roots of modern psycho-social practice there is a valuable opportunity for social workers to build on a solid theoretical foundation with skills and techniques that can feel relevant to many service users. An example here is in the use of interpretation. This is one of the most powerful aspects of a psychodynamic approach that can be seen mirrored in the family therapy technique of a reflecting team conversation.

Feminist approaches evolved more overtly during the 1980s as female family therapists began to discuss and write about power and gender relations within families (Perelberg and Miller, 1990; Goldner, 1991; Hare-Mustin, 1991). Their feminist analysis of therapeutic work revealed that couples were strongly influenced by assumptions about gender roles and expectations within relationships and families. Despite thirty years of feminist theory and practice in other contexts, these writers and many female family therapists began to articulate a challenge to the gender-neutral concepts in orthodox family therapy theory and practice. Instead of assuming a parity between partners or married couples they incorporated an understanding of the inequality conditioned and socialised into relationships that explained domestic violence at one extreme or at the other a stereotype of the passive/nurturing female and assertive/emotionally distant male.

Where problems do occur in relationships these can often be better evaluated through a gendered lens that highlights the contradictions and dilemmas between people who are constrained by powerful concepts of maleness and femaleness. When individuals fail to conform to the societal norm of working man and child-caring female this is usually expressed as a female failing. Orthodox family therapists however well-intentioned would try to reverse this stereotype by seeking to engage the male partner in more child-care duties, but in many cases this may simply reinforce the female's sense of failure. This attempted intervention neglected to understand that for many women success in child care was an important defining characteristic of their femininity from which they gained enormous self-esteem and role satisfaction. The intervention also unwittingly reinforced the male as the problem-solver and the more successful partner.

Social workers using an empowering anti-oppressive framework for their practice will find these concepts resonate with their way of working with women who are abused by violent partners or left to cope with children on their own. By combining feminist systems concepts with social work skills you can overtly address the wider social context of the difficulties and dilemmas faced by women by challenging the prevailing patriarchal assumptions that undervalue child care and women's relationship/nurturing skills. Helping women to recover from such traumas and build self-confidence requires patience as well as the ability to reframe them away from notions of individual fault/blame/failure and towards an understanding of the social constraints affecting relationship patterns. Using a feminist approach also means making explicit throughout your work with clients the power differences between genders and enabling them to tackle the consequent dilemmas in their relationships.

Constructivism and *social constructionism* are two related but different concepts linked to postmodern theories that have recently begun to challenge some of the orthodox thinking and techniques surrounding family therapy practice. The postmodern thesis rejects the notion that there is a fixed truth or single reality about family process (Walker, 2001c). The postmodern view suggests that each individual constructs his or her personalised views and interpretations of what the family might be experiencing together. Family therapists with a constructivist or social constructionist perspective emphasise the importance of cultural diversity and multiple realities and the acceptance of a wide range of belief systems (White and Epston, 1990; Goldenberg and Goldenberg, 2004). Constructivism stems from the study of the biology of cognition which argues that individuals have unique nervous systems that permit different assumptions being made about the same situation. Social constructionism is similar in that it argues that there is no such thing as objective reality, but that what we do construct from what we observe arises from the language system, relationships and culture we share with others. In practice therefore the constructivist and social constructionist family therapist would be recognised by their more collaborative style of working. The focus will be on helping the family examine and reassess the assumptions individuals make about their lives rather than focusing on family patterns of communication. Using these approaches involves taking a position of uncertainty and not knowing; here instead the therapist joins in the search for workable solutions on an equal basis with the family.

Narrative therapy recognises the natural ability that people have to possess, to generate and to evolve new narratives and stories in order to make sense of their experiences (Freeman et al., 1996). The focus of interest is the meanings that families generate to explain and shape possible courses of actions. Traditions within families and cultures are used to guide interpretations of events. Making these more explicit in the more conversational style of the therapeutic process helps to validate the family experience rather than seeking to impose a solution or follow a therapist-determined path. The nature of the conversation is key to this approach. Social workers will note some similarities with an exchange model of assessment, empowering and service user focused work. The approach challenges the way clients are labelled because these usually encompass superficial, negative and one-dimensional descriptions. Clients can begin to accept these limiting descriptions and by believing they are 'true' will start to behave in ways that will confirm those labels. Narrative therapy aims to help families by collaborating in developing alternative stories about their lives and replacing a single, problem-saturated belief with a number of different, complex beliefs that will open up various possibilities.

The activity that follows has been designed to develop your critical thinking skills and your capability to distinguish between the different ways of working that you will encounter in interprofessional work.

- Compare the information opposite with the previous section on established methods and models.
- What difference do you feel these new developments would make?

Commentary

The challenge in taking on a therapeutic stance that uses systems theory is that it requires you to partly relinquish the often bureaucratic, formalised inspectorial role with all its dull paraphernalia of reports, meetings, procedures and legal requirements. Fortunately, this is now a hallmark of the Munro recommendations. These aspects of the social work role are exactly the opposite of what will engage families or parents struggling to survive on income support, in bad housing, with poor health and a raft of emotional and behavioural problems. The negative image conveyed by the trappings of power and officialdom only serves to alienate and distance you from those who are desperate for help and a way out of their difficulties. By immersing yourself in the nitty-gritty of family life (who does what; what causes arguments; how do jobs get allocated; when do children go to bed; why is someone not going to school, etc.) both you and the family can explore new solutions and strategies. By tackling the small issues the family will be able to learn to think and act differently and in so doing will be better equipped and more able to tackle the bigger issues confronting them.

THE INTRINSIC VALUE OF SYSTEMS THEORY AND PRACTICE

The attraction of family therapy and systems theory for many social workers using the techniques or pursuing advanced training to gain formal registration is no more or less than that which can be found for any other method of practice. It will suit some people while also repelling others. Social workers interested in employing therapeutic work with service users and recognising the limitations of working with individuals will find it offers a more comprehensive theoretical knowledge base that can incorporate both elements of the psychosocial paradigm. Family therapy immediately brings into the picture of information gathering and assessment questions about the *context* of the presenting problem. This can appeal to social workers who feel modern managerialist approaches to practice ignore or discount the political, economic and social policy impact on family functioning.

It offers an explanatory tool and conceptual resource with which to give voice to people who are oppressed and victimised by a patriarchal capitalist system. On the other hand, family therapy can offer the most psychodynamically-oriented social worker a theoretical and practical resource with which to explore the micro level of interpersonal transactions within and between kinship relationships that defy straightforward advice and support. Unique techniques such as those mentioned earlier can release bottled-up feelings and promote new conversations between partners or parents and children that were previously repressed or displaced. Self-defeating patterns of behaviour or dangerous acting-out can also be identified and understood in a different context from that of orthodox individual fault and blame explanations.

The advantage here is that in family therapy everyone can be harnessed to tackle the problem/s and with this collective investment everyone can be identified with a positive outcome. In child protection contexts a careful balance has to be struck between the therapeutic potential and a risk assessment. Joint working with another colleague or agency can help, as can your capacity to wear two hats at once provided you have access to good quality supervision. Social workers can therefore properly adopt a different position from that prescribed by the statutory role. By adopting a position of not knowing the solution and committing yourself *with the family* to the search for that solution, you can be released from the burden of dual responsibility that can stymie practice manoeuvrability. This is particularly relevant in the contemporary context of the ethnically rich and culturally diverse society in which myriad family forms, traditions, and beliefs exist. Thus systems theory offers practitioners a vehicle for adopting a partnership and empowering approach which requires the family to be firmly in the driving seat.

THE EVIDENCE BASE

There have been increasing numbers of studies of family therapy attempting to measure the effectiveness of this particular therapeutic intervention since it began to be more comprehensively established in the 1970s (Lask, 1979; Campbell and Draper, 1985; Reimers and Treacher, 1995; Dallos and Draper, 2000). On the whole the evidence is consistent that family therapy is a valuable and effective approach to use in a variety of contexts. Before examining some of the studies to gain some detail about how family therapy helped it needs to be acknowledged that most of the studies have been undertaken in 'clinical' settings: there have been relatively few studies of family therapy employed in social work agency contexts. Indeed generally speaking the valid evidence base for social work interventions is rather thin but it is also improving.

However, even within the confines of clinical practice it is clear that family therapy has now established itself alongside some of the older and more orthodox therapeutic methods and models of intervention as a reliable and acceptable approach. A meta-analysis of the findings of 163 published and unpublished outcome studies on the efficacy and effectiveness of marital and family therapy concluded that the clients did significantly better than untreated control group clients. Based on a substantial literature search of the available research findings recently some clear findings demonstrate (Friedlander, 2001; Goldenberg and Goldenberg, 2004):

- Compared with receiving no treatment, non-behavioural marital/family therapies are effective in two thirds of all cases.
- The efficacy of systemic, behavioural, emotionally-focused, and insight-producing family therapies has been established for marital and adolescent delinquent problems.
- Structural family therapy appears to be particularly helpful for certain childhood and adolescent psychosomatic symptoms.
- There is evidence for the efficacy of family therapy in treating childhood conduct disorders, phobias, anxieties, and in particular autism.

A major review of consumer studies of family therapy and marital counselling analysed various research, including large- and small-scale studies, individual case studies, specific therapeutic methodologies and ethnographic studies (Treacher, 1995). These are particularly valuable sources of evidence because whilst they do not have the same methodological rigour as 'clinical' research studies, they nevertheless reflect a more realistic experience of families in front-line working contexts. The review concluded that practitioners who neglected the service user perspective and undervalued the personal relationship aspects of their family support work in favour of concentrating on inducing change ran the risk of creating considerable dissatisfaction among service users. This reinforced findings from an earlier study into the effectiveness of family therapy which advised that advice and directive work needed to be balanced with reflective and general supportive elements (Howe, 1989). In particular the following conclusions are worth highlighting:

- Families needed an explanation of what the therapy was about and how it differed from regular social service contact.
- Families felt they were being investigated, judged, manipulated and maligned and were unable to discuss the issues they felt were important.

These studies point up the dilemmas faced by social workers trying to employ therapeutic techniques in the context of a statutory remit which often includes a coercive element to family participation as well as an inspectorial/monitoring aspect to the work. Assessment in social work is expected to include a therapeutic element but in the context of determining whether a child is in need or there are child protection concerns, it is understandable if both parents and social workers lose track of the purpose of such assessments. These dilemmas also reflect the time constraints which the Munro Report criticised as imposing artificial timescales which would prove inherently anti-therapeutic. As with similar studies in other health and social care organisations, it is difficult to draw substantive extrapolations from the data examining family therapy in social work practice because these rarely meet the research validity and reliability criteria. Thus attempts to compare findings usually run into methodological problems that will negate any meaningful meta-analysis.

This activity below is experiential in nature which will give you the chance to reflect on any changes that are happening or about to happen in your working context and enable you to develop some strategies for coping.

ACTIVITY

- Reflect on the above information and consider what impact this evidence has on your thinking and feeling about systems theory.
- Make two lists (one positive and the other negative). Discuss these with a colleague/supervisor.

In a sense these findings will confirm the view that attempting to use family therapy approaches in social work needs to be thought through, planned and introduced in a way that best fits with the context of service users. Families who have had regular contact with social service departments regarding child care issues will have learned a number of responses to their patterns of contact with, and relationships towards, social work staff. Parents could also have a perception of social workers as interfering, undermining, nosey parkers which then contextualises their behaviour and communications with them. On the other hand, they could perceive social workers as rescuers, troubleshooters, or mediators between them and difficult teenagers. In either view a number of roles may be prescribed which will affect the emotional dynamics between families and social workers. This could range from parents infantalising themselves, resulting in behaviour that elicits an authoritative/parental response, through to aggressive/hostile behaviour that elicits a compliant or collusive response from the social worker, as has been highlighted in many child death enquiries.

These patterns of interaction need to be thoroughly understood using systems theory in order to figure out the most appropriate way of using a family therapy approach. Fortunately, as a flexible approach, there is a wide range of options to select from as we noted earlier. It is also vital to take account of the natural history and environmental context of children's problems in relation to their developmental stage and acknowledge that there are no standardised ways of measuring childhood functioning. As discussed earlier, many of these classic measures have been based on white Eurocentric models that nowadays are no longer consistent with our culturally inclusive practice. What is consistent in all the major studies is the general absence and rarity of service user evaluations of, and involvement in, the design of child and family research. The implication here is that by enlarging the focus for effectiveness measures it is possible to see children not just with problems but also as having positive and constructive elements in their family lives and building on these and amplifying them wherever possible. They also have much to tell us about how they feel about research into their lives and how methodologies can become more child centred.

This view is echoed in recommendations based on thorough research into interventions targeted at the child, teacher and parent which demonstrate that the combined effect produces the most sustained reduction in conflict problems, both at home and at school, as well as in peer relationships (Webster-Stratton, 1997). Recognising and building on the children's own perspectives provides new opportunities for social work with children and families that would be guided by possibilities which adults are not yet aware of or have failed to pay enough attention to. Thus it is possible to adhere to the Children Act tenets of the paramountcy of every child's welfare whilst also employing a systems theoretical paradigm that permits an effective analysis of children's emotional, psychological and environmental family context.

PART II

DILEMMAS AND CHALLENGES IN APPLYING SYSTEMS THEORY IN PRACTICE

4

PREVENTION AND EARLY INTERVENTION

INTRODUCTION

This chapter seeks to explore and develop preventative work with children and families which should be one of the more noticeable consequences of the Munro reforms. More time spent with vulnerable families means we have a better opportunity to get involved early on and stop situations deteriorating. Relationship-building can begin from a position of supportive involvement rather than within the context of fractious child protection procedures. This will immediately impact on the perception and early impressions parents/carers will get of social workers. When work does become difficult these early impressions will help us get through them. Professionals have great statutory authority/power in their work with carers and children. It is therefore important that this mantle of power is wisely used in order to avoid oppression and abuse.

Practitioners are required to have a critical awareness of government policy and must strike a balance between their authority, the methods for early intervention, and the rights of children and their families. The emphasis in what follows will rest on the importance of our knowledge and understanding of relevant skills, which will enable our work with families to be conducted in a way that builds on strengths and promotes partnership within a framework which seeks to empower and protect every child. By promoting such a partnership you will be empowering parents/carers and thus protecting children. Good practice endeavours to ensure that appropriate interventions are organised to support the child and in the majority of cases the family as well (Walker and Thurston, 2006).

Research on child protection with families (MacDonald, 2002; Buckley, 2003) suggests that the use of certain skills by practitioners is likely to be related to positive outcomes. Effective work is more likely when staff make use of the following skills:

- Helping families to understand the role of child protection workers.
- Working through a problem-solving process which focuses on families' rather than workers' definitions of problems.
- Reinforcing parents' pro-social expressions and actions.

- Making appropriate use of confrontation.
- Fostering a collaborative parent/worker relationship.

Since the financial crisis of 2008 and subsequent change of government as well as the introduction of budget austerity measures, funding for preventive services has been cut: this represents a short-term saving but one with long-term negative consequences for children's welfare.

THE UN CONVENTION ON THE RIGHTS OF THE CHILD 1989

The UK was one of the last countries to sign up to this UN Convention, so Munro's call for social work to be child centred reminds us about the overall social and political context of children's rights and the way in which childhood is constructed. In the United Kingdom's case, the above fact speaks volumes about the society in which children are perceived and the powerless position they were placed in for centuries and remain in many respects. Children's rights to health and overall well-being were first raised as unique and different from those of adults within the Declaration of Geneva (1924) (cited by Corby, 2000): this highlighted the importance of several mainstays to supporting children and young people:

- Welfare.
- The means necessary for normal development.
- Food and medicine.
- Relief in times of stress.
- Protection against exploitation.
- Protection against socialisation to serve others.

The Convention indicates on a human rights basis the rights children ought to enjoy and what the obligations of signatory states must be. Three principles underpin the Convention:

- All the rights covered by the Convention must be available to all children without discrimination of any kind.
- Every child's best interests must be a primary consideration in all actions concerning them.
- Every child's views must be considered and taken into account in all matters affecting them.

In some ways the Convention goes beyond the principles contained in the Children Act 1989. To begin with the Children Act established that courts have to regard children's welfare as the paramount consideration. However, under Article 3 of the Convention children's welfare is a primary consideration across a wider range of settings where decisions about child welfare are made. Therefore decisions about school exclusion or asylum hearings could be appealed under this article. Secondly, Article 19 seeks to protect children from all forms of maltreatment or neglect. This conflicts with the current UK legislation that permits the physical chastisement of children by smacking. Three other main principles enshrined in the UN Convention reinforce the philosophy of safeguarding children and young people:

- Children have unique needs which set them apart from adults.
- The best environment for a child is within a protective and nurturing family.
- Governments and adults in general should be committed to acting in the best interest of the child.

These rights are categorised into general rights to life, expression, information and privacy. More specifically every child should have protective rights against being exploited or abused. Civil rights are also highlighted, including the right to nationality and personal identity as well as the right to stay with the family. Alongside these is an acknowledgment that children should be in an environment that encourages their development and offers them a foundation for welfare (Moules and Ramsey, 1998). Special circumstance rights include children in war zones or other challenging situations where the need for safety must be considered. The Children Act (1989) confirmed many of these ideas in British law and the Children Act 2004 continues this defence of children's rights, including the right to protection from harm and to education, growth, health and wellbeing.

To ensure that child-care professionals are able to follow this through into their support for the family we need to start by defining what is meant by the term 'family'. Each family is unique, however one popular definition suggests that 'The family is a social group characterised by common residence, economic co-operation and reproduction. It includes adults of both sexes, at least two of whom maintain a socially approved sexual relationship, and one or more children, own or adopted, of the sexually co-habitant adults' (Murdock, 1949, cited in Haralambos and Holborn, 1991: 454). The concern with this definition is that it does not relate to family circumstances in the twenty-first century, rather it is a media-contrived idea that is narrowly focused.

The multiplicity of modern family structures is not acknowledged in mainstream discourse: very little recognition is given to gay or lesbian couples with or without children and alongside this there is a lack of realisation that cultural family groups may be cross-generational. The definition could also be seen as paternalistic in that a family is not acknowledged to be complete unless there is a man present and therefore this makes the assumption that lone parents, and especially women, are not able to maintain a family.

The conventional nuclear family makes up only a small number of families in the UK today. The rise in divorce rates, the increased time children and young people have to stay at home, and the number of individuals who prefer to live alone, shatter the traditional definition. Families, then, can be said to be a collection of individuals who contribute to the collection of common characteristics and are accountable for each member of the group. This is greater than their responsibilities to others outside the group and this may or may not be linked to heredity, adoption or marriage (Fulcher and Scott, 1999). On the whole, when exploring how to safeguard children, we can see the child or young person present in a variety of family groups or other systems, usually with responsible adults acting as carers or parents.

The following activity is designed to challenge any pre-conceptions you might have about family structure/organisation, encourage you to be flexible and non-judgemental about the way others live, and prepare you to manage other attitudes among some professionals.

ACTIVITY

- Reflect upon the families that you work with; spend some time highlighting the different styles of family structure.
- Analyse each structure, exploring its strengths and weaknesses. Are there any common themes for the families?

Commentary

> The parenting children receive is a cornerstone for the development of their emotional, interpersonal and social well being. The quality of relationships they form with others, including their own children when they become parents, will be shaped by their care taking experiences. (Reder and Lucey, 1995: 3)

Families may have common themes related to shared budgets and residency, however it is the bond between members which truly reflects the spirit of a family and the desire to support, care for and love each other. Now that the details of what constitutes a family have been explored, it is necessary to discuss how to keep children safe in the wider arena of the community.

'Community' can be defined as a group of individuals who have a common situation, which may be that of class, geographical location, or culture. The people within that community may share common activities, these individuals may have a shared identity which could be related to their culture, religion or sexuality (Fulcher and Scott, 1999). When examining the role of society and its responsibility to safeguard children and young people who are its members, issues will arise around promoting a child-friendly community.

Poverty, poor housing and unemployment all make the situation more challenging not only for the family but also for the local community, both with regard to health and social care. In addition children and young people do not often have the opportunity to express their needs and perceptions (NSPCC, 1996). Since *The Black Report and The Health Divide: Inequalities in Health*, by Townsend, Davidson and Whitehead (1988), and updates by Micklewright and Stewart (2000) and the House of Commons Health Committee (2009), it has been clear that families with less money and education endure more morbidity and higher mortality. This has been related to many concerns, including general lifestyle, health and child protection risk factors.

FACTORS AFFECTING SAFEGUARDING CHILDREN IN THE COMMUNITY

- Lack of social integration.
- Cultural or religious tension.

- Attitudes towards children and young people by the local community.
- Limited awareness of the specific needs of children and young people.
- An imbalance of power.
- Poverty.
- Inconsistent patterns of employment.
- Limited access to services.
- Difficulty in obtaining information, especially if English is not the first language.
- Inadequate transport services, as well as places to play, exercise or socialise.
- Inadequate educational provision.
- High crime rates (especially violent crime).
- The lack of a forum to hear a child's or young person's voice.
- Poor housing provision.
- Neglect, decay and litter in the local environment.

While some of the factors affecting the wellbeing and safety of children require resources, other factors relate to the public's opinions about children and young people, with more emphasis now being placed on enabling children and young people to influence government policy. The creation of the role of Commissioner for Children is meant to progress this aspiration and this may result in a change in the way children's opinions are viewed (Children Act 2004). In order to explore how society and child-care workers in the community can keep children safe and stop abusive situations from occurring prevention needs to be examined and we need to evaluate how it relates to child care.

Both health and child-care professionals can see the need to highlight the different levels of prevention required, confirming that the prevention of abuse is the ideal solution but if this is not obtainable then early detection and intervention is the next best thing. Intervention is the practice of coming between or interacting with other humans. Trevithick (2005: 6) described it as:

> the purposeful actions we undertake as professionals in a given situation, based on knowledge and understanding we have acquired, the skills we have learned and the values we adopt. The process that occurs during intervention therefore utilises our skills and experience to enhance our professional practice.

While it has been commonly acknowledged within health and social care settings that interventions are required, there are commonly three levels of prevention that will support the process: primary, secondary, and tertiary. Smith (1999: 129) cites Fuller (1991), who describes the levels as:

> primary prevention would prevent the emergence of a problem, secondary prevention would refer to working on a problem in its early stages and tertiary prevention would limit the damaging effects of a problem already established.

Hardiker et al. (1991) also acknowledge a fourth level, arguing that the secondary level can be separated into mild and easily supported risk situations as well as more serious situations which may require more intensive long-term support and this needs to be contained, whereas a fourth level would encompass work undertaken with a child when they are under the care of the local authority. Therefore all four levels would need to be defined and explored and then related to ways to safeguard children.

Primary prevention can be seen to work at the societal level: this offers universal services, acknowledging the general needs of the population and influencing individuals and families to make positive lifestyle decisions. This can be promoted via media campaigns and encouraging individuals to protect the wellbeing of themselves and their families. It can include advice on education, health and employment and may reduce the risk of families requiring more specialist services (Hardiker et al., 1991; Moules and Ramsay, 1998; Smith, 1999; Wilson and James, 2002).

EXAMPLES OF PRIMARY PREVENTION

Self-help groups

Community project working with children and families

Good quality day-care

School-based activities

Universal financial benefits for children (family allowance)

Family tax credit

NHS Direct

Good quality social housing

Easy access to health care

Easy access to local government and library services

Family centres

Literacy and parenting classes

Strong links between schools and the local community

Guidance services linked to schools, hospitals and health centres

Organised play or leisure activities (especially during school holidays)

Well-resourced preschool nursery provision (Rising 4 programmes)

The following activity encourages you to perceive the depth and breadth of the community in which you practise and to foster collaborative interprofessional work.

ACTIVITY

- Compile a list of the useful primary preventive resources you can access in the community you work in.
- Highlight the most popular resources used.
- Compare these services and find the similarities that make these services popular.

Services that do not appear to have a secondary function, and especially those around surveillance, will be more popular as families may not feel comfortable if they believe the details they submit may be used for more intrusive purposes. With programmes such as SureStart this acknowledgement will have been given to the issues surrounding poverty and the effect these can have on an entire family.

Secondary prevention is normally understood as early detection and short-term intervention where children and families are offered more focused support from professionals involving home visiting, clinics and counselling. Browne (2002: 61) states 'such professionals can be instructed to screen routinely all families who come into contact with the service they are providing and identify predictive characteristics'. While predictive factors can be difficult when trying to confirm the potential for abuse, some tools have had more success than others. Post Natal Depression (PND) is a general depressive disorder that includes symptoms of clinical depression. These can result in tearfulness, insomnia, difficulties in eating, mood swings and general apathy. If a mother's resources and support are inadequate they may not have the emotional ability to be patient when their baby cries continually or will not sleep.

What has been agreed on by all the professionals is that the earlier a detection of PND occurs, the more successful the outcome will be for both mother and child (Murray, 1997). One predictive tool developed which has been shown to be appropriate is the Edinburgh Postnatal Depression Scale (E.P.D.S.), where the mother grades herself on how she feels emotionally following the birth of her baby. The use of tools such as the E.P.D.S. seems a valid method of assessment which encourages awareness and helps to empower the mother rather than labelling her as mentally ill. However, the assessment and subsequent score which highlights the presence of depression will only be successful if they lead to support, either in the form of individual counselling or through group support. Women who are nervous about admitting to PND, and fearful of being referred to social workers by health visitors who are concerned about safeguarding, may disguise their symptoms and answer the E.P.D.S. falsely in order to avoid intrusive and undermining attention from child protection social workers.

EXAMPLES OF SECONDARY PREVENTION

Parenting helplines

Home visits

Child surveillance clinics

Drug and alcohol programmes

Anger management programmes

Parental support programmes in the home

Youth services

Parent support groups

Child development programmes

Community mothers' programmes

Parent training programmes

Preschool programmes

Duty services to provide rapid response

Family centres and support services

Counselling individually or in groups

For secondary preventive work to be successful it has to occur in a supportive environment rather than in isolation, so dealing with a child's behaviour difficulties would not be so successful if their family's circumstances were ignored. MacDonald (2002) comments that short-term solutions may often produce good results, however for some families the intervention may require further input, especially when parents are learning new skills in order to support their child. In addition, as a child becomes older different skills will need to be learnt: this is especially true for parents who have learning disabilities and will need long-term support and are thus more likely to have their child removed.

Tertiary prevention is described as an increased level of input over a longer period of time when it has been proven that abuse has occurred and especially as regards more complex and long-term difficulties within a family. The idea here will be to stop the worst effects happening to the child and to avoid, if possible, placing that child in care. Individual work with a child and their family may still produce positive outcomes, however these interventions will require commitment on the part of both the child-care professional and the child and their family to stay the course. The best interests of the child in legal terms and local government and work practices will enable a model to function which focuses on the child and family while still being accountable for the long-term outcomes.

EXAMPLES OF TERTIARY PREVENTION

Play therapy
Cognitive behavioural therapy
Parent training
Group and individual work for parents
Direct work with children focusing on the abuse
Abuse specific programmes for the child and non-offending parent
Brief focused casework
Short-term fostering

Respite care
Utilisation statutory framework
Task-centred casework
Family Centres with focused work by centre workers
Family therapy
Family case conference
Family support groups
Refuges

MacDonald (2002) highlights high attrition rates and the inconsistency of the research undertaken within this area as presenting a problem in determining how successful these supportive services have proven to be in the long run. Alongside this is the reality that the longer you leave a child in an abusive environment the more likelihood there will be that the effect will be greater on their emotional wellbeing. Therefore there needs to be a clear time-frame for when the intervention is deemed to have been unsuccessful and the child must be removed from that environment.

The activity that follows aims to focus your attention on the bureaucratic and professional boundaries that can hamper effective child protection work.

- Find a copy of your job description and reflect upon which parts of your practice are undertaken at a primary, secondary, or tertiary level. Consider any areas you are working in where you may be able to start preventive work earlier.
- If you are working at the primary preventive level, how can you utilise services and child-care practitioners at the higher levels to reduce the risk of progression for the children and families you work with?

Commentary

The focus for individual child-care workers may be based around a particular level of intervention, however by working together in an integrated way it should be possible to offer more opportunities for families to access services before a crisis intervention is required. This could be in the guise of offering social service advice and guidance on benefit entitlements, etc. at a mum and toddler group arranged by a health visitor, or youth workers from Connexions could attend a senior school assembly to showcase the services they offer, or family planning practitioners could perhaps be present at a baby clinic for example. The permutations are endless here, with the main aim being to provide families with some opportunities to ask for help on their terms before a professional intrusion becomes a necessity.

While exploring prevention and the different levels of intervention, various beliefs surrounding the types of intervention need to be acknowledged. While health workers on the whole will wish to prevent or reduce the effect of illness or disability, a social care worker will focus on the needs of an individual and attempt to reduce the risk of a family breakdown. Culturally sensitive approaches also take on board the wishes and views of ethnic groups when planning services (Chapter 8 explores this further).

A combination of these perspectives will ensure that the appropriate intervention for a child and their family will take on board the risk to that child's health, disability, family function and cultural diversity. Now that a clear understanding of levels of preventive work has been explored, some reflection is required on the individual skills and practices that can be undertaken to promote the physical, psychological and social wellbeing of the child and their family.

EARLY INTERVENTION SKILLS

Social workers need to possess formal knowledge/technical skills which they will begin to develop during training and when newly qualified. New policies are now in place to help NQSWs to have a planned, controlled caseload that has been designed to maximise their learning and confidence and maintain their safeguarding priorities. Social workers, and this is probably also the case among most professionals involved in the care of children and young people, have to be able to manage their own work and time schedules which can change dramatically, fluctuate, and involve intense periods of stress and anxiety.

Good interpersonal skills with children, young people and their families are a pre-requisite but these cannot be learned from a dry textbook or even with excellent practice supervision during training. Time and continuous professional development (CPD) are critical in this and another powerful expectation voiced within the Munro reforms. These developing skills should be harnessed to offer help and advice in a non-patronising, non-judgemental way that is consistent with social work ethics and values. However, under strong workload pressures, personal anxiety and poor supervision it is not surprising that our best intentions can fail. Self-awareness and proper non-administrative supervision should provide a safe place in which we may explore our vulnerabilities and spot signs of stress.

Being able to teach, model, or guide parents, children or junior colleagues is a skill that will develop naturally and be part of our interpersonal work where unconscious or subtle communication takes place. Having some problem-solving abilities is helpful here but not to the point where we begin to undermine parents or colleagues. It is more a case of examining all the possibilities that are open to us, even the most unlikely, and considering their potential (Trevithick, 2005):

- To be able to utilise reflection both during interventions with families and afterward in order to continue to improve our practice.
- To be able to make appropriate arrangements to care and support a family.
- To establish clear priorities so that time is spent with a family to enable them to feel empowered in a partnership with child-care practitioners.
- To listen actively to a family and respond appropriately, remaining calm and trying to contain anxiety even when others are showing signs of distress.
- To be able to develop and draw upon a network of other child-care professionals when necessary and to reciprocate as and when requested to do so.
- To have an understanding of an individual family's coping strategies.
- When the situation requires it to use counselling skills (referring to a counsellor if more input is required).
- To be an advocate for a child and interpret complex situations as necessary.
- To manage professional boundaries, constructively challenging and acknowledging the need for supervision.

The following activity has been designed to enhance your continuous professional development and enable you to progress your reflective practitioner skills.

- Drawing from the list above highlight which skills you use most often.
- Reflect upon any areas that you need to work to improve.
- Develop some strategies to employ these more frequently and imaginatively and ensure that you are able to use your skills to the best of your ability.

Commentary

All child-care practitioners will endeavour to place children centrally, both within their work and during time spent with colleagues discussing the children and young people under their care. Encouraging children and families to be empowered is a way to enhance their lives and reduce the risk of abuse. In the normal run of events planned play for a child sets up that child for grown-up gender responsibility. Play thus acts as a rehearsal of ways to behave in real-life situations and within its construction the development of empowerment (Skidmore, 1994). However, many children and families will have learnt helplessness which will cause them to become powerless.

This may be due to the view they hold of child-care professionals, especially if communication is a problem, or it could be related to their fear of the unknown and therefore a reliance on others to take responsibility. Families can learn to become helpless because events have occurred outside their control such as unemployment or disability, or because their previous experience has shown them that any action they take will not rectify the situation (Bentovim, 2002; Ruch, 2009).

This notion of learned helplessness appears to be related more to people who express the view that negative things occur because they are incompetent rather than an external force causing the problem. People who are more able to work through the helpless phase will be aware both that the event occurred and that it was outside of their control. If we relate this to children who are at risk in the community, a child could believe that they caused the abuse. If this is the case they will need to be supported to work through their feelings in order to understand they are not to blame and can start to acknowledge that there are ways to become empowered.

Skidmore (1994) advises practitioners to help children and their families to find areas in their lives that they can control and to encourage each child and family to make well-informed decisions about their future. This has to be seen as a reciprocal relationship where the child-care practitioner is able to let go of their power and the child/young person and their family have a desire to take up that power.

While persuasion may be a useful tool any attempt to force a person to take up this reasonability will prove more disempowering than the situation that individual may have originally been in. The way forward is to work in partnership with children and their families at all levels of prevention. This ability to work in partnership enables

(Cont'd)

the family to decide on their level of input, for the parents and the child themselves to acknowledge their rights. Not only that, the boundaries will become more flexible, enabling the child-care worker to move in and out of the arena of care as the family requires.

In order for us to work closely and satisfactorily with families we require good communication skills: to work as advocates demands that we are able to negotiate with other members of the inter-professional team, which once again requires communication and co-operation. Finally, empowering children and families means having sufficient awareness to give information freely and thereby to ensure there is informed decision making. In short, good interpersonal skills are the lubricant which enables the inter-agency team to function successfully for and on behalf of children.

REVIEWING THE WORK PROCESS

Reviews are everybody's business: they are not the responsibility of a particular child protection professional or agency and they should involve children and parents as much as possible, consistent with the particular circumstances and needs of every child as emphasised in the Children Act 1989 and the Human Rights Act 1998. Reviews should not be considered unusual or convened in haste in order to allocate blame when things go wrong. They should be regarded as routine and no less important than any other part of the child protection process. They must also relate and link explicitly to the current child protection plan.

The way in which reviews and endings are thought about will affect the attitudes and behaviours of everyone involved in child protection cases. A review might be thought of as an ending in itself, as a way of taking stock and summarising the work to date so that a neat ending can be arrived at. If practitioners feel this way then they may inadvertently close their minds to new information or changed circumstances that would suggest further involvement. If on the other hand a review is considered as a staging post in a journey where evidence can be weighed, evaluated and compared against baseline data recorded at the start of an intervention, then it ought to be seen as a temporary punctuation. In the context of safeguarding children a review must examine the existing child protection plan and measure any progress (or the lack of it) against just that. The purpose of the review will be to ensure:

- that action plans, programmes, targets, aims and objectives are being kept to;
- that the work involved is consistent with participants' personal expectations in terms of values, ethics, the paramount safety of children and the commitment to family welfare;

- it examines the child protection plan and assesses whether each person is carrying out their part of it within the agreed timescale;
- it determines whether the intended results of an intervention have occurred according to the identified outcomes for each service or action in terms of its impact on a child's needs;
- the review complies with agency policy, practices and administrative structures;
- that best practice guidance, research, and national and international legislation is used to inform, but not to detract from, making judgements.

There should be no assumptions about the outcome of a review beforehand and practitioners and parents will need to approach these with any prejudices or preferences put to one side. Self-fulfilling prophecies do happen and the need to close what might be a messy, unhappy and wearing case riddled with uncertainty and frustration could be powerful. The review itself need not be a formal meeting of several professionals as part of statutory requirements: it could be an informal reflective process undertaken by the worker themselves as part of their own self-management. This could mark the beginning of a subtle process that could continue in the form of a semi-formal review with a headteacher, supervisor or senior nurse for example, in which evaluations and assumptions could be safely tested and examined within a supportive relationship. A review could also be more formal within the context of inter-agency meetings or case conferences, where written and verbal reports will be collated, minutes will be recorded, and specific decisions and action plans will be formulated.

The common theme in each of these review contexts will be that they are understood *as part of a process* rather than an event, and that the review must be explicitly related to the plan for the children and the intended outcomes in relation to their needs. Practitioners and parents will need to focus sharply on whether actions, services and interventions are having the desired effect: for example, a health visitor may be helping a parent to improve their interactions with a very young child in order to achieve certain developmental milestones; a teacher and educational psychologist may be working with an older child to improve their classroom behaviour; or a housing official may be attempting to advocate for larger accommodation in order to relieve family stress and enable older children to experience greater privacy by having their own bedrooms.

Each practitioner in addition to evaluating their own contribution must consider the impact this is having on other interventions. The review might assume a level of co-ordination and complementarity between interventions but in reality a particular combination might prove contradictory: for example, an educational welfare officer might be aiming to improve school attendance in order to enable a withdrawn child to improve their social skills and self-esteem, but a child and adolescent psychotherapist might assess this child as phobic and unable in the short term to cope with an enforced return to school. This contradiction could be highlighted in a review where agreement on the way forward could be negotiated with amendments being made to the current plan. Table 4.1 illustrates

Table 4.1 Changes required to the current child protection plan (as agreed at the review meeting) (DH, 2002)

Identified child's developmental needs and strengths and difficulties in each domain	How will the child's developmental needs be responded to: *actions or services to be taken/provided*	Frequency and length of service: *e.g. hours per week*	Person/ Agency responsible	Date service will commence/ commenced	Date service completed *(if appropriate)*	Planned outcomes: *progress to be achieved by next review or other specified date*
Child's developmental needs						
Parenting capacity						
Family and environmental factors						

how the Integrated Children's System can be used to identify any specific changes that need to be made to the current plan, thereby avoiding duplication and divergent tasks.

This circular process of assessment, planning, intervention and review is common to all practitioners but in child protection work, because of a variety of factors, reviews and endings will tend to impose an artificial finality on the process – as Munro discovered. This can be due to the need to cease an unwelcome involvement by professionals; to make decisions regarding registration/de-registration; to reach conclusions regarding a risk assessment; or a move to reduce the delay in placement decisions. These factors combined with high workloads impose a timescale on contact between families and practitioners that can serve to heighten anxiety, increase pressures, and neglect the critically important issues around review and closure that will require just as much attention as the earlier processes of screening, investigation and assessment. For example, earlier research (Farmer and Owen, 1995) showed that:

- reviews that highlighted areas of risk previously overlooked often failed to influence senior managers who were expected to make the necessary decisions;
- once a pattern of case management had been established this was usually endorsed at subsequent reviews, even when it was deficient.

The assumption at many case conferences will be that a case can be closed because a child's name has been removed from the child protection register. This is however a false and potentially fatal assumption. The focus should always be on the child and their needs: a child is likely to still be defined as a child in need and as requiring on-going help. The evidence strongly suggests that such de-registration often results in a withdrawal of the very resources that were maintaining a child's safety and the essential support required by many families.

A combination of worker impatience to close cases and parents' desire to avoid scrutiny could jeopardise an opportunity to establish healthy trusting relationships and pave the way for family support intervention that will better safeguard children's safety in the long run. So why is this so? Partly it is a question of resources, but it is equally and perhaps more importantly about the way child protection and family support are perceived as separate areas of work rather than seamless parts of a continuous process.

'It didn't bother me either way, whether they kept her name on it or took it off. I was just more concerned with getting some help and getting things sorted out.' (Parent quoted in Farmer and Owen, 1995: 288)

'Support needs to last for a long time. Contact and support needs to be kept up so if the child or young person needs help in the future, they'll know where to go/who to see and they won't be back to Square One.' (Parent quoted in DfES, 2003a)

CHANGE AND OUTCOMES

Reviews should be seen as part and parcel of the process of change. The review itself aims to establish what if anything has altered in a family's situation. Changes can take place in people's behaviours, perceptions and feelings. The act of reviewing may also in itself provoke changes: it can serve to motivate families to try harder or plunge them into despair and hopelessness. In other words, it is not just an administrative or procedural exercise. It is crucial that everyone understands the feelings and dynamics generated during reviews and before endings because these can inform their understanding of the work at hand. This applies just as much to families as to workers. Certain feelings may provoke false hope or equally false fears, leading to actions that will be unsupported by hard evidence. A variety of responses to the prospect of change may be detected at this point: for example, a worker and parent/carer might both feel:

- *relief* at the prospect of some decision being made;
- *guilt* at the need for a review due to plans failing;
- *sadness* at the potential for loss;
- *confusion* at the mixed messages being given;
- *anxiety* at the negative consequences;
- *anger* at feeling judged;
- *happiness* at knowing something is going to happen;
- *ambivalence* at wanting help but not what is being offered.

Parents can often feel abandoned once a child is assessed as not at risk of significant harm, yet this is probably the most important time to continue work to support them and help build those skills necessary to meet their child's developmental needs. It is equally crucial that practitioners in supervisory or conference contexts are aware of the impact that powerful feelings are having on their judgement. What do these feelings tell us about the way a family is managing the protection of the child/ren of concern? If there is a great deal of anxiety in the professional system and does this mirror the same feelings in the family that is facing the withdrawal of a professional involvement? Understanding these complex processes can enable workers to reflect back on the plan and the previously identified needs of the child/ren to see whether a change has occurred, to what degree this has happened, and if it is being sustained (Walker and Thurston, 2006).

Until 2008 the issue of removing a child from the old child protection register used to represent an important official indicator of improved child protection, a reduction of risk and by implication a greater safeguarding of children. However, research has demonstrated that in 17 per cent of cases where de-registration had occurred due to a change in the official perception of risk, there was no real improvement in child safety. A deterioration in risk factors also occurred in 11 per cent of de-registered cases. Evidence of the ambivalence and ambiguity surrounding endings was revealed in 20 per cent of cases, with parents being unclear over whether their children's names had been removed from the register or not (Farmer and Owen, 1995). Meanwhile a meta-review of risk assessment instruments designed to predict future child maltreatment only served to stigmatise parents and demonstrated poor levels of accuracy and reliability (Peters and Barlow, 2003).

In addition the evidence demonstrates that it is common for the needs of the main carer to be neglected in child protection work (Brandon et al., 2008). Parental needs tend to go unmet when important areas of difficulty remain unrecognised, such as domestic violence, drug and alcohol abuse, and children's mental health needs, or because of parental alienation during the investigative child protection process. Where parental needs *are* recognised, however, children's needs are in danger of being sidelined when parents are the main focus of intervention. In effectively safeguarding children we should aim to include both parties rather than constructing a false and dangerous dichotomy between the two.

> 'You stop being violent – hurting yourself or someone else. You don't need to cry for help – but that doesn't mean you don't still need support.' (Parent quoted in CRE, 2003).

This jeopardises the future prospects for children's safety, especially when their developmental needs go unmet when reviews focus on incidents of abuse rather than taking an ecological and developmental approach. For example, there may be an absence of incidents of abuse in the period under review but the harm inflicted could still be happening in terms of missed developmental milestones, weight loss, poor school attainment, disturbed behaviour or a lack of social contact. It is vital to consider the wider picture and not rely on a limited range of indicators.

Organisational needs do impact negatively on service delivery in relation to safeguarding children. Workload stresses, targets, inspections, unallocated cases, plus unexpected illnesses or vacancy covering might increase the pressure to close a case that parents would prefer to remain open. The review process should identify the expected outcomes to an intervention plan that will then provide concrete measures for evaluating whether or not an ending is feasible.

Managers in all agencies taking the decision to close cases now have more explicit accountability in child protection work, which while leaving individual workers feeling less vulnerable should also act as a prompt to ensure that alternative services are put in place. Every individual involved needs to consider what part they can play in continuing to focus on meeting the needs of the child. And while the ending may feel abrupt for a family all concerned must ensure that an ending meeting with the family is undertaken in a way that enables and actively encourages them to seek further help if this is needed. Staff in schools, nurseries, health centres and family centres can be crucial here by supporting and encouraging parents at this time. The balance between imposing a support structure and motivating the family to ask for this will be reflected by the degree to which they are reluctant or more enthusiastic about receiving help and support.

CASE CLOSURE

The criteria for leaving the child protection system are not well defined for workers or families. It is important to understand that leaving the child protection system is not the same as closing a case. Parents may expect no further contact and be confused when told they will still be receiving help. This can provoke feelings of persecution in parents and stress in staff trying to evaluate issues of safety, risk and on-going support. It is critical in these circumstances to maintain a focus on children's needs. Health visitors, for example, will often occupy the pivotal role of maintaining a continuing involvement throughout the various phases of child protection and family support interventions. A systems approach can enable us to remain connected.

The evidence from previous child abuse enquiries suggests that it is in cases where the focus on the children's developmental needs has been lost where there is a risk of further abuse or death (Laming, 2003; Fawcett et al., 2004). Therefore the planning to end a contact should commence at the beginning of contact when solid baseline data can be established upon which both you and the family can measure any progress, or the lack of it, towards clear outcomes. The following questions may be helpful in this:

- How will the family know that your presence in their life has been useful and that the family is better off now than before the child protection involvement?
- How will the parents know that the family has reached the point where its members feel capable of going on without you?
- How will the family know they have reached the point where they can conduct their own lives without you and the child/ren will be safe?

Such planning needs to be handled especially carefully when dealing with families where child protection concerns have been raised but have subsequently proved to be unfounded. Getting the balance right here is tricky. Openness and clarity should be the hallmark of your involvement but not to the extent where a child's safety may be put at risk. Deciding when and how much information can be shared will depend on a fine risk assessment and the judgement of all practitioners involved. Parents will rightly feel upset and angry that they have been excluded to some extent but this should all be planned for in advance (Walker and Thurston, 2006).

A careful explanation of the reasons for your actions, combined with documentary evidence that any allegations that were unfounded have been officially recorded, will go some way to easing their distress. It is crucial to ensure that the family is not labelled and work is undertaken to rebuild trust so that they will feel able to use the services that are open to them in future. However, even disproved cases and unfounded suspicions may need to be considered in a future intervention because not all disproved cases will necessarily mean children are safe. Table 4.2 illustrates how a closure record might look so that in the event of a family transferring to another area the receiving agencies can instantly see where their responsibilities fall in terms of the current plan.

Table 4.2 Summary of interventions and actual outcomes from the date of the most recent referral

Child/young person's identified developmental needs, strengths and difficulties	Actions and services provided: both planned and unplanned services and actions	Frequency and length of service: e.g. hours per week	Person/agency responsible	Date services commenced	Planned outcome: progress to be achieved during the course of social services involvement	Date services ended	Actual outcome: progress made, reason services ended or were not provided
Child/young person's health							
Child/young person's education							
Child/young person's emotional and behavioural development							
Child/young person's identity							
Child/young person's family and social relationships							
Child/young person's social presentation							
Child/young person's self-care skills							
Parental capacity							
Family and environmental factors							

Researchers have found that clients believed that decisions on whether to remove children, when children will be returned home, what they need to do before their children are returned and when workers will make monitoring visits, were all made with no understandable logic or proper explanation (Berg and Kelly, 2000). This leads to adversarial, coercive and non-productive encounters that will cause a battle of wills to ensue that will be to no-one's benefit. Small attainable goals that include solutions rather than an absence of problems will help to instil feelings of success that can be built upon to achieve outcomes. For example, nursery staff could show a parent how developmental changes such as increased language skills can be attributed to them playing more with the child, or a teacher could praise a parent whose child is behaving less disruptively in class as a sign of their improved parenting skills.

Setbacks in child protection plans are normal and should be expected and planned for. Unrealistic goals that fail to be attained undermine confidence and contribute to a spiral of disillusion and discouragement. For example, evidence suggests that parenting classes have high drop-out rates due to staff incompetence and inappropriate referrals and therefore it should never be assumed that dropping-out means a parent is not committed to change or the protection of their child (NFPI, 2010). We must remember that change is hard and this is especially the case with long-term, entrenched problems. Here are a few strategies to help you respond to setbacks (after Berg and Kelly, 2000):

- *Keep hopeful*: chronic difficulties take time to respond to help and setbacks are part of the process of change.
- *There is no magic pill*: the harder you and the family struggle, the sweeter the taste of success will be.
- *Ask how the parent stopped when they did*: rather than focusing on the setback behaviour, ask why it did not get worse, last longer, or be more destructive. In other words, emphasise the control exercised by the parent and build upon that.
- *Ask how this setback was different from the last one*: find out the tiny details and distinctions between events and how the family decided to end the setback this time, then decide whether it is worth repeating this as a tactic.
- *Each setback is a learning opportunity*: find out how the family intends to incorporate this new information into their life. Be specific here.
- *Review the difference that achieving a parent's goal will make to their life*: what would the children notice was different? Who will be the first to notice that the parent is making changes to their behaviour?
- *Help the parent to assess their progress*: use scaling questions for this, such as where the parent would place themselves on a 1–10 scale where 10 equals meeting the agreed goal and 1 equals the point at which you both started working together.

Reviews and endings are the occasions (like beginnings) that can set the tone for future contact and activity. Conducted properly, openly and honestly, these offer an opportunity for everyone to be clear about their responsibilities and the consequences of not contributing towards their part of the protection plan. Evaluating that plan effectively and drawing reasonable conclusions from it will depend on everyone's judgement and opinions about the relative importance attached to a variety of factors. A positive factor may be judged to outweigh several negatives and vice versa. Keeping all the lines of communication open is crucial here, not just when there is agreement but when there is disagreement as well. Families never stand still and positive changes may occur regardless of planned interventions. Negative changes can also happen in spite of interventions that are aimed at helping. Be alert to these events and ready to respond flexibly, creatively and decisively. Never forget how hard being a parent and safeguarding children are.

5

CHILDREN AND YOUNG PEOPLE AT RISK

INTRODUCTION

In this chapter consideration will be given to the issues that social workers need to be mindful of and must examine in order to offer a service that is both supportive of the child and their family and ensures that that child's needs and safety remain centre-stage. This will be in terms of the child who suffers abuse as well as children who abuse or become young offenders. Each child is unique and therefore, as Munro confirms, blanket policies and procedures will not support every child. Rather, a focused approach is required that acknowledges a child's right to access holistic and optimum growth and development within a systems perspective.

Children therefore primarily need to feel safe enough to communicate with professionals, which may lead to issues of confidentiality for the parents/carers living with a child. What follows is a menu of resources focused on risk where information will be provided to enable practitioners to enhance their skills, which may then support an investigation of concerns raised about a child's physical, emotional, cognitive, social, and spiritual health. At the same time, a systems approach will offer a different context from the orthodox, narrowly defined tick-box approach to risk assessment, with all its time constraints that work against rather than with practitioners' intuitive skills and families' own capacity to engage with social work services.

An increase in professional interest during the last century in children's wellbeing has led to an examination of every aspect of children's lives. Foucault viewed this extensive interest in people's lives as a 'clinical gaze' (Smart, 1992). While this had already emerged earlier in the century with the public health movement, it was perhaps in the early 1970s that the ideas surrounding children's emotional issues came sufficiently to the fore with the result that professionals examined not only their physical and intellectual development but also their psychological wellbeing (Walker and Thurston, 2006).

As a result of this interest producing a clear picture of what the 'normal' child developmental progression should be at every age, using quantifiable analysis, meant children on the edge of normality came under increasing scrutiny. Paradoxically the more defined this picture became the greater was the increase in the numbers of children and families who were continuously monitored. The positive benefits of this meant that children's problems could be resolved earlier through early interventions. The negative aspect to this has been an over-standardisation of what was held to be 'good enough parenting'. As Munro has argued, the child protection system has become so overwhelmed with templates, procedures, impractical databases and bureaucracy that these actually make it more difficult to detect child abuse.

REASONS FOR ABUSE

When discussing child abuse and how to protect children and young people it is important to touch upon the various views on why abuse occurs. There are three main groups of perspectives surrounding the theories of abuse (Kay, 1999; Calder and Horwath, 1999; Corby, 2000; Wilson and James, 2002).

- *Psychological theories* focus on the instinctive and psychological qualities of the individuals who abuse. This approach argues that there is some innate characteristic within an individual which places them at greater risk of abusing, their motivation being linked to biological or instinctive features of human behaviour. Child abuse may also be seen to be the result of the deprived learning experiences of a carer which might lead to inadequate controlling techniques when trying to manage children's behaviour.
- *Social psychological theories* focus on the dynamics of interactions between the abuser, the child, and their immediate environment. This approach appears to be positioned between focusing on the individual and broader social factors and therefore how that individual is able to relate to their immediate environment is seen as the cornerstone for these perspectives. While explanations are given to the relationships within the family, individuals are often seen in isolation and separated from the wider social influences and stresses. As a result, the political and wider social implication in the deterioration of neighbourhoods or social networks is often ignored (Kay, 1999; Corby, 2000; Wilson and James, 2002).
- *Sociological perspectives* emphasise social conditions and the political climate as the principal reason for the existence of child abuse and neglect. Feminist theorists highlight the strong connection between abuse which is overwhelmingly perpetrated by males against females and the patriarchal gender power disparity in society. Exploring the sociological perspective of child abuse is unsettling as it raises the issue of safeguarding children and young people to the level of society rather than the individual. This includes professional child-care workers who, when acknowledging this approach, can feel that the daily intervention which they offer to families is often not enough to support family stress. This can lead to frustration as the worker cannot remove the family from poverty or the challenging social environment.

While all these main groups have strengths and weaknesses each approach on its own is unable to fully encompass the reasons for the occurrence of child abuse. Corby (2000) cites the Ecological Framework (Belsky, 1980) as a four-level approach that recognises these different perspectives and how they interlink with each other. This is not dissimilar to a systems framework and is yet another resource you may draw from in your work. Thus as we saw in Chapter 3 in Figure 3.1:

- The *Ontogenic* (inner) *circle* explores what the individual parent or carer brings to their interaction with the child.
- The *Microsystem* in the next ring highlights how members of the family interact with each other.
- The *Exosystem* investigates how the family interacts within the immediate environment.
- The *Macrosystem* in the outer ring acknowledges the broader factors such as society's view on poverty and welfare and the impact this may have on the family.

Appreciating the way these different systems interact with each other enables child-care professionals to offer support that is not just targeted towards the individual level for a child and their family, but also support that can incorporate the broader requirements that that family and the local community may have, including the need for appropriate housing, better street lighting, community centre or medical care.

GENERAL RISK FACTORS

To embark on an exploration of how children and young people can be at risk a clear understanding is required of risk and the factors involved. The media are sometimes responsible for encouraging the belief that all children are at risk as soon as they emerge from their home environments. While it may be the case that children are abused by strangers it should be acknowledged that they are *more vulnerable to abuse within their home environments* by known male relatives than they are in the street. However, as Rogers (2003) highlighted in her report for the National Family and Parenting Institute, when commentating on the government policy surrounding children and young people at risk, there are difficulties in defining a child at risk whether they are in the street or in their home environment.

A child at risk may present in a similar fashion to their peers, both in relation to physical appearance and mental wellbeing, and therefore may be difficult to assess. In reality, abuse usually occurs in an environment that a child is familiar with, whether this is within the home, school, or indeed their local community. Therefore all professionals, regardless of their work setting, need to be aware of the risk factors involved. A child or young person can be at risk of abuse by male family members or family friends, but for some children and young people their peers may be the ones carrying out the abuse, or that child or young person may be an abuser themselves, or they may place themselves in danger by willingly taking part in risk-taking behaviour. It therefore becomes crucial initially to explore the risk factors which may produce circumstances within the family and local community that will result in an inability to safeguard children and young people. The following risk factors have been adapted from Rogers (2003) and Gregg (1995).

SPECIFIC RISK FACTORS

Family violence/abuse

Drug or alcohol abuse (child or parent)

Changes in family structure

Parenting difficulties

Poor parenting history

Unwanted pregnancy (difficult birth)

Family conflict

Child living away from home

Child or parental disabilities (including learning disabilities)

Child or parental mental illness

Changes in family finances

Physical environment and accommodation

Availability of services

Attitude of local community towards child and family

Child or family isolation (either geographically or culturally)

Poverty

These risk factors provide a broad outlook and only offer potential features, which may lead a child or young person to be at risk of abuse, carrying out the abuse of others, or indeed undertaking risk-taking behaviour. When reflecting on ways to safeguard children and young people a consideration of the accumulative effects is required. It is also worth noting that while risk and protective factors and clear assessment frameworks can offer guidance to child-care professionals when supporting children, it is difficult to draw up a photo-fit picture of what an abuser may look like and their background.

Some families who have accumulated a number of factors may in consequence be unable to fully care and support their children. However, it is also the case that for other families there can appear to be no predisposing factors. Kay (1999: 15) comments that 'there are no prescriptions for detecting that child abuse will take place in any particular family, but it may be that these factors can be taken in conjunction with other information to help identify the vulnerable families who may need support'.

The activity that follows will prompt you to understand how external factors are just as important as internal factors in child protection and put yourself in the shoes of other professionals involved in the safeguarding system.

- Spend time reflecting on the community and families you work with, highlighting both the general and the environmentally specific factors which may lead to children and young people being at risk.
- Would this list contain different risk factors if a colleague from a different agency or organisation undertook this activity?

ACTIVITY

Commentary

When exploring the record you have compiled it will be worthwhile to remember that this is also a potential list. Some children and families may live through and survive emotional, physical, or financial traumas with their family life intact, while other families may not be able to endure relatively minor changes in family circumstances. This can be due to the number of resilience factors an individual or family may have. Werner (2000: 116), when exploring studies which have investigated the concept, defined resilience 'as an end product or buffering process that does not eliminate risks and stress but that allows the individual to deal with them effectively'.

She goes on to cite Garmezy et al. (1984) who surmised that there were three main mechanisms which enabled these protective factors to occur. *Compensation* offers a framework where stress and protective factors counterbalance each other and personal qualities and support can outweigh the stress. *Challenge* as a protective mechanism, highlights the strength that a moderate amount of stress can add to levels of competence. Finally *immunity*, as the protective factors within the child or their environment, moderates the impact of the stress on the child and they then adapt to the changing environment with less trauma. These models are not mutually exclusive, rather they can work together or in sequence depending on the age and stage of a child's development. A health visitor, youth worker, community police officer, school nurse, or CAMHS worker may identify other risk factors in the community, or if these are similar they might rank them in a different order of priority concern. And while there are a number of specific protective factors, these may vary over time depending on a child's age and the resources available.

PROTECTIVE FACTORS

Low distress
Low emotionality
Sociability
Good self-help skills
Average intelligence or above
Impulse control
Strongly motivated
Keen interests or hobbies
Positive self-image

Self-confident
Independent
Good communication skills
Good problem-solving skills
Reflective learning style
Assertive
Positive set of values
Supportive peer group

(Adapted from Werner (2000), Corby (2000), and Buchanan (2002))

CHILDREN'S CONCERNS

The latest DfE school exclusion figures released in 2011 show that overall exclusion numbers have continued to fall. This could be interpreted as a measure of success in keeping children in school, indicating improved behaviour and potentially less abuse. On the other hand evidence also suggests that league table sensitivity, OFSTED reports, and other indicators present a less clear picture. Schools can juggle the concept of exclusion to influence the numbers permanently excluded, temporarily excluded, or even internally excluded from lessons. However, pupil numbers, especially in secondary schools, have fallen since the previous figures were released. The percentages excluded from this smaller population matter and these have not changed significantly. This is why certain pupils, such as those from Irish Traveller or Black Caribbean communities or those with special educational needs, remain over-represented in school exclusions. The consequences of being permanently excluded from school matter enormously for any child. For example, 40 per cent of 16 to 18 year olds who are not in education, employment or training (NEETS) have been permanently excluded. As the Ministry for Justice (2011) recently noted, nine out of ten of incarcerated young people who had offended had been excluded from school before the age of 14 and had never again re-engaged. This emphasises further the need for a systems approach to be applied across and within agencies which have been corralled into their own separate, isolated system by structural and financial constraints that are preventing inter-agency communication.

Alongside risk factors, the individual circumstances for each child and young person also need to be considered. In the Green Paper *Every Child Matters* (DfES, 2003b), children and young people commented that they wished to be fit and well; to feel protected and secure; to enjoy pleasurable experiences; reach their potential ability; give something back to society; and not to be poor. The Commission for Social Care Inspection (CSCI, 2004) also asked children and young people about the concerns they had about feeling safe. Their report highlighted children's awareness of risk in their communities and schools with regard to abduction, bullying and muggings. It concluded that most children did feel safe, however some of the issues raised included worrying about being believed if they spoke out and concerned that the offender would not be appropriately punished. This clearly shows a need to acknowledge any issues raised by children and young people and to follow through their concerns. One of the enduring problems for social workers is encountering children and young people who, from their many experiences, feel they will not be believed or that it is wrong to disclose the abuse happening to them. Thus they will not open up until and unless the right conditions are created that will enable them to share distressing information or details. The Munro changes should maximise the potential for this to happen with social workers if they have been given the opportunity to work more closely and more frequently directly with children.

While abuse is a concern for every child and young person with regard to their individual experiences, O'Hagan (1993) and Bifulco and Moran (1998) argue that it is more complex as the effects of such abuse will be influenced by other factors. The type of association between a child and an abuser will have an impact on this. For example, if a child sees that person every day and consequently develops a constant fear of abuse this may prove more harmful than a child who sees their abuser infrequently. And when the abuse is brutal, this could be more damaging than if the abuse is perceived as being more restrained.

A child's age and developmental stage must also to be taken into consideration, as it may be argued that a young person who already has a clear picture of who they are may be less affected by abuse, no matter how severe, if compared to a young child who is still discovering their own self worth and value. Finally, it could be argued that the duration of the abuse and how often it occurs may also have a bearing on the long-term outcome for a child or young person. However, each child and young person is unique and their level of resilience to the effects of abuse will also be individual to them. This is an area of great uncertainty, one that calls on a social worker's capacity to 'hold' this uncertainty and the anxiety that accompanies it. This can only be done through constant reflective practice and sophisticated supervision skills.

TYPES OF ABUSE

Types of abuse, as defined by the DH (1999a), are divided into four categories: physical, emotional, sexual, and neglect. The first important point here is that these rarely occur in isolation or separate from one another. Physical abuse has profound psychological consequences and even minor abuse can unsettle a fragile child or a young person with low levels of resilience. Emotional abuse is hard to detect other than in surface behaviour or 'acting out' behaviour. Key to this is interpreting the presenting behaviour and fathoming out what may be the underlying cause. Sexual abuse by its very nature is the most difficult to detect and listing the signs and symptoms could be an endless task. Using systems theory you can, however, begin to paint a broad and deep picture of a child who has come to your attention or has been referred by another agency worker. CAMHS staff are also more than likely to be working with sexual abuse without even knowing it because their perspective and training will lead them to treat a presenting mental health problem. Rising thresholds in this time of austerity mean that only severe cases will be prioritised, so this means that self-harming, suicide attempts, complex cases and early onset psychosis will be at the front of the queue.

From a systems perspective these can be seen as sentinel symptoms of child sexual abuse that may have been suffered for many years. Skilled social workers with good training and supervision ought to be sensitive to these possibilities, but staff shortages, time pressures and a defensive medical culture will militate against exploring deeply or initiating child protection procedures that are counter-therapeutic. Neglect is always cited as being difficult to detect and provide evidence for (Jowitt and O'Loughlin, 2005). In the social work literature it seems to be often seen as a given in the context of socio-economic factors, or impossible to quantify in the context of middle-class family lifestyles and 'surface' characteristics. Yet the evidence we have shows that it can be just as deeply harmful as direct, violent physical abuse (Calder, 2003).

> Physical abuse can be seen as physical injury to a child or young person presenting with an unconvincing story for the injury, and can been seen on a continuum from slight to severe and in a number of cases fatal. Bruises are the most generally seen symptom followed by fractures and head injuries. (Kay, 1999)

COMMON FORMS OF PHYSICAL ABUSE

Table 5.1

Shaking the child violently	Hitting, punching or beating the child
Throwing the child	Kicking
Throwing objects at the child	Scalding and/or Burning
Grabbing, squeezing or crushing parts of the child's body	Fabricated or Induced Illness(FII) (Munchausen by proxy)
Scratching, pinching or twisting parts of the child's body	Poisoning (this could include prescribed drugs)
Drowning	Smothering or suffocating the child
Breaking bones	Beating the child with an object
Biting	Stabbing or cutting

Emotional abuse can be seen as the constant negative emotional behaviour of a parent/carer towards a child, causing relentless and continual undesirable consequences on that child's emotional progression (Bifulco and Moran, 1998; O'Hagan, 1989; Corby, 2000). Emotional abuse by its very nature is implicated in every abuse a child endures, as the words used by the abuser before, during, or after the abuse will be used to hurt, coerce or frighten that child. It is important to recognise that emotional abuse may occur on its own. Survivors of abuse often highlight the long-term effects the emotional trauma will have had upon them: while the wounds from physical abuse can heal in a relatively short period of time, emotional scars can run deep and may require intensive psychological therapy to aid recovery (Bifulco and Moran, 1998). While these are the characteristics shown by abusers, it can be more of a challenge to assess the effects that such abuse is having as we noted earlier.

CHARACTERISTICS SHOWN BY ABUSERS WHO EMOTIONALLY ABUSE

Table 5.2

Deprivation of emotional needs	Humiliation
Persistent negative attitude	Verbal abuse
Inappropriate development expectations	Inability to recognise child's individuality
Emotional unavailability and rejection	Telling the child, they are unloved
Frightening the child	Threatening the child
Inability to recognise child's psychological boundaries	Cognitive distortions and inconsistencies
Corrupting and exploiting the child	Ridiculing the child
Lack of warmth	Denying the child's achievements

The following activity will help develop your capacity to empathise and comprehend the emotional pain and turmoil suffered by abused children which you can then convey to other professionals who are unable to do so.

ACTIVITY

- Using the meanings of the above behaviours give examples of how you think these are acted out in families you are working with.
- When exploring the behaviour of a person emotionally abusing a child, spend some time reflecting on how this probably makes the child feel.

Commentary

It is worth bearing in mind that the fear which often accompanies emotional abuse can be just as traumatic as physical violence and not only affects a child psychologically but can also delay their development and physical growth.

Remember that some of the effects on the child may not initially be linked to the abuse; rather the child will be seen as the individual who has problems, especially when these are linked to behavioural problems or disruptive difficulties. Teachers can miss this because of their prime concern to manage a large class with possibly several disruptive children and those with special educational needs. Paradoxically it could be the quiet, compliant, conscientious child who is most at risk.

Sexual abuse can be seen as forcing or enticing a child or young person to take part in sexual activities, whether or not the child is aware of what is happening (Corby, 2000). There are several definitions with subtle differences available in specialist texts that have been modified over the years, especially in the context of internet pornography, child trafficking and on-line grooming. The activities may involve physical contact, including penetrative and non-penetrative acts, and below is a list to assist in their recognition and your understanding.

Table 5.3

Sexual assault	Child pornography, where sexual abuse is recorded
Sexual intercourse vaginal or anal	Showing children pornographic material
Rape	Involving children in sexual activities
Masturbation of the child or of the adult by the child	Touching, fondling, or kissing the child in a sexual manner
Oral sex with the child or by the child	Indecent exposure
Child prostitution	Sexual activity with other children
Coerced sexual activity with animals or objects	Images of the abused child on the Internet

While many individuals within society and indeed childcare professionals would like to believe that sexual abuse is a rare phenomenon (undertaken by sick or evil individuals), professionals need to be realistic about the number of children and young people who are abused: the NSPCC (2010) have commented that sexual abuse is a significant form of abuse. The numbers of individuals who are survivors of sexual abuse are considerable. Some authors such as DeMause (1998) believe that there has been an historical global epidemic of sexual abuse which is now slowly improving.

However, Corby (2000) comments that depending on the definition the number of children and young people who claim to have been sexually abused varies in American studies from 6 to 62 per cent for females and 3 to 16 per cent for males. Corby also cites Mrazek et al's (1983) finding that 48 per cent of young college women reported being abused sometime in their childhood or teenage years. Yet statistics can be seen as the tip of the iceberg: many authors and researchers have confirmed the difficulties they had in detecting and supporting the child and their non-offending carers following disclosures of sexual abuse (Bifulco and Moran, 1998; Kay, 1999; Violence Against Children Study Group, 1999; Corby, 2000; Wilson and James, 2002).

Children and young people who have been affected by sexual abuse can have concerns that no one will believe them even if they are able to discuss what has occurred. They also tend to have feelings of guilt because in some cases the perpetrator will have groomed them over a number of years in a caring relationship and the sexual assault may not have been particularly painful. They may also have received gifts that were given as bribes in exchange for the abuse or financial rewards for them and/or their family and finally the physical act itself may have felt pleasurable and in some cases the child or young person may have reached orgasm.

A child or young person who has been groomed and manipulated physically and emotionally may have been led to believe that this is normal, loving family behaviour, until they discover that someone touching their body in an inappropriate way is abuse. Further guilt and emotional trauma may potentially occur following a disclosure due to professionals' attitudes:

> ... for example, it may be that not all abused children are traumatised by the sexual abuse in ways that continue to have an impact on their behaviour or to limit their outlook on life ... however, it is also possible that children can be traumatized by the manner in which professionals react and attempt to address their experiences of abuse. (Bagley and King , 1990: 220, cited by Trevithick, 2005: 210)

Neglect can be defined as the continual inability to care for a child's needs, which may lead to gravely harming that child's physical condition or holistic progress. This delay in development should be recognised in contrast to that of a child of a similar age and stage of development. Kay (1999) comments that neglect is a subjective category and professionals need to take care when citing neglect as occurring for a child. Some individuals may see the handling of a child by a parent as neglectful but this view may not be held by others. Inappropriate clothing in cold weather may be seen as neglectful, however this may be due to a parent's lack of finances rather than a failure to protect due to their inability to see that child's physical needs.

NEGLECT

Table 5.4

Inadequate or inappropriate food	Inadequate or inappropriate clothes
Denying or failing to provide the child with adequate warmth and shelter	Not responding to the requirements of the child's developmental stage e.g. not toilet training the child
Failing to wash or bath the child	Failing to provide the child with clean clothing and a hygienic environment
Failing to supervise the child in potentially dangerous situations	Failing to seek medical attention when the child is ill or injured
Faltering growth (was Failure To Thrive (FTT))	Failing to ensure attendance at school

The following activity challenges you to think outside the organisational system boundaries and overcome the impediments to interprofessional work.

ACTIVITY

- Saleha is four months old and was born one month premature. Her mother, who speaks very little English, has brought her to the health centre, as she is concerned that she is not really gaining any weight. She looks pale and withdrawn and appears thin: she is also dressed in inadequate clothing. Mum says she is always hungry and constantly afflicted with minor illnesses.
- How can support be offered to Saleha's mother that ensures this child's and the entire family's needs are taken into account, including health promotion advice, its interpretation, and a health and social assessment?

Commentary

It is crucial when exploring the issues surrounding neglect to acknowledge that an inability to safeguard the welfare of children and young people is often not a conscious act. Rather, some parents may be adrift in a world filled with stress, isolation, depression or mental illness which will then inhibit their ability to care for themselves let alone their children. While other parents may not have the knowledge, cognitive ability or information to support their children, while trying to offer the best for their children they may therefore lack the capability to carry out appropriate child care. A significant number of parents may not have the personal or material resources to support their children. Systems thinking can enable you to embrace the bigger picture and the entire context of what is happening and where you are working.

This may mean that the whole family system displays a detrimental lifestyle, one that is due to deprivation rather than conscious neglect. This leaves a small number of parents who may wilfully neglect their children, through a lack of care or thoughtfulness; these parents will place their own needs and desires above the needs of their children. Social workers who are liberated from form filling and the tyranny of the Integrated Children's System in the Munro model will have an opportunity to explore how a child is coping and how their family is dealing with their day-to-day lives. This will then highlight if the child is in need and the resources that will need to be made available to meet this need. This should be done in co-operation with the family and all other relevant agencies in order to ensure that a consistent and co-ordinated approach is obtained within a systems framework.

The current inter-agency tool for assessment designed to avoid repetitive questioning from different professionals is the Common Assessment Framework. Used thoughtfully this can be utilised to support Saleha and her mother. (Details of the CAF follow in Chapter 6.) It is important to explore her health needs so as to exclude any physiological reasons for her poor weight gain, however in order to ensure her mother is part of this process the relevant interpreters need to be utilised. While in the main cities this can be straightforward as services for foreign language speakers are relatively easy to access, this is often not the case in more rural areas, small towns or villages. Over-the-phone services can have some value, but it is vital not to use family and friends if possible as this can lead to confusion and mixed messages as they will have an emotional link to the child and family involved.

The Violence Against Children Study Group (1999) have commented that children who are black (they include all children who are non-white in this title) will often receive an inadequate service compared to their white peers, due to the colour-blind approach of many child-care workers who would claim they offer an equal service to all while ignoring the specific context for institutional racism. This can be linked to language, culture and traditions, where stereotypes are employed as a reality when assessing the family, rather than taking on board the unique issues for individual children and their families.

Use of an inter-agency team will be paramount in Saleha's situation, as the collaboration and co-operation will ensure that her health needs are explored, and following paediatric input, including investigations and health assessments, the team will need to ensure that the support continues seamlessly into the community. While the health visitor will continue to monitor her weight and give her mother advice on her diet, nutrition and clothing, social work colleagues will need to follow up with social support and financial advice. Housing colleagues may also be involved to explore issues related to Saleha's health and the accommodation available, while support groups (which may be religious or culturally based) or the education service may offer some support in her mother acquiring English language skills.

SIGNS OF ABUSE

When reflecting on abuse of any kind including neglect, some types of abuse may seem obvious and easy to detect while others may not be so clear. A child may cover up injuries with clothing, or have plausible explanations for the cause of their injury. It is therefore necessary that individual judgements are made to decide whether the abuse needs further investigation. Another way to assess the situation is to observe other changes in a child's behaviour: these are not necessarily indicators of abuse, rather they are symptoms for that child (which may be due to abuse).

- Stress-related symptoms, self-harming, headaches, stomach aches, panic attacks.
- Eating disorders, regression to wetting and soiling, sexually explicit play.
- Clinging behaviour, poor concentration, self neglect.
- Mental health problems such as depression/anxiety/OCD, nightmares, disruptions in sleep pattern.

RISK ASSESSMENT OR RISK MANAGEMENT?

In attempting to fulfil the requirement to protect allegedly vulnerable others, a worker may unwittingly reinforce a client's perception that they are being remorselessly labelled as the problem. Systems theory points to the way in which family and social systems may manage problems by identifying these as caused by individuals but which are in fact a result of dysfunctional systems and not because of any particular individual within them. In focusing too narrowly on an assessment of the alleged problem person, this theoretical insight and the practice which should result from it are placed to one side while never excusing the responsibility or the dangers posed by one powerful individual within a system.

The result of this is that the scapegoating which may have been contributing to the client being identified as the problem in the first place is reflected on the client in the assessment process. This client may then respond (as they perhaps may have done in their social context) with aggression. Thus, by neglecting the client's systemic context, the worker becomes part of the dysfunctional system and any therapeutic potential within the professional encounter is reduced dramatically, sometimes to the extent of verbal or physical violence occurring or retribution being exacted upon their partner/children once social workers have exited the scene.

This is a further example of the necessity of integrating theoretical knowledge with the skills and values of social work if practice is to be effective. It is also a necessity if the well documented dangers which social workers encounter are to be minimised. Partnership practice can contribute to the effective assessment and management of risk. However the aspiration of partnership practice can lead, in unskilled hands, to the loss of professional boundaries which in itself can put workers in danger.

FAILING TO MAINTAIN BOUNDARIES

Unfortunately partnership practice can easily be narrowly misinterpreted as workers standing in their clients' shoes. Our attempts to empathise with clients are often described in these terms, but empathy or understanding is not about standing in someone's shoes. This, in any case, is impossible and more than that it can also be misperceived by clients as the creation of a mutual acceptance of their position and their response to it. This can be a flawed position in the sense that inevitably such a misperception, if this is shared by both worker and client, will result in the worker eventually having to belatedly affirm the difference of their position. This, in turn, can then give rise to feelings of rejection and betrayal in a client and the resultant danger of aggressive reactions (Walker and Beckett, 2011).

Because our professional role must entail empathy and an understanding of all the participants' positions in the system, we cannot create an alliance with any one participant. The acceptance and acknowledgement of this difference between workers and clients is the skill of working in partnership, one which involves not only empathising with clients but also negotiating the differences between them in terms of roles and relationships. Failing to establish this difference as well as the boundaries that exist is a potential source of risk to workers.

Well-intentioned but ill-informed attempts at partnerships in risk assessment can therefore be dangerous for both clients and workers. If serious aggression occurs, a client will be left with yet another experience of failure and a worker may not only have been ineffective but also physically harmed. The process of effective partnership practice involves risk but should not invite danger. Tension and ambiguity are inherent when working with risk, but it is unambiguously unprofessional to court such danger. This is further evidence that systems-informed assessment cannot be understood as separate from the wider process of social work intervention.

The difference between danger and risk and the importance of regaining an understanding of the social work process in risk assessment are important. It is simply not possible to provide unambiguous checklists that will help workers to identify dangerous people, or rules that will reliably eliminate any risk to the self or others. What is possible however is to acquire the knowledge, skills and values of the social work profession and to integrate these in a social work process in order to minimise the danger and manage risk as effectively as possible.

One of the consequences of pressures to reduce risk and eliminate danger from social work has been an obsession with the production of checklists, such as eligibility criteria, assessment schedules and risk assessment scales. As Munro reports this has been at the expense of paying attention to the process aspects of social work interventions. The tendency here has been for practice to become narrowly focused on aspects of the individual such as dependency or dangerousness, rather than concentrating on the whole person-in-context. This is counter to (and in extreme cases can threaten) the established values and effective practice of social work which emphasise individualisation, respect for the person and an holistic approach which takes full account of the social and cultural context.

The activity below will enhance your understanding of the complexities that surround the concept of risk assessment and also enable you to articulate these before an interprofessional audience.

ACTIVITY

- Make some brief notes describing several of the disadvantages of viewing risk solely as danger and intervention as being about risk control.

Commentary

Ironically the danger of such practice is that in pursuing the ultimately unattainable goal of achieving entirely risk-free practice workers may overlook the risks attached to interventions. Removing a child who is allegedly in danger from its family opens that child up to other dangers which can be equally damaging. The rights of young people could be neglected in order to control the risks they pose to themselves or others. It is also possible to lose sight of the individual-in-context, their strengths as well as the creative potential for development and growth that this brings. Social work values include recognising individuals' uniqueness, diversity and strengths. Focusing too narrowly on one aspect of an individual (e.g., their dangerousness) may limit the opportunities for interventions that can enable children and young people to build on their strengths to become less dangerous. As workers we may also overlook the risks to ourselves. An over-eagerness to control the risks posed to others can expose workers to unacceptable levels of risk to themselves. This can result not only in serious harm being inflicted on workers, but can also add to the guilt and other problems experienced by clients who are involved in being violent towards workers.

DEFINING RISK

Social work's occupational standards and competencies guidance demonstrates the tension that exists in risk work between care and control. Some of the requirements seem to have been based on a risk perspective that suggests it contains positive opportunities for personal development. Other requirements argue that risk must be viewed as something which is entirely negative and as such it must be controlled and eliminated. In order to be able to achieve a balance in our practice between these apparently conflicting requirements, it would be helpful at this point to consider these perspectives in more detail. We can do this by thinking about two approaches to risk in our work. As the profession has developed its understanding and practice in relation to risk, two contrasting approaches have emerged. The *safety first approach*, which can be paraphrased as CYB (Cover Your Back), and the *risk-taking approach*, which subscribes to the view that risk is an inherent part of social life. If individuals are to be fully engaged in social life some amount of risk will be inevitable. Both terms are however problematic:

- Competent social work should not be entirely 'defensive' and preoccupied with covering your back.
- Risk taking carries connotations of an advocacy for taking risks which is counterintuitive to many and easily misconstrued as irresponsible in view of the vulnerability shown by many service users.

CHARACTERISTICS OF THE RISK CONTROL PERSPECTIVE

- *Definition*: risks are negative – they are dangerous and/or threatening.
- *Priority principles*: professional responsibility and accountability.
- *Practice priorities*: identification (assessment scales) and elimination (procedural, legalistic).

CHARACTERISTICS OF THE RISK MANAGEMENT PERSPECTIVE

- *Definition*: risks are part of life and balancing risks and benefits is part of every individual's development, as well as being self-determining and personally responsible.
- *Priority principles*: self-determination and anti-oppression.
- *Practice priorities*: solution-focused, partnership practice, empowerment.

The benefits of the risk management perspective are that it is in keeping with the values and practice of modern social work: it emphasises the process of maximising benefits as well as minimising risks, rather than the procedure for identifying and eliminating risks, and builds on strengths as well. The drawbacks are that it relies heavily on a highly developed professional competence and judgement and requires a client commitment to the partnership. It also necessitates a client possessing sufficient intellectual/cognitive competence. In addition to this it involves ambiguity and uncertainty, is poorly understood by the public, and requires a supportive management practice and organisational policy. The risks to social workers are virtually ignored. As understanding and practice in relation to risk develop it becomes clear that there needs to be an integration of the best elements within both approaches. Eliminating or totally controlling the risks that are inherent in social work is impossible. It is therefore undesirable to think of risk and the social work task in relation to it in this way because:

- evidence and intuition suggest this is impossible and thus valuable resources are wasted;
- risk is part of social life;

- practice which is effective in terms of promoting individual responsibility and social competence cannot be reductionist: instead it must recognise the person-in-context and build on their strengths;
- social work agencies have responsibilities in law in relation to certain client groups: individual social workers must neither neglect these responsibilities nor accept unlimited liability, whether or not there are already legal requirements in place;
- the social and individual costs of control can outweigh the social and individual benefits;
- social work routinely brings its practitioners into contact with dangerous people and entails them making professional judgements which can potentially be castigated by management, organisations and the media.

It is however possible to minimise risk: for example, by appropriately employing well-validated risk assessment scales where these are available. Other ways of minimising risk would include being aware of the meaning of risk and its role in the personal development and social life of service users; ensuring that practice is evidence based and in accordance with statutes, government guidance and agency policy; and managing decision calls (don't be rushed, ensure the immediate safety of all parties involved, be appropriately assertive, and be sure that a decision has to be made and if so by whom). The capacity to share responsibility, to involve where possible and support the subject of the decision, to report back to the referring agency, to ensure continuity, and to debrief as soon as possible with a manager/supervisor is crucial here.

Clearly identifying specific risks and the contexts in which these might occur is a helpful skill to develop. Fully engaging clients and significant others in risk assessments and managing and recording these accurately is vital also. A multidisciplinary sharing of such risk management with other involved professionals, while clearly recording risk assessments and management plans and relating these to specific legal requirements as appropriate, is a necessity. You should always ensure the availability of supervision and record the key decisions that come from this. Finally, never forget that managing the risk to oneself is a priority within professional practice.

The following activity will further develop your understanding of risk and link it to the new Working Together guidance that will enhance your interprofessional practice.

ACTIVITY

- What do you feel are the shortcomings in your practice guidance and legislative context for the effective management of risk in your agency service?
- Review the material above and list three priority factors you consider could improve your current risk assessment and risk management practice.

Commentary

A generic framework for risk assessment practice which can take into account the two perspectives on risk and the tensions between the various practice requirements has been influential since it was first described by Brearley **et al.** (1982). His framework has been based on a clear definition of danger, risk, predisposing and situational hazards, and strengths as follows:

- Dangers: undesirable outcomes.
- Risk: the chance of a loss or the occurrence of an undesirable outcome as a result of a decision or course of action. The chance of a gain and a desirable outcome.

Social work, for the reasons discussed above, can focus too narrowly on potential losses and will thereby miss the potential for making gains. Competent practice involves weighing up the pros and cons of both possibilities, which Brearley described in terms of hazards and strengths. A hazard is an existing factor that introduces or increases the possibility of an undesirable outcome. He identified two types of hazard:

- Predisposing hazards: these are factors in the person's background, such as their experiences and personality, which will make an undesirable outcome more likely.
- Situational hazards: these are factors that are specific to the current situation which will make an undesirable outcome more likely.

This distinction between the two types of hazard is useful because it can help you to focus on those aspects of a risk situation which may be more amenable to intervention and change:

- Strengths: any factor which reduces the possibility of an undesirable outcome occurring. The dangers we have discussed of a too-narrow focus on hazards is reduced by this requirement to identify strengths. This may seem to be an obvious requirement of an holistic assessment which fully takes account of the person-in-context, but it is one that can be easily neglected in the pressured environment of risk work.

Listing these hazards and strengths provides a way to quantify the balance between them. You will need to identify what other information can be obtained to help analyse the whole situation, before reaching a conclusion and making a judgement about any decisions that must be made. Decision making needs to be more explicit while plans should flow logically from the assessment. There is a need here for a guiding framework. If the decisions are not clearly linked to the assessment findings the accountability for actions will be difficult to support. In the event of an unsuccessful outcome there will be no way of analysing which aspect of the situation could account for this and how future interventions could be amended in light of it.

Following local custom and practice rather than agency procedures will result in inconsistencies in our practice and therefore we will be open to complaints from service users on the grounds of an inequity of treatment, which is in any case insupportable in terms of professional accountability.

Risk assessments should take account of any relevant information about predisposing and situational factors, of which the relevant database is a readily accessible source. Neglecting this basic source would be subsequently indefensible in terms of professional accountability. Not notifying referrers of the outcome of their request for services can result in disillusionment among colleagues from other agencies (and concerned members of the public) about the worth of such referrals, leading to potentially hazardous situations for vulnerable individuals who should indeed be referred. Its value is essential in continuing multi-disciplinary risk work. Ignoring it is also professionally impolite (Jack and Walker, 2000).

Failing to convey decisions affecting families' welfare undermines the potential for partnership practice both currently and/or in the future. Doing so (as with the above) also means that there is no clear audit trail linking the referral, assessment, intervention and outcome. Managers failing to indicate their endorsement of a social worker's action means there is no record of the agreed intervention which is mutually binding and this may lead to disagreements later on about what was in fact agreed. This can be potentially hazardous to a worker in situations where harm occurs to clients or others. This exploration of the complexity of risk in relation to child care can provide a summary of some of the general implications for practice that may be drawn from the discussion so far. Competent practice in risk work should:

- adopt an holistic systems perspective on need (as well as identifying risk);
- appropriately employ well-validated criteria of risk within a coherent framework of assessment and a consequent, clearly related intervention;
- explicitly involve parents and children in recording their perceptions and opinions;
- avoid a gender bias in the assessment, recommendation and intervention (attention will often focus unreasonably on mothers in abusive situations);
- utilise multi-disciplinary processes of assessment and decision making;
- be explicitly shared in supervision and recorded and endorsed at every stage by managers.

THE SOCIAL CONSTRUCTION OF RISK

Risk is an inherent part of safeguarding children and young people. Definitions of concepts such as risk, dangerous and significant harm are ambiguous and widely agreed to be determined by social, cultural and historical factors. There is no absolute definition of dangerousness that is independent of any social and cultural context. Similarly, the definition of significant harm is relative. The legal debates about the acceptability of the physical chastisement (i.e., smacking) of children are an example of this. In some European states this is illegal though this is currently not the case in England and Wales: however, there is an ongoing debate about whether it should be considered so. Many hold that such parental behaviour is indeed physical abuse with the potential for significant harm to be done to the developing child: others believe that sparing the rod spoils the child. This lack of absolutes and the ambiguity it brings with it has profound implications for safeguarding practices in relation to risk. This is epitomised in the tension between care and control.

The final activity below focuses on risk in order to provide you with a comprehensive and multi-faceted understanding of the concepts behind critical decisions in interprofessional child protection work.

- Make some brief notes describing several disadvantages of viewing risk solely as danger and intervention as about risk control.

ACTIVITY

6

USING SYSTEMS THEORY
IN ASSESSMENT

INTRODUCTION

The previous government received a critique of their policies for safeguarding children and young people which suggested that there had been an extension of state
intervention in families' lives, primarily within a project designed to get poor parents to fulfil their responsibilities towards their children that was too focused on
instrumental approaches to assessment which produced self-reliant citizens. The
authors argued that these policies neglected to analyse how children were harmed
in a variety of settings and what their views were about what should be done about
this (Fawcett et al., 2004). Their conclusions underline the importance of taking
notice of the process of assessment and using a systems model, making sure that
multiple perspectives are embraced. This view was recently echoed by Helm (2010)
who argued that social workers were continuing to fail to establish, and establish a
regard for, children's views in their analysis. The experiences of children and young
people have been captured in a number of studies which reveal a stark gap between
the rhetoric of official guidance and the reality of children's and young people's
experiences of assessments (Ofsted, 2008).

Social work assessment is often taken for granted and sometimes the subject of
unwarranted attention, but it is always a potentially liberating and empowering
experience for workers and service users. It is vital that we understand how effective
assessments take into account people's needs, rights, strengths, responsibilities and
resources. Recent research concluded that the implementation of unified assessment
procedures highlighted the ways in which these have facilitated positive changes in
practice and foregrounded aspects of unified assessment where their translation into
practice has proved difficult. The authors suggest that unified assessments promote
a more consistent application of the eligibility criteria and encourage more creative
approaches to both care and service delivery planning.

However, considerable variability in the nature and volume of information collected by practitioners, who expressed reservations about the domain approach to assessment, was also noted and problems relating to the sharing and management of information were highlighted (Seddon et al., 2010). We need to reflect on how our individual practice can enable us to identify clients' strengths rather than weaknesses and work with their existing systems, networks and communities. Organisational restrictions and resource constraints will militate against creative child-focused practice, but we need to overcome these: the Munro changes should enable this to happen.

Recent research confirms the trend for neglecting the voice of the child in the assessment process (Buckley, 2003). The literature in general tends to suggest the following reasons why social workers encounter problems when trying to communicate with children and young people about their needs:

- Values about children and childhood.
- Professional socialisation and role.
- Resistance to a children's rights agenda.
- Motivation.
- Practical opportunity.
- Dealing with children's views.

What emerges from this is a process whereby social workers will employ adult language and concepts along with crude question-and-answer techniques in order to elicit information: these do not work. Open-ended work, involving songs, play or child-centred tools to chat about the child's day, or creating drawings, is much better for relating to and understanding a child's perspective. Building an assessment from this material takes time but this does pay off in the long run. An apt example from a child protection practitioner illustrates this: the social worker, during a visit to a woman who had suffered domestic violence, heard her child say 'Where's Daddy?' This could have been interpreted as meaning that the child was missing him and should, despite the context, be able to see him (especially if the father was demanding access). However, in time the social worker was able to ascertain that in asking this question the child was expressing her dread that he would return to inflict more harm on the family and wanted to know that he was not returning (Helm, 2010).

Understanding how oppression and discrimination can influence contemporary assessment practice and people's ability to function is a crucial task within practice development. The following descriptions and analyses of the policy guidance on work with clients in the context of children and families' work have been designed in order to illuminate areas for creative potential.

UNDERSTANDING ASSESSMENT

Assessment has been defined as a tool to aid us in planning future work, as the beginning of helping another person to identify areas for growth and change. Its purpose is the identification of needs: it is never an end in itself (Taylor and Devine,

1993). Assessment is the foundation for the social work process we adopt with service users: it can set the tone for further contact; it will be our first opportunity to engage with new or existing clients; and it can be perceived by people as a judgement on their character or behaviour. However the research evidence demonstrates how children's voices still tend to remain unheard (Thomas and Holland, 2010). The authors noted that practitioners displayed a broad understanding of identities when discussing their own identities in interviews and reported a practice commitment to learning about the details of children's lives in an attempt to 'get to know' individual children. However, their assessment reports also tended to convey only narrowly defined and negative aspects of the children's identities, with many descriptions standardised and replicated between reports. It was suggested that bureaucratic constraints, along with the need to argue a case in adversarial legal circumstances and defensive practices, may have impeded change.

A good experience of assessment can make people feel positive about receiving help and will thus define their attitude towards both you and your agency. A bad experience of assessment can make matters worse, offend clients, and make any problems harder to resolve in the long term. We know that children feel excluded from the process and there is firm evidence to support this (Brandon et al., 2008). You can regard assessment as little more than a paper-chasing exercise, involving form filling and restricting peoples' aspirations. Or you can see it as an opportunity to engage with service users in a problem-solving partnership where both of you can learn more about yourselves (Martin, 2010). A good way of measuring your progress during your assessment practice is to use the concept of systematic practice (Thompson, 2005). This requires that you ask yourself three questions:

- *What am I trying to achieve?* This involves considering what needs remain unmet and acts as a focus for the assessment, helping you to avoid the pitfall of simply gathering a lot of information with no clarity about what needs to be done.
- *How am I going to achieve it?* This relates to the need to develop a strategy for achieving the identified objectives, namely how you intend to get to where you want to be.
- *How will I know when I have achieved it?* This helps you to bring clarity to what can invariably be vagueness in the work process and enables you to envisage the outcome of the work and to recognise when this has been achieved or not.

There are three types of assessment that most of us will encounter in some form or other in whatever agency we practise in. These will have been designed to indicate the level of perceived need and seriousness and the complexity of a service user's situation.

INITIAL ASSESSMENT

This provides a good basis for short-term planning and can be used as part of the eligibility criteria to determine the level of need and priority. In child-care situations it is used to effect immediate child protection, with a general requirement of a two-week time limit.

COMPREHENSIVE ASSESSMENT

This takes over from where an initial assessment finishes and when more complex needs have been identified. Alternatively it will have been initiated following changes in a service user's situation where some basic, but limited, information already exists.

CORE ASSESSMENT

This is used in child-care cases and was a specific requirement under the Children Act 1989 guidance for a time-limited assessment in order to help inform the decision-making process in legal proceedings. Its key aim is to enable all stakeholders to contribute as much information as possible consistent with effective outcomes. The coalition government has already discarded the timeframe following the Munro recommendations, thus allowing for more flexibility and the reality of different situations to determine timescales.

The following activity aims to enable you to better implement the new Working Together guidance and to distinguish between the changes as well as reflect on the reasons behind them.

- Write down the ways in which you think the above material will help in your assessment of a child and family you might be working with, as well as the ways in which this will hinder your assessment.
- Discuss in supervision the dilemmas and challenges these pose for you individually and how you can manage them.

ACTIVITY

Commentary

Such broad concepts and a lack of specifics can seem daunting to social workers working under pressure with their available resources. Time is crucial in many situations and it is often difficult to obtain full information in risky circumstances. Interventions undertaken in one set of circumstances can impact on the quality of subsequent assessments and vice versa, as systems theory recognises. It is vital to consider the purpose of assessments and the relationship between assessments and interventions which can make it hard to separate their functions. The danger here is that social workers will feel impelled to conduct lengthy, detailed assessments, following the framework rigidly

(Cont'd)

rather than using it as a framework to guide their practice across a multitude of different circumstances. Their skill will be in focusing on the most important aspects of the framework relevant to particular situations.

Knowing the level or depth required from an assessment is a starting-point. But we will need to proceed with a framework or guide to the different elements making up the assessment. If we move beyond some of our agency constraints and believe in service user-focused assessment as an interactive process rather than an administrative convenience, then as Milner and O'Bryne (2009) describe we will need a helpful framework as a base for effective assessment in a variety of practice contexts:

- *Preparation*: deciding who to see, which data will be relevant, what the purpose is and what the limits of the task are.
- *Data collection*: people are met and engaged with, difference gaps are addressed, and empowerment and choice are safeguarded as we come to the task with respectful uncertainty and a research mentality.
- *Weighing up the data*: current social and psychological theory and research findings that are part of every social worker's learning are drawn on to answer the question 'Is there a problem and is it serious?'
- *Analysing the data*: these are interpreted in order to seek out and gain an understanding of the service user in order to develop ideas for the intervention.
- *Utilising the data*: this stage is used to finalise any judgements.

Milner and O'Byrne (2009) have offered a very useful way of navigating the potential complexities in assessment practice by suggesting five theoretical approaches or 'maps' to guide the modern practitioner. These have been based on psychodynamic, behavioural, task-centred, solution-focused and narrative theories. These maps, combining knowledge from sociology and psychology, enable social workers to engage in collaborative work while maintaining a focus on the essential values that will result in effective and appropriate interventions.

PRACTICE GUIDANCE

The Social Care Institute for Excellence focused on social work assessment in a definitive document (SCIE, 2003) which reinforced the importance of three key assessment skills:

- *Critical thinking*: this means being able to critically analyse underlying assumptions when conducting assessments and developing the thinking skills to assess unfamiliar scenarios and generate plausible hypotheses from these.

- *Research skills*: this means having an advanced ability in seeking out existing reliable research evidence and developing the skills to undertake research itself. Evidence suggests that learning skills in ethnographic research or discourse analysis can enhance cultural competence.
- *Knowledge*: the ability to conduct assessments requires not just skills but also a relevant knowledge base. The demands placed upon social workers are often multi-factoral and highly complex, involving several interlocking and multiple domains. No social worker can have knowledge of every conceivable situation they may be presented with, but it is possible to acquire specialist expertise and experience or to have the ability to locate and access such expertise.

Acts of Parliament and associated practice guidance illustrate the wealth of material that has provided the framework within which your assessment practice takes place. These are the rules of engagement that permit you to take some of the most important decisions that will affect the lives of a great many people, possibly for years and generations to follow. Some of this is prescriptive and written in an administrative language that probably feels alien to your caring, compassionate instincts. You might feel comfortable with the power and authority offered within the law and guidance. Or you may feel distinctly uncomfortable within the constraints imposed on your practice and better judgement. This is however the framework in which your practice takes place and what legitimates your social work role (Walker and Beckett, 2011).

Your task in managing this material will not be helped by the artificial distinctions and divisions in your agency that will compartmentalise families and communities into specialist areas of practice when in reality these are effectively linked in all sorts of ways as Munro argues. The various national priorities guidance is another central government prompt to steer local authorities and other providers towards those services and service user groups that it deems should receive particular attention: this usually comes with financial incentives or penalties. This *one-size–fits-all* guidance can also be criticised for being insensitive towards particular regions or local area needs. Therefore we are already able to detect a number of layers to the various pressures that go towards affecting our assessment practice:

- Prescriptions for what we are meant to achieve in assessment practice occupational standards.
- Legislative injunctions setting out the legal powers and responsibilities that define our practice.
- Practice guidance documents based on research studies that offer some evidence of effectiveness and good practice examples.
- Central government budget allocations for local government that will determine the scope of what an agency can provide.

The activity that follows aims to allow you to familiarise yourself with key documentation and improve your continuous professional development using a critical and reflective perspective.

- Review the previous material and make a list of the legislative and practice guidance that is relevant to your work context.
- Now look for evidence of how these are translated into your particular agency eligibility criteria and service specification.

THE COMMON ASSESSMENT FRAMEWORK

Government guidance (DfES, 2005b) indicates that this should be the main, and sometimes the only, assessment instrument to be used at the first sign of the emerging vulnerability in a child or young person and this is to act as a marker for a referral to another agency or specialist service. Assessments have hitherto been used to make decisions about whether or not a child meets the threshold criteria which will then trigger the delivery of a service. The concept of the Common Assessment Framework (CAF) is that this should lead to a common approach to needs assessment, as an initial assessment for use by statutory or voluntary sector staff in education, early years, health, police, youth justice or social work. It is intended that this will reduce the number of assessments experienced by children and foster improved information sharing and thus help dissolve professional boundaries. However, recent research illustrates that such efforts at standardisation and categorisation are highly problematic and likely to fail (White et al., 2009; Gillingham, 2011).

The framework (DfES, 2005b) is expected to contribute to the wider culture change across the children and young people's workforce by offering:

- general guidance on its use;
- a common procedure for assessment;
- a methodology based on the Framework for the Assessment of Children in Need and their Families;
- a focus on child development and communication skills with children, carers and parents;
- the gaining of consent;
- how to record findings and identify an appropriate response;
- how to share information when a child moves between local authority areas;
- an explanation of the roles and responsibilities of different agencies and practitioners.

The framework needs to be familiar to all staff whose work contributes to achieving the five outcomes for wellbeing laid out in *Every Child Matters*. The assessment should be completed with the full knowledge, consent and involvement of the children and their parents. It should be child centred, ensuring an equality of opportunity; solution- and action-focused; and an ongoing process rather than a one-off event. Using it competently demands skilled practice. Evidence shows however that the impacts of CAF as a technology on the everyday professional practices in child welfare are problematic. There are descriptive, stylistic and interpretive demands placed on practitioners in child welfare who tend to make strategic and moral decisions about whether and when to complete a CAF and how to do so. These are based on assessments of their accountabilities, their level of child welfare competence and their domain-specific knowledge, as well as their moral judgements and the institutional contexts in which these are played out (White et al., 2009).

The framework must be centred on children and the whole spectrum of their potential needs, rather than the policy focus and statutory obligations of particular services. Outcomes from the CAF should include the identification of the broader needs of vulnerable children without additional support. Earlier interventions are also expected from practitioners who are looking outside their usual work area for additional support. This should reduce the number of assessments undergone by children and families by improving the quality of referrals between agencies.

THE PROCESS OF THE COMMON ASSESSMENT

PREPARATION

Talk to the child and their parents. Discuss the issues and what you can do to help. Then talk to anyone else you need to who is already involved. If you decide a common assessment would be useful you must seek the agreement of the child and their parent as appropriate.

DISCUSSION

Talk to the child and their family and complete the assessment with them. Make use of additional information from other sources to avoid repeated questions. Add to or update any existing common assessments. At the end of the discussion seek to understand better the child's and family's strengths and needs and what can be done to help. Agree on the actions that your service and the family can deliver. Then agree with the family any actions that others will be required to deliver and record these on the form.

SERVICE DELIVERY

Deliver on your actions. Make referrals or broker access to other services using the common assessment to demonstrate evidence of need. Keep an eye on progress. Where the child or their family needs services from a range of agencies a lead professional must be identified to co-ordinate these.

ELEMENTS OF THE CAF

DEVELOPMENT OF THE BABY, CHILD, OR YOUNG PERSON

- *General health*: this includes health conditions or impairments which significantly affect an individual's functioning in everyday life.
- *Physical development*: this includes means of mobility and the level of physical or sexual maturity or delayed development.
- *Speech, language and communications development*: this includes the ability to communicate effectively, confidently, and appropriately with others.
- *Emotional and social development*: this includes the emotional and social responses a baby, child or young person gives to parents, carers and others outside the family.
- *Behavioural development*: this includes lifestyle and the capacity for self-control.
- *Identity*: this includes the growing sense of self as a separate and valued person, as well as self-esteem, self-image and social presentation.
- *Family and social relationships*: these include the ability to empathise and build stable and affectionate relationships with others, including family, peers and the wider community.
- *Self-care skills and independence*: these include the acquisition of practical, emotional and communication competencies to increase independence.
- *Understanding, reasoning and problem solving*: these include the ability to understand and organise information, as well as to reason and solve problems.
- *Participation in learning, education and employment*: this includes the degree to which a child or young person has access to and is engaged in education and/or work-based training and if they are not participating the reasons for this.
- *Progress and achievement in learning*: this includes the child's or young person's educational achievements and progress, including in relation to their peers.
- *Aspirations*: these include the child's or young person's ambitions, whether their aspirations are realistic and how they will be able to plan to meet these. Note that there may be barriers to their achievement because of other responsibilities at home.

PARENTS AND CARERS

- *Basic care, ensuring safety and protection*: this includes the extent to which a baby's, child's or young person's physical needs are not met and they are protected from harm, danger and self-harm.
- *Emotional warmth and stability*: this includes the provision of emotional warmth in a stable family environment, thereby giving the baby, child or young person a sense of being valued.
- *Guidance, boundaries and stimulation*: this includes enabling the child or young person to regulate their own emotions and behaviour while promoting the child's or young person's learning and intellectual development through encouragement, stimulation and promoting social opportunities.

FAMILY AND ENVIRONMENTAL FACTORS

- *Family history, functioning and wellbeing*: this includes the impact of family situations and experiences.
- *Wider family*: this includes the family's relationships with relatives and non-relatives.
- *Housing, employment and financial considerations*: this includes living arrangements, amenities, facilities, who is working or not, and the amount of income available over a sustained period of time.

SOCIAL AND COMMUNITY RESOURCES

- *Neighbourhood*: this includes the wider context of the neighbourhood and its impact on the baby, child or young person, as well as the availability of facilities and services.
- *Accessibility*: this includes schools, day-care, primary health care, places of worship, transport, shops, leisure activities and family support services.
- *Characteristics*: these include levels of crime, disadvantage, employment, levels of substance misuse/trading.
- *Social integration*: this includes the degree of the young person's social integration or isolation, peer influences, friendships and social networks.

The conventional way in which the Framework for the Assessment of Children in Need and the subsequent Common Assessment Framework were depicted diagrammatically was either as a triangular shape, or in the case of the CAF, a pentangle. Thus each domain could be seen separately and linked using a linear line. Unwittingly these diagrammatic representations and linear lists of their individual elements emphasised separateness rather than connectedness and interactivity which are the hallmarks of systems theory. So if as social workers we are going to manage systems theory and practice we need to find better visual representations for the holistic information we collect when undertaking assessments with children and families. This will show a less straightforward picture, one that will not look neat and tidy but will more realistically represent the reality of human organisation. Three examples of such a visual device can be seen on the following page.

The following activity will ensure that you make time to reflect on your level of professional knowledge and will provide you with evidence to inform your annual appraisal and address your training needs.

- Review the above material and make a note of those elements that are less familiar to you.
- Make sure you make some time soon to discuss these in supervision or with your manager in order to help you understand these and integrate them into your practice.

ACTIVITY

(a)

(b)

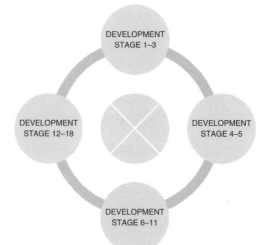

(c)

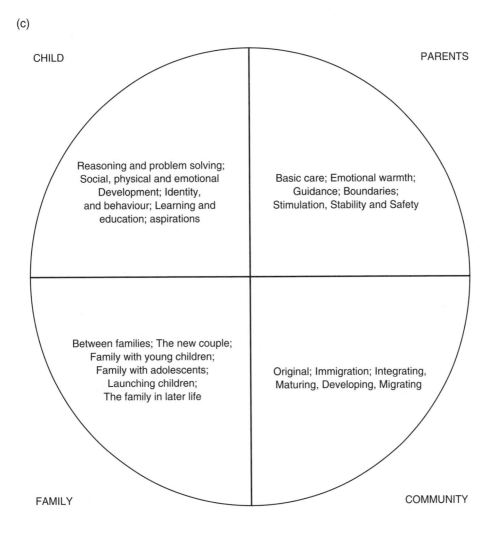

Dev stages	life cycle 1	life cycle 2	attachments	CAF elements
1–2			infant	development
2–3				
4–5				parents/carers
6–11			child	
12–18			adolescent	environment
				community

Figure 6.1

THE IMPORTANCE OF ATTACHMENT

The place of attachment theory has been well established in social work educa-tion, training and practice. It is probably one of the foundation elements of assess-ment that most engages social workers and it can set the scene for how work progresses. Social workers can feel pressured into making quick judgements and this element is most influential as it touches on some primitive emotions and feel-ings within us about child safety. Figure 6.1 and Table 6.1 both offer a useful quick reference to help you understand and assess the attachment trajectory of the child or young person you might be working with. In the context of systems theory and ensuring the needs of the child are determined from their perspective this is impor-tant. What then follows is a more detailed explanation of these behaviours and patterns (Ainsworth et al., 1978; George, 1996; Simpson et al. 1996; Crittenden, 1997; Howe et al., 1999).

Table 6.1   Attachment behaviours and patterns in children and adolescents

	Secure– autonomous	Avoidant– dismissing	Ambivalent–preoccupied– entangled
Infant	Secure	Insecure–avoidant	Insecure–ambivalent–resistant
Child	Secure–optimal	Defended– disengaged	Dependent–deprived–coercive
Adolescent	Autonomous–free to evaluate	Dismissing	Preoccupied–entangled– enmeshed

SECURE AND AUTONOMOUS PATTERNS

INFANT

Parents/carers of secure infants tend to be good at reading their children's signals. There is synchrony between them involving mutual reciprocal interactions. Clear patterns begin to be perceived by infants that will help them to make sense of their own and their parents'/carers' behaviour. A parent/carer who is available emotion-ally, as well as responsive and comforting can generate a soothing, comfortable environment. This helps infants locate and support their own understanding of their own and others' emotions and behaviour. It also:

• enables the child to access, acknowledge and integrate their thoughts and the full range of their feelings;
• allows the child to acknowledge the power of feelings in affecting behaviour.

CHILD

Instead of using crying, following and protesting to signify emotional arousal and distress, the young child begins to learn to deal with their feelings cognitively using language and mental processes. Emotional competence develops so that secure children will show good affect recognition. The child has increasing confidence in acknowledging and managing difficult and anxiety-provoking emotions. Secure children function well in family life, in their classroom behaviour, and in peer relationships.

They are reasonably co-operative and able to draw upon a range of strategies to cope with the demands of social relationships. They show less emotional dependence on teachers and are more likely to approach them in a positive manner.

- The secure child is generally popular with their friends. They show good empathy, tend to be included in group activities, and exhibit low levels of conflict in their play.
- Secure children are less likely to be victimisers or victims, have higher self-esteem and be skilled at conflict resolution.

ADOLESCENT

Secure autonomous adolescents will acknowledge the value and impact of attachment relationships. The influence of such relationships on personality development has long been recognised. They can tolerate imperfections in themselves, their parents and those with whom they are currently in a close relationship. When describing attachment experiences they are able to provide specific, concrete examples that are coherent and reflective.

- They remain constructively engaged with a problem rather than attempting to avoid it or becoming angry at its apparent intractability.
- They feel comfortable with closeness and enjoy good self-esteem.

AVOIDANT-DISMISSING PATTERNS

INFANT

Carers who feel agitated, distressed or hostile towards their infants are less likely to respond to those infants' distress. They may try to control the situation by ignoring them or will attempt to convince the infant they are not 'really' upset. This undermines the child's confidence in their own perceptions. The pattern that develops is that the parent/carer becomes emotionally less available and psychologically distant. They withdraw when the child shows distress and indeed are more available the quieter the infant is. In turn the infant learns to become subdued and to downplay feelings of upset, need or arousal in order to remain in an emotional proximity to the carer.

CHILD

Avoidant children are less likely to seek support from their carers/teachers. Their attachment style becomes more detached and cool, perhaps even socially accepta-ble. They have learned that their carers feel more comfortable with behaviour that is low in emotional content. Achievements are valued more highly than emotional closeness.

Avoidant personalities tend to modify their own behaviour as a way of defending against social rejection. Some children may become compulsively compliant with high anxiety levels about getting tasks 'right'. If parents or teachers display unhappiness or disapproval the child feels responsible, unsettled, ashamed or guilty.

ADOLESCENT

Avoidant-dismissing patterns can be demonstrated here ranging from being socially reserved to being compulsively self-reliant. They tend to minimise the emotional effects that relationships have on them. There is if anything a systematic avoidance of negative experiences and memories. The adolescent has a strong need to keep focused on practical tasks. Anything or anybody who distracts them will make this adolescent feel agitated, anxious or angry. Aggressive behaviour is likely to erupt at these moments. Equally this adolescent will be keen to keep to the rules and seems over-vigilant when other people appear to break rules. Thus a heightened sense of justice, right and wrong can be observed.

AMBIVALENT-PREOCCUPIED-ENTANGLED PATTERNS

INFANT

Carers who are inconsistent with their babies needs are experienced as unpredict-ably unresponsive. Infants feel emotionally neglected and when they begin to explore and seek independence their parents/carers feel uncomfortable. These infants have to increase their attachment behaviours in order to break through the lack of carer responsiveness. The infants' behaviour will be characterised by crying, clinging, making constant demands and shouting or tugging. Their sepa-ration anxiety may be pronounced. The parent is, in behavioural terms, 'non-contingently responsive' (i.e., their responses bear no relation to the behaviour of the child).

Thus the clinging, demanding behaviour will increase as the infant learns that their persistence here will gain a reaction. However, this might be a biscuit or a physical assault. As a result the infant compensates by becoming hyperactive, maximising the opportunities to gain comfort and attention whenever the carer feels able to provide it. The infant begins to construct a self image using feelings of worthlessness, of not being liked or valued. This then leads to feelings of doubt, despair and inadequacy.

CHILD

As a child increases in age it can raise the level of demands and persistence. A parent may threaten to leave the home or will request the child is looked after by the local authority. This only further increases that child's levels of distress, anger and despair. Alternatively, where severe physical neglect occurs, a child may lapse into passivity, helplessness and depression.

Family relationships can be characterised by high levels of active, demanding behaviour by parents and children. Threats and counter-threats will be traded about who cares and who loves who in an impulsive, disorganised atmosphere. Relationships can feel emotionally entangled and enmeshed, with parents and children learning how to lie, deceive and coerce in order to survive.

Ambivalent children will show poor levels of concentration. They might suggest they are feeling unwell in an unspecified way in order to secure a socially acceptable attachment. They will be characteristically lacking in self-reliance, their failures will always be the fault of others, and they will see themselves as perpetual victims. These children can quickly become known to teachers.

ADOLESCENT

In adolescence the more extreme coercive behavioural strategies become increasingly disruptive, attention-seeking, and difficult to control. Life is lived at a heightened pitch of dissatisfaction and anger. Antisocial behaviour, conflict, control problems and poor concentration are observed. Feelings of guilt and personal responsibility are largely absent.

Parents and peers can be subjected to threats and intimidation to make them respond and provide. There will be a struggle taking place between anger with, and seeking approval from, parents. These adolescents will exhibit a need to be close, but to be dependent on someone who may abandon them will arouse strong feelings of anxiety. They will feel a strong sense of powerlessness and describe parents/carers and practitioners as either wonderful and loving or hateful and cruel: there will be no grey areas in this regard.

It is important to recognise that these characteristics are distilled from practice and research evidence covering a wide variety of working and professional contexts.

Complexity has been sacrificed to some extent to assist comprehension, therefore it is crucial to also recognise:

- that within these generalised characteristics there is a range and overlap;
- that some children are reserved and will show mildly avoidant-dismissing patterns;
- that some children are prone to reactive characteristics with mildly ambivalent-preoccupied patterns;
- that we should not be fooled by our first impressions;
- that these classifications are based on white, ethno-centric assumptions;
- that research studies tend not to distinguish between girls' and boys' differentiated socialisation;
- that poverty, unemployment and homelessness are important mitigating factors;
- that the effects of sexual, physical or emotional abuse can be mistaken for attachment problems.

Using a systems perspective should enable you to accommodate as much evidence/information as possible in order to help you broaden and deepen your understanding of the complete situation you are beginning to interact with. Table 6.2 opposite is a summary of the key human growth developmental stages from four different authors whose work will be familiar to most social workers. In this systems context these stages need to be applied or considered in conjunction with the above tools as an aid to your intuitive, interactive relationship with families and the wider system.

ASSESSMENTS AS A SYSTEMS PROCESS

Organisational arrangements within social care agencies are driving the way assessment is conceptualised by social workers as we have already noted. It is therefore a requirement that you adopt a wide definition of assessment if your practice is to be empowering and anti-oppressive. It is important to think of each assessment as a process rather than a one-off event. There should be a seamless transition from assessment to intervention in a circular process that includes the crucial elements of planning and reviewing. Once completed, the circle will begin again at the assessment stage of the process and so on. Think of it as a continuous, perpetual movement, punctuated by a range of activities involving major or minor interventions in the lives of service users. Rather than adopting a one-dimensional view of assessment you could also perceive it as an intervention in itself: the very act of conducting an information-gathering interview could have a significant positive impact on a person's wellbeing. The simple idea that someone cares and is prepared to listen to their story could be enormously comforting to an individual who is lonely, isolated and with low self-esteem.

No discussion of assessments can be complete without addressing the concept of need, as it is a word that frequently appears in much of the legislation, practice guidance and service providers' documentation. There are universal needs expressed in global documents like the UN Declaration on the Rights of the Child and there are special needs which although clearly discriminatory appear to be accepted as a useful signifier for certain groups in society. What this does is to permit rationing to

Table 6.2 Summary of Developmental Concepts

Theory		Age range			
	1	2–3	4–5	6–11	12–18
Erikson's psycho-social stages of development:	The infant requires consistent and stable care in order to develop feelings of security. Begins to trust the environment but can also develop suspicion and insecurity. Deprivation at this stage can lead to emotional detachment throughout life and difficulties forming relationships.	The child begins to explore and seeks some independence from parents/carers. A sense of autonomy develops but can combine with feelings of shame and self-doubt. Failure to integrate at this stage may lead to difficulties in social integration.	The child needs to explore the wider environment and plan new activities. Begins to initiate activities but fears punishment and guilt as a consequence. Successful integration results in a confident person, but problems can produce deep insecurities.	The older child begins to acquire knowledge and skills to adapt to surroundings. Develops sense of achievement but marred by possible feelings of inferiority and failure if efforts are denigrated.	The individual enters stage of personal and vocational identity formation. Self-perception heightened, but potential for conflict, confusion, and strong emotions.
Freud's psycho-sexual stages of development:	The oral stage during which the infant obtains its' principle source of comfort from sucking the breast milk of the mother, and the gratification from the nutrition.	The anal stage when the anus and defecation are the major sources of sensual pleasure. The child is preoccupied with body control with parental/carer encouragement. Obsessional behaviour and over-control later in childhood could indicate a problematic stage development.	The phallic stage, with the penis the focus of attention is the characteristic of this psycho-sexual stage. In boys the oedipus complex and in girls the electra complex are generated in desires to have a sexual relationship with the opposite sex parent. The root of anxieties and neuroses can be found here if transition to the next stage is impeded.	The latency stage, which is characterised by calm after the storm of the powerful emotions preceding it.	The genital stage whereby the individual becomes interested in opposite-sex partners as a substitute for the opposite-sex parent, and as a way of resolving the tensions inherent in oedipuls and electra complexes.

(Cont'd)

Table 6.2 Continued

Theory		Age range			
	1	2–3	4–5	6–11	12–18
Bowlby's attachment theory:	This stage is characterised by pre-attachment undiscriminating social responsiveness. The baby is interested in voices and faces and enjoys social interaction.	The infant begins to develop discriminating social responses and experiments with attachments to different people. Familiar people elicit more response than strangers.	Attachment to main carer is prominent with the child showing separation anxiety when carer is absent. The child actively initiates responses from the carer.	The main carer's absences become longer, but the child develops a reciprocal attachment relationship.	The child and developing young person begins to understand the carer's needs from a secure emotional base.
Piaget's stages of cognitive development:	The sensori-motor stage characterised by infants exploring their physicality and modifying reflexes until they can experiment with objects and build a mental picture of things around them.	The pre-operational stage when the child acquires language, makes pictures, and participates in imaginative play. The child tends to be self-centred and fixed in her/his thinking believing they are responsible for external events.	The concrete operations stage when a child can understand and apply more abstract tasks such as sorting or measuring.	This stage is characterised by less egocentric thinking and more relational thinking–differentiation between things. The complexity of the external world is beginning to be appreciated.	The stage of formal operations characterised by the use of rules and problem-solving skills. The child moves into adolescence with increasing capacity to think abstractly and reflect on tasks in a deductive, logical way.

occur under the guise of benign motives. If you consider the idea that every person has special needs, in the sense of their individual uniqueness, and replace this with the notion of rights then the concept of special needs becomes redundant. Within our social work context the concept of need can have a powerful impact on assessment practice. It has been categorised in the following way to help us distinguish the subtleties in meaning and the ways in which need can be defined (Bradshaw, 1972):

- *Normative need*: this is decided by professionals or administrators on behalf of the community. Standards are set to minimum levels of service with stigma attached.
- *Felt need*: this is limited by the individual's expression of wants based on their perceptions, knowledge and experience.
- *Expressed need*: these are felt needs translated into service demands but restricted by what the client feels is likely to be offered.
- *Comparative need*: this is a comparison of need between two areas or service user groups in order to reach a standardised provision. This results in a levelling-down rather than a levelling-up.

It is useful to bear these definitions in mind during the process of your assessment practice. They can help guide you and enable you to position yourself as you move from the role of client advocate articulating their needs through to the agency representative who is expected to place a boundary or limit on resources. Social workers employed as care managers are to some extent insulated from these twin pressures by being separated from assessment, but they also know what is required by clients in particular circumstances, understand the inadequacies of minimum provision, and appreciate the negative consequences for service users.

You will need to integrate a multi-faceted knowledge of child development into your assessments from learning acquired from studies in human growth and development in order to be able to use this framework confidently (Beckett, 2003). Systems theory and a psycho-social perspective are especially useful tools for this context. In addition, two key concepts that are critical to the interrelationship between the inner and outer worlds are attachment and self-esteem. Children who are securely attached to significant adults in their early childhood have been shown to develop good peer relationships and to cope well with problems. Social work practice that is concerned with helping children who have lost their attachment figures places great emphasis on providing these children with continuity in good, alternative parenting experiences.

The following activity has been designed to provide you with an opportunity to develop some insights into the underpinning knowledge base you are using unconsciously and to reflect on how this fits with your interprofessional work.

- Think about how often attachment theory features in your child protection work in an explicit way.
- Now see how well or how badly you feel this fits with systems theory.

ACTIVITY

Commentary

It is crucial that we avoid being deterministic about some of these theoretical resources or assuming that adverse childhood experiences can automatically cascade down through subsequent generations. Modern research has demonstrated the complexity and diversity of different children's responses to similar experiences. It is vital that we seek to understand what may act as protective factors in children's lives and can then mitigate the effects of negative experiences and promote resilience. It is noteworthy that there are children who are with ample social and family support who have little capacity to cope with small amounts of stress.

Children will vary in their vulnerability to psycho-social stress and adversity as a result of both genetic and environmental influences. Family-wide experiences tend to impinge on individual children in quite different ways. The reduction of negative chain reactions and an increase in positive chain reactions will influence the extent to which the effects of adversity will persist over time. New experiences that open up opportunities can provide beneficial turning-point effects. Although positive experiences in themselves will not exert much of a protective effect, they can be helpful if they serve to neutralise some risk factors and the cognitive and affective processing of experiences is likely to influence whether or not resilience develops (Rutter, 1985).

Evidence-based practice requires the gathering, testing, recording, and weighing of evidence on which to base decisions and the careful use of knowledge gained during work with a child and family. This helps with the task of determining what is most relevant in a family's situation, what is most significant for the child, the impact the intervention is having, and making the judgement about when more or less action is required in the child's best interests. It is important to pay equal attention to all three domains in the framework and to not be deflected by a child's behavioural symptoms to the extent that parental capacity and environmental factors are neglected.

Research demonstrates that assessments can come to be dominated by the agendas set by social services departments, thereby undermining the concept of inter-agency co-operation (Howarth, 2002). Also, in the drive to complete recording forms within specified timescales, anti-oppressive practice is given a lack of attention while the pace of an assessment is inconsistent with a family's capacity to cope. In the case of fostering and adoption work research has highlighted practice based on a diagnostic assessment of foster carers using psychodynamic theories, contrasted with practice based on task-centred, functional analysis which applicants found more useful (Berridge, 1997). The key point here is that we can locate and justify our chosen practice orientation and demonstrate how it fulfils the task requirement within a systems framework while also remaining child centred.

McLeod (2008) offers the following suggestions for making it easier for children and young people to have their views heard and understood and for social workers' practice to become more child centred:

- Stop, look and listen.
- Keep an open mind.
- Give the child some control.
- Start from where the child is.
- Give them permission to talk.
- Avoid direct questions.
- Offer prompts and triggers.
- Provide information and explanations.
- Encourage questions.
- Check out their understandings.

POST-ASSESSMENT ISSUES

The choice of interventions open to social workers in safeguarding children work is necessarily broad because of the wide variety of physical, psychological and social factors influencing the child or young person being helped. The social work literature itself offers a sometimes bewildering array of methods and models of intervention, apart from the wider psychiatric, psychological and therapeutic texts available to guide the helping process with individuals, families or groups. Public health, education, social and fiscal policy interventions by local and central government agencies can also impact on children's welfare generally and these will need to be taken into account.

One way of conceptualising this mosaic of influences on children and adolescents and capturing a *meta* view of such panoramic concerns is the idea that the variety of influences can be classified into different systems. The notion of a systems approach to formulating interventions was developed thirty years ago and it has been enshrined in the classic (1974) text by Pincus and Minahan which illustrates the various systems influencing service users/clients. Within each system of influence there exists a number of factors which the Munro Report has further elucidated.

Before embarking on any one form of intervention however, social workers need to reflect on the ethical questions raised by the choices made and their potential consequences. The legal contexts for intervening in children and young people's lives were considered in Chapter 2 and these are relevant to the discussion here because of their link with the consent and competence to understand the choices offered. For example, individual counselling or therapy may succeed in helping a young person to develop a sense of self, but in so doing the experience may alienate them from their family. Family therapy may also result in improvements in a child with emotional difficulties, but in the process of the work siblings may be adversely affected or the parental marriage/partnership could be exposed as problematic (Sharman, 1997).

And even though a social worker may not deliver the work themselves, the act of referring to a specialist resource offering specific help means they are sanctioning a potentially powerful intervention in the life of the child and their family system.

A social worker who feels that a child is bottling up their feelings and needs to learn to express these via counselling may be causing additional stress to that child who is expected, within their community or cultural context, to be developing self-control and some containment of their emotions. A young person who is displaying destructive obsessional behaviour, or self-harming as a means of managing stress caused by abuse, may be referred for family therapy or given an individual behavioural or psychodynamic intervention by a social worker depending on the particular practitioner's preference, resource limits, or the child's choice. However, each intervention will come with its own set of assumptions and potential consequences in terms of generating other stressors. This is the other side of risk assessment, namely the risk we pose to families. The same intervention could be given to two children with the same problem, but only one of them might benefit. These ethical dilemmas are important as we must acknowledge and reflect upon these before proceeding with any course of action. The crucial point here is to ensure the *most* effective support is offered to the *right* child for an *appropriate* problem.

PART III

CREATING THE DIFFERENCE THAT MAKES A DIFFERENCE

7

COLLABORATIVE SYSTEMS OR COMBATIVE SYSTEMS?

INTRODUCTION

Over many years professionals have been encouraged by government legislation, local and government inquires and local policies and procedures to work together to support the child and family. This has recently been reinforced with the Victoria Climbié inquiry (DH, 2003c), *Every Child Matters* (DfES, 2003b), the Baby Peter inquiry, the Munro Report (2011b) and the new Working Together Guidance (DfE, 2011). However, in reality this appears to be a belief that is valued but not always obtainable. Therefore an exploration of the barriers to working together and the solutions to reducing or removing the barriers in this chapter will offer resources to the individual professional who is concerned about the need for greater collaboration and co-operation consistent with systems practice and theory. This will include exploring ways of networking, working successfully in a group, and highlighting the relevant individuals and systems required to safeguard the wellbeing of children and young people.

The Colwell Report (DHSS, 1974a) repeatedly emphasised the need for a suitable system that would enable practitioners to communicate and interact in a more effective way: 'The overall impression created by Maria's sad history is that while individuals made mistakes it was the "system", using the word in the widest sense, which failed her' (1974a: 86). It would be up to the government to suggest the outline and legal boundaries of such a system, and then up to the inter-agency group of agencies to make that system work, with a key co-ordinating role going to the social services department.

The search for the ideal system began shortly after the publication of the Colwell Report. The guidance for this system was contained in the same series of circulars that established responsibility within the inter-agency field. The hypothesis behind this development was that such a system would make up for individual errors, a lack of training, and difficulties in the inter-agency system. The Laming inquiry similarly emphasised the need for a system that could make up for individual errors.

Although the advice of the government was to become more prescriptive in terms of the system (for example, the Working Together documents defined the categories for registration and the criteria for registration and de-registration), the actual working of the different local systems showed a stubborn local variation (Bingley-Miller et al., 1993; Murphy, 1996a, 1996b, 2003).

According to Murphy (2004), despite the considerable development of child protection systems, inquiries into child deaths still showed that a lack of expertise and poor inter-agency communication and performance heightened the possibility of child deaths or injuries. What the search for an ideal system failed to address was the need for improved training and professional performance within the system. That system, no matter how foolproof, was not, on its own, sufficient. The 1990s saw the same three themes (communication, responsibility and systematisation) being developed in the British inter-agency system. The Children Act 1989 introduced a new era where the family welfare perspective gradually regained its ascendancy over the child protection perspective. This meant that the need for communication between agencies was matched by an insistence on the need to communicate with parents as well as children. The publication of *Messages from Research* (DH, 1995) led some systems into a process that became known as *refocusing*, where children were held outside the child protection system and worked with as children in need (Jones and O'Loughlin, 2002). In 2003 the Laming inquiry report was to comment specifically on how badly the child in need/child protection duality had been handled in Haringey's social services department.

In the area of responsibility, the government intervened with legislation and guidance that continually re-shaped the inter-agency system. After the Children Act 1989, decisions that were to be made about forcible interventions into families' lives (i.e., concerned with abuse) were to be made far more under the supervision of the legal system. One of the problems associated with this growth in power of the legal system was that it presumed that better child-care disposals and judgements would consequently be made. *Every Child Matters* was able to locate child protection work firmly within the wider child in need framework and make suggestions for how the themes of communication, responsibility and systematisation should be handled in the future (Murphy, 2004).

POWER WITHIN SYSTEMS

The hierarchical power structure and the influential role of the four main agencies (health, police, education and social services) are significant. In child abuse work, practitioners may hold positional power over a particular part of the process. Therefore, a paediatrician can hold sway over the interpretation of the signs of physical abuse; the police can offer advice on the likelihood of a successful prosecution for sexual abuse; and the health visitor can interpret the developmental signs of a failure to thrive. But the child protection process holds a special role for the social worker who will have the job of facilitating the child protection process from referral to review. And even where the process involves many other practitioners, it will be the social worker who holds the responsibility for coordinating this work, particularly with regard to the crucial protective intervention. This position can give the impression that *social workers hold too much control and influence* within the system.

Differences in organisational structure (or how the work is managed and controlled) can prove a considerable block to inter-agency working. The organisational, financial and legal bases of the network of professionals are evidently very different here, ranging from the independent contractor status of the individual GP to the quasi-military command structure of the police (Hallett and Birchall, 1992). This means that when a practitioner from a flattened or non-existent hierarchy (for example, a GP) is communicating with a worker from a very structured hierarchy (the police) their understanding of the discretion or choice available to the other will frequently be inaccurate. A certain tension also exists between the exercise of individual professional judgement and what is agency permissible. This tension is easily compounded by the attitudes of other professionals, who may express frustration about delays in decision making while being unaware of the processes that must be gone through (Calder, 2003). In practice, this equation between control and discretion can prove to be complicated. And even when two practitioners come from broadly similar organisations, the same problem of structural difference applies. Although a social worker and a teacher will come from large, well-defined hierarchies, their relationships with their managers can be very different.

The final step in improving power imbalances afflicting inter-agency co-operation might involve challenging those factors that led to an imbalance within the system. The British system suffers from a chronic imbalance between the protective and legal interventions on the one hand and the preventative and therapeutic interventions on the other. This can also lead to dysfunctional differences in how much power exists between the different practitioner groups involved in the process. Good practice should lead to a recognition that all interventions, whether preventative, protective, legal or therapeutic, are essential for good practice. Good practice may mean a move to equalise interventions by emphasising the neglected interventions (preventative and therapeutic) at the expense of those that are already powerful (protective and legal). This will result in a change in the relative power of those groups that currently work in the less powerful interventions.

THE INDIVIDUAL WITHIN THE SYSTEM

One of the reasons often given for failures in inter-agency co-operation is that a key individual within that system failed to fulfil their part of the process and this resulted in a breakdown in the protective intervention. This hypothesis can be commonly seen in child abuse inquiries where individual key personnel are allocated blame: staff were never called to account by their supervisors in respect of the two children at risk (Blom-Cooper, 1987) was the specific criticism of the health visitor and senior nursing officers in the Jasmine Beckford case. In Victoria Climbié's case, Lisa Arthurworrey (the social worker) and Karen Jones (the police officer) were much criticised in the media. Arthurworrey was initially dismissed, even though the senior managers in her department went undisciplined, and it was only much later that the spotlight fell on the paediatrician who was the last professional to examine Victoria and the *systemic historic failings in her department* that were revealed by a whistleblower.

There is a temptation in this to track down difficult individuals in child protection systems, blame them for poor inter-agency relationships, and then to speculate that, when they move on, these inter-agency relationships and their practice will improve. In the Kimberley Carlile case Blom-Cooper's team recommended the removal of Martin Ruddock (the senior social worker) from any future role in the child protection system (Blom-Cooper, 1987). Their inference was clear: in any child protection system it would be Martin Ruddock, as an individual practitioner, who would be unable to help protect children.

Systems theory reveals that it is not the individual within the system but the structure of the system itself that is of key importance. Thus, when that individual does move on, we will find that the problems in inter-agency relationships frequently remain unchanged. The Colwell Report concluded that a system should, so far as was possible, be able to absorb individual errors and yet function adequately, it being quite impossible, and indeed unfair, to lay any direct blame upon any individual or indeed upon any small group of individuals (DHSS, 1974a). The very idea that one individual within a system can be blamed for a child's death or injury denies the whole concept of collective inter-agency decision making and responsibility. Unfortunately, on some occasions, even the concerned agencies themselves can adopt this convenient practice of finding a scapegoat. In Britain, when things go wrong, the system encourages the blaming of individual agencies and practitioners (Murphy, 2000).

As well as bringing all our perspectives and individual aspects from our lives as practitioners, we also bring to our child protection work our personal histories of being a child, an adult, and perhaps a parent as well. Child protection can cut across our feelings and experiences in some of the most personal parts of our lives; those experiences and feelings can in turn have a powerful effect on our professional behaviour. As child abuse work encompasses some of the most painful and private aspects of some people's lives, the work can evoke powerful responses in a practitioner's inner, private self. The pain and the stress of the child or the family can thus be mirrored in the practitioner's feelings (Murphy, 1997).

The following activity could apply to all professionals involved in child protection and provides space for reflecting on the human cost of such stressful work. Knowing that other professionals feel the same should help break down some of the barriers erected by bureaucratic systems.

- Prior to your next planned supervision session let your line manager know that you want some extra time at the end of the agenda. Avoid explaining any specifics.
- In that extra time express how your work in general or a specific high-risk case is affecting you emotionally. Stop your manager from attempting to provide a quick-fix or reverting to a bureaucratic mode involving procedures for stress management.
- Explain that you need them to listen, absorb what you are saying without comment, reflect in silence, and resist feeling that you are criticising them.

Commentary

There is a myth, subscribed to by most agencies and professional groups involved in child protection work, which suggests that while we are at work we can leave the self or the personal part of ourselves at home. However, our personal histories and feelings will travel to work with us each and every day. Unless we work with our conflicts, confusions, disgusts and deep satisfactions they will skew our work. Nothing makes us so aware of our sexuality and anger as sexual abuse (Moore, 1992). Moore reminds us that this split between the professional and the personal is largely false and the myth of the personal-professional split is likely to reduce rather than increase our individual and collective effectiveness.

Child protection procedures implicitly presume that staff will leave their individual selves at home and become truly selfless parts of the child protection machine. It is assumed that there is no need to care for staff who are engaged in child protection work, as that comforting process should take place solely within the private life of the individual concerned, or will somehow dissipate while they are in the office or absorbed in supervision (Murphy, 1997).Our current understanding of personal history and personal reaction is more complicated than this (Dale et al., 1986). The severity of an individual's reaction will not just be based on whether, or how badly, an individual has been abused. It is important to move away from the linear, compartmentalising way of understanding, towards one where we may recognise that a multiplicity of personal factors will affect our personal response to a given child protection case, something which systems theory informs us of.

MULTI-DISCIPLINARY AND INTER-AGENCY WORKING

Partnership practice is not restricted to how you work with service users, it also encompasses how you should follow best practice guidance in relationships with other agencies. Governmental and professional expectations are far more integrated and therefore more effective joint working across professional boundaries in safe-guarding contexts. Research shows there are still barriers to effective working which will have a negative impact on clients and hinder integrated practice. These include:

- financial constraints;
- differing organisational and managerial structures;
- different priorities.

Joint working can be improved and is influenced by intentional approaches as well as informal evolutionary factors. The intentional approach may formalise joint working arrangements but these can neglect the more personal and creative aspects of a partnership. Embedding such approaches can take a long time, constrain opportunities into restrictive prescriptions, and result in relatively unresponsive mechanisms. An evolving approach, on the other hand, allows for informal net-working but can become over-reliant on key personalities and historical associa-tions. Charismatic individuals may be highly effective in the short term but might also prove impossible to replace and will thus leave a void when they move on. A combination of formal and informal strategies can optimise the conditions for effec-tive joint working via:

- joint planning meetings;
- the creation of joint posts;
- the development of joint strategies;
- individual initiatives;
- shared goals and visions;
- a track record of joint working.

Interprofessional or multi-disciplinary care is a contemporary term that is often used synonymously to mean joint working between staff from different professional backgrounds. Staff may work in the same team location or operate from separate uni-professional teams. Within the same agency they may represent different disci-plines or client groups. In whichever configuration joint working has always been recommended as the best way of delivering coherent and effective care in health and social work practice. Every social or health care textbook features injunctions for closer working between agencies, better communication, and clearer lines of accountability.

When these elements of practice are absent this is usually highlighted in all-too frequent inquiries into deaths involving child abuse. The government's practice guidance emphasises these ideas in slick, managerialist terms and appeals to systems-level co-ordination, enhanced procedures, and strategic planning. Translating these ideas into practice skills is more difficult than creating rhetorical slogans. There have been some attempts to identify the key and common skill and knowledge elements that inform our work with children and young people for example (Tucker et al., 1999).

The conclusions so far have been that different workers from different professional contexts can share a common perception of what needs to be understood about a child or young person's life in order to intervene effectively:

- The social and environmental context.
- Gender, class, ethnicity, disability.
- Articulating a human rights perspective.
- Recognising the individual characteristics of every person.
- Developing reflective practice.

These are recognisable as being consistent with social work practice knowledge and skills, however they are also operationalised within different legal and organisational contexts which is where problems will arise when trying to foster better inter-agency working. Staff in any agency context will be hampered and hindered to some extent by the constraints imposed by budgets, resource limits and service specifications. One way of mitigating against these factors is to promote more joint education and training opportunities and to foster moves towards shared professional qualifications.

Social workers are often reminded of their pivotal role in multi-disciplinary working and the core skills of social work practice are cited as a major asset in helping to achieve better interprofessional work (Parsloe, 1999; Smale et al., 2000; Adams et al., 2000). The care manager role has perhaps institutionalised this concept where social workers are employed to organise and monitor care plans using a variety of other agency staff, often in multi-disciplinary settings. In other situations you may be directly or indirectly involved in work in which your contribution, *however small*, could make a big difference to a successful outcome. In the context of child and family work for example, the social work role will be pivotal in the following circumstances:

- As child and family workers involved in assessments.
- As convenors of inter-agency planning meetings.
- At case conferences involving child protection concerns.
- In long-term care planning and reviews.
- In the formal care management role.
- As contributors to multi-disciplinary interventions.
- As referrers to specialist and community resources.

In whichever context of practice you will need to examine the complex web of agencies and staff available that will be able to contribute to clients' needs. Look at the front cover of this book to remind yourself of the complexity. This offers you an opportunity to reflect on the potential for success, spot any potential areas of professional disagreement or confusion, and clarify the social work contribution. The unique professional profile of social work embodying psycho-social principles, as well as a social model of human growth and development, finds expression in the values enshrined in the latest social work code of ethics. Together with the national occupational standards and new competencies described earlier, these offer a power-ful intellectual *corpus* that can be brought to interprofessional and multi-disciplinary work (BASW, 2012).

THE CHALLENGES IN WORKING TOGETHER

The range of staff involved in the delivery of health and social care services is broad and the potential for disagreement, confusion or poor communication is high (Koprowska, 2005). The benefits of working together cannot be overstated but this should not happen at the expense of proper professional debates that can sometimes be difficult. However, before considering the diversity of professional and voluntary backgrounds engaged in this work, it is worth remembering that parents/carers provide over 90 per cent of the care of their children. They are the people who will be most in contact with the child or young person at the centre of concern. Therefore they must be seen as partners with whom an appropriate alliance may be formed, even in the face of profound disagreements about the way forward.

There is growing interest in the further development of interprofessional and multi-disciplinary working in order to maximise the effectiveness of interventions to meet the diverse needs of multi-cultural societies and service users (Magrab et al., 1997; Oberheumer, 1998; Tucker et al., 1999). The evidence suggests there are cost-benefit advantages if a duplication of tasks can be avoided, if relationships between staff are improved, and if there is a greater opportunity to maintain the child as the centre of attention rather than the needs of various organisations.

Other professionals do not experience the same level of supervision or the same type of supervision that permits reflective practice and the opportunity for stress management as well as an exploration of strategies for coping with difference. The tradition in social work for such supervision is constantly brought under pressure by managerialist prescriptions for brief, task-centred working practices, risk assessments and the prioritisation of caseloads. However, supervision that enables a worker to understand and learn from the interactive processes experienced during work would be a valuable tool that would encourage you to reflect on practice that can be emotionally draining.

Some social workers may find the experience unsettling while others will draw immense comfort from it. Both will benefit and have their practice enhanced as a result. In multi-disciplinary and interprofessional contexts a culture of such enlightened supervision for all staff can create a rich climate for professional growth and an improved quality of service for service users. The evidence suggests there is also an appetite to incorporate this social work model of supervision into the new multi-disciplinary teams that are becoming more common in health and social care (Debell and Walker, 2002).

Social workers bring a distinctive contribution to interprofessional and multi-disciplinary work. Effective multi-disciplinary teamworking or inter-agency working requires the notion of power to be addressed and shared more equally between staff. It also demands that this power is shared via more participative practices with service users and the community being served. Your skills in advocacy and empowerment are therefore crucial in making this happen. As workers we also bring a concept of oppression and how discriminatory social contexts can blight the lives of children and families. This wider social and political perspective can raise awareness among other staff and inform and enrich the intervention practices of other professionals (Middleton, 1997).

The activity that follows illustrates the complex nature of your work with children and families which will test the principles of partnership working and interprofessional relationships.

ACTIVITY

- The case study below gives an example where the partnership appears fraught with difficulties and may appear unachievable. You have just been allocated this case.
- Think about how you would try to work in partnership with the family, taking into account the concerns voiced by other professionals.

Father (Seamus), aged 45, unemployed.
Mother (Mary), aged 32, left family six months ago, whereabouts unknown.
Daughter (Anne-Marie), aged 11, at a special school for children with learning difficulties.
Son (Liam), aged 6, attends primary school.
Twins (Sean and Sinead), aged 38 months: Sean is brain damaged and Sinead has a hole in the heart. Both children have developmental delays.

The case was transferred from another local authority and has been dealt with on a duty basis. The father, Seamus, has been unco-operative with many agencies concerned about his children. He has been rude, hostile and racially abusive. Hospital appointments for the twins have been missed and your concerns have been increasing over time. Anne-Marie and Liam bed wet and both have missed a lot of schooling. Seamus feels there is nothing much wrong with them and focuses his attention mostly on the twins. He feels that professionals are exaggerating and he is determined to care for his family on his own.

The following questions might help in your planning:

- What are your feelings about working with members of this particular family?
- What are your anxieties about this case?
- How would you handle Seamus's anger?
- How would you propose to share your concerns about the children with Seamus?
- What strategies would you hope to develop in order to work in partnership with the family?

Commentary

Reflecting on your feelings may produce elements of fear, disapproval, and frustration, or you may perhaps be aware of a certain admiration for Seamus's tenacity and self-sufficiency. You may also feel protective towards the children and angry that Seamus is not putting their needs first. As a black worker you may want to discuss whether you should be allocated this case given his racist language, but on the other hand you may feel quite challenged to work with him.

Your main anxieties may come from Seamus's lack of co-operation and from concerns about the children's needs being neglected. The long-term consequences of this on their development, together with the impact on Seamus of soldiering on, heighten your concerns. His anger could be explored to tease out the cause and help him manage it more usefully. Is it due to his wife's exit? Being perceived as an inadequate parent? Professional interference? His feelings of helplessness and his own needs being eclipsed?

Being open and honest with Seamus about your concerns for the children is important but tricky. If you are less open you are likely to be disempowering Seamus by not sharing the same information about the reasons for your involvement. So the issue is how you will share your concerns and whether you can achieve this in a supportive manner, avoiding being patronising or accusatory. You might find joint working with a colleague helpful here when managing his anger and protecting your own safety.

Arranging a multi-agency case conference might be useful for planning and using resources and could offer a chance to share concerns and measure the level against other perspectives. You might find it worthwhile to explore the family's wider system as a possible source of support, however some thought also needs to be given to the significance for the children of Mary and her absence. You might think about using a contract with Seamus. This could set out the purposes of your involvement and what is possible or not in terms of support, help and resources. This could then give him sufficient space to outline his concerns, need and goals.

As part of the planning work, it might be helpful to list the needs of each child in the family as well as any concerns and to then identify areas of agreement and disagreement between yourself and Seamus. You may however decide that he cannot be worked with and that a legal intervention is the only way to secure the children's welfare. If this is the case, it is important that such a judgement is soundly based on evidence from other professional's research, and that it only comes after all the other possibilities for engagement have been exhausted.

Imagine you have a supervision session arranged with your team leader. Supervision should be part of a consultation and thinking process. Explore with your team leader, peer group, tutor or a colleague, some of the issues that have arisen when considering how to work in partnership with service users in practice. This might include managing your own feelings, dilemmas and conflicts. You can also consider the challenges in trying to work in an anti-discriminatory way in partnership with other professionals and colleagues.

Supervision is a good opportunity to explore those issues and feelings that you are uncertain or unconfident about. It should give you enough space and time to think and work through the issues raised. You might find asking yourself the questions listed below useful in helping you identify areas for further exploration, self-development and awareness.

- What particular dilemmas does partnership working present for me?
- What are the advantages and disadvantages of working in partnership with clients?
- Do I find it easy or difficult to be open and honest with service users about my concerns?
- What strategies do I need to develop to handle difficult feelings?

THE ROLE OF ADVOCACY

Advocacy is associated with a rights-based approach to planning intervention and arises from a recognition that social work has not always empowered service users. At its simplest it is about speaking up for, or acting on behalf of, another person. The aim of advocacy is to make sure each client's voice is heard; to make sure that person gets the services they need; and to make sure they know their rights so they can work towards obtaining what they are entitled to. It should be part of your integrated practice knowledge and skills so you will need to recognise that:

- the service user's voice and views are paramount;
- good advocacy leaves the person more able to do it themselves;
- advocacy should help people to make informed choices;
- the user feels in control of the process and trusts the advocate;
- advising, assisting and supporting are vital, not pressurising or persuading.

There are three main types of advocacy and these are as follows.

CITIZEN ADVOCACY

This works on a one-to-one basis where volunteers will usually act on behalf of those who require services. A citizen advocate will primarily perform an instrumental role which can focus on welfare benefits problems or negotiating a care plan. There is also an expressive role for volunteers which involves meeting emotional needs, befriending people, and providing support.

SELF-ADVOCACY

This involves training and group support to help people learn skills and gain sufficient emotional strength to advocate for themselves. It is also about personal and political needs, focusing on participation in all areas of service planning and delivery. The aim is not just to improve services but also to improve the status of service users. Self-advocacy has the important function of facilitating collective action as well as making it easier for individuals to be assertive.

GROUP ADVOCACY

This brings people together who have similar interests so they can operate as a group to represent these shared interests. Similar to self-advocacy, the aim is to influence service delivery decisions and reframe how certain problems or groups of clients are perceived by professionals. Group advocacy may be part of campaigning organisations that are operating in the voluntary sector. People with learning difficulties and mental health problems have been in the forefront of group advocacy as they have responded to depersonalised and institutional services failing to meet their needs in safeguarding children situations.

The following activity extends the concept of partnership and interprofessional work and will enable you to reflect on the difficulties in trying to practise advocacy.

ACTIVITY

- Think about some recent practice you have been involved in and reflect on whether there were elements of advocacy in your work.
- How might you evaluate whether your approach encompasses principles of advocacy?

Commentary

The following questions might be useful in helping you decide whether and how you might incorporate an advocacy approach in your social work practice. How do service users have a say in these areas, what is the evidence that their contribution is valued, and what helps or hinders advocacy? Look at the following and decide how far and how much service users are involved in these activities:

- Collecting and sharing information.
- Meeting the training needs of staff and service users.
- Policy making and planning.
- Implementing policy and running the service.

Providing service users with enough resources to enable them to meet and discuss policy and practice issues is evidence of a genuine effort to engage and facilitate empowering strategies. Training in committee skills is required to help demystify official ways of working that are unfamiliar to those who are outside of the power system. It is crucial that as workers we support and sustain people who may falter, feel nervous and appear ready to withdraw when they meet the earliest obstacle to their participation. Try to resist assuming this proves they are not capable and instead try to build their confidence and have a strategy in place to deal with their anxieties about competence.

The smallest detail can make a big difference. For example, remember to invite a user group to send a representative rather than submit to the temptation to select someone yourself with whom you feel comfortable. It is also probably better to invite more than one person because an individual can easily feel outnumbered in a meeting that is full of professionals. Two people can support each other and give each other confidence when speaking. It is also important to pay them to attend and offensive to expect them to do so regularly as the only unpaid people in a roomful of salaried professionals.

INTERPROFESSIONAL CARE

Case Example

Jason is a white, working-class young man with a history of family violence, disruption, offending behaviour and failed care placements. He is currently in residential care and on the cusp of moving on to independent living. His engagement with child and adolescent mental health services has been sporadic and there is concern he will need input from adult mental health services. His behaviour has worsened in recent months as discussion of his future is more often mentioned. He uses alcohol and drugs and knows people who deal drugs, one of whom is his girlfriend. Trying to organise a seamless multi-agency plan for his transition to independent living is proving hard, as the various institutional age limits for involvement are reached, and adult services cannot see him as a priority.

Using systems theory map out a grid showing on one side what, in partnership with him, Jason's needs will be after discharge from care. On the other axis of the grid show which agencies are best able to meet those needs.

Using the risk assessment/management tools identify potential problem areas, anticipate how they might manifest themselves and put together an action plan before he leaves care.

Commentary

Jason like any other young person will usually wish to become more independent as they reach their middle to late teenage years, they may also at times have a problem with non-co-operation. These issues may vary from the need to undertake further education and reflect upon career opportunities, to the exploration of adult relationships and the wish to have families. The professional has a requirement to ensure that individual's need for information is also met.

Jason will need help to make decisions with various degrees of support from their family and professionals depending upon age and level of independence and on-going relationship with family members. Young people leaving care or young offenders units will need further support from professionals as they may lack support from family members to discuss issues. The concerns about inconsistency of support from services may be due to where the young person lives and is also reflected in the support that can be offered by specific youth practitioners whether within Youth Services, or Youth Offending Teams.

While some parts of the country have well established teams who offer a service often via specialists who are experts in young people and their needs, there are still a significant number of individuals who have minimal input from specialist youth services unless they are offenders. These young adults who have been involved in the criminal justice system are trying to live as normal a life for themselves as they can, however it is very difficult for them to find and hold down a job or continue in full time education.

While this specialised service gives the individual the physical support and an intervention if required, it might not always take into account the uniqueness of the person and their family. In addition, while the opportunity may arise for some individuals the reality is for many young people that the resources are not available in their geographical area for this to occur. Even when the service is available, the time and financial restraints may make the service difficult to implement. Research with nurse specialists in practice demonstrates this was clearly highlighted. While nurses and doctors acknowledge the value of progression services for young adults before they reach adult care, practically this is much more difficult to plan.

PARTNERSHIP PRACTICE

Parents who have been socially excluded will have greater difficulty in promoting the safety and wellbeing of their children, obtaining help if problems arise, and participating in the helping process (Audit Commission, 1994). The concept of partnership may be quite alien to some parents who will expect to be told what to do and how the situation will be put right. Others will want to prescribe precisely what needs to happen. Making explicit and keeping in mind that *partnership does not mean equal* will help clients and social workers to form a more effective relationship.

Working in multi-disciplinary contexts means addressing the different knowledge and value base of other staff, but it also means encountering a variety of views about service user participation and empowering strategies. Not all staff (and that includes other social workers) will be comfortable with notions of participatory practice and empowerment. The following list provides an indication of the potential reservoir of professional and voluntary resources available, several of whom may be involved with the same family at the same time.

- *Primary care*: this is based around GP practices and providing a child health service to enable, advise, and support parents; it offers diagnoses and access to help with the mild and early signs of problems; it is located within a Primary Care Trust boundary.
- *Child health*: this is based in specialist units or clinics in acute or community settings; paediatricians, health visitors, school nurses and other specialists will be involved in physical and developmental problems that include a mental health component.
- *Teachers*: these will be based in schools together with other support staff and educational psychologists in special units such as EBD schools; they can offer an early identification of learning difficulties, SEN and/or behavioural problems, as well as deliver a personal and social skills education to promote mental health.
- *Social work and probation*: these are based around local authority structures and special-ist units with children and family client groups; they offer family support, child protec-tion, and work with young offenders, including the identification of, and help with, mental health problems in co-operation with other agencies.
- *Voluntary sector*: this will be based in family centres or peripatetic home visiting as a growing part of the mosaic of provision for children and young people where statutory services are inaccessible or inappropriate; this sector offers a preventive role, less stigma, and a flexible response to local needs such as counselling, parent support, or advice and information.
- *Mental health specialists*: these are based in outpatient, inpatient, or specialist centres together with multi-disciplinary staff such as social workers, psychotherapists, child and adolescent psychiatrists, psychologists, and family therapists; they offer assessments, management, and therapeutic interventions with individuals, groups or families.

INTERPROFESSIONAL SYSTEMS AND RELATIONSHIPS

The increased use of voluntary agencies, unqualified family support staff and even unpaid volunteers is one facet of the government's strategy to provide more people who can help parents rapidly while concerns escalate. However, without adequate training, supervision and support these staff can be ineffective and, at worst, may do more harm than good. Efforts put into improving relationships between staff can benefit both them and clients. The limited knowledge base of some staff may prevent them from assessing individuals accurately and then lead them to interpret a child's behaviour, for example, as wilful rather than perhaps a reaction to abuse. The evidence suggests, in essence, that bringing services closer to children and families who require them is essential. At the same time it is a necessity that we make sure there is a good fit between the expertise of the staff involved and the complexity of the problem (Davis et al., 1997; Durlak and Wells, 1997; Ouellette et al., 1999; Dulmus and Rapp-Paglicci, 2000).

This means more integrated provision at the primary level, with multi-disciplinary staff receiving training and support to intervene in ways that will meet the needs of the local community. In addition, a systems-wide dimension is required here to energise and mobilise the latent strengths of those individuals and groups who can act as grassroots facilitators to help create preventive resources when and where these are needed. Such an organisational model requires a systems-level method of evaluation in order to test its effectiveness in delivering better outcomes for children and young people. A system of care that is made up of multiple agencies working together acknowledges that children have multiple needs which will require at various times different combinations of a broad range of health and social care agencies.

However, there is some evidence that suggests simply altering the service delivery configuration of services will not in and of itself translate into improved outcomes for children (Morrisey et al., 1997). The focus of the research needs to embrace an evaluation of both the organisational and the supportive impact and how these two variables interact. The strain imposed on professional relationships can impact adversely on relationships with service users. The increasing demands for service provision are producing pressure to spread staff thinly across a range of needs, even though this may not in the long run prevent the abuse of some children and young people and only scratch the surface of underlying causes. The social work task is to research the local community in order to identify naturally occurring systems/resources/networks of people who, with suffient support and encouragement, will be able to bring their expertise to the search for solutions.

We mentioned previously there is growing interest in the further development of interprofessional and multi-disciplinary working in order to maximise the effectiveness of interventions to meet the diverse needs of multi-cultural societies and service users (Magrab et al., 1997; Oberheumer, 1998; Tucker et al., 1999). The evidence suggests there are cost-benefit advantages if a duplication of tasks can be avoided, if relationships between staff are improved, and if there are more opportunities to maintain the child as the centre of attention rather than the needs of the various organisations. The suggestion is that rather than passing the young person round the system of costly service provision for repeated assessments, it would be preferable to sustain work over a *consistent* period with as few staff as *need* to be involved. Research with young people has supported this proposition (Sinclair et al., 1995). What young people say they want is:

- a continuity of input from the same social worker;
- persistence on the part of the social worker working on their behalf;
- social workers engaging with them in direct work;
- social workers being less dependent on input from other professionals.

The terminology employed by staff in key agencies is one of the factors militating against more effective interprofessional work. For example, in the case of a child exhibiting disturbed behaviour health professionals will tend to talk about mental health problems and psychiatric disorders, while education staff will talk about children who are presenting challenging behaviour, emotional or behavioural problems, or who have special educational needs, and social workers will talk about children in need, at risk, suffering significant harm, or some of the above. All these terms are used to describe children with broadly similar problems. A psychiatrist can describe a child as having a conduct disorder, while a teacher might say they are aggressive and attention seeking, and a social worker might describe the same child as emotionally disturbed due to neglect and/or abuse.

The characteristics of successful multi-disciplinary work occur within a framework that is familiar to social workers. This begins with assessment and then proceeds through decision making, planning, monitoring, evaluation, and finally to closure. It has been argued that this common framework which is employed by most health and social care staff offers the optimum model for encouraging reflective practice to be at the core of contemporary social work (Taylor and White, 2000). This can occur in an examination of the impact of the intervention in meeting a child's needs; in the evaluation of staff inputs and strategies; and in the relationship between organisational demands, resources, objectives and priorities. Each agency involved can measure effectiveness against this basic framework and find some common ground on which to consider the best way of helping that child.

Reflective practice offers the opportunity to shift beyond functional analysis to making active links between the value base, policy-making process, and the variety of interventions conducted. Combined with this practice-led motivation for interprofessional working, there is evidence that government policy imperatives requiring closer co-operation between professionals coming into contact with children and families are having an effect (Eber et al., 1996; VanDenBerg and Grealish, 1996; Sutton, 1999). Social workers' skills in relationship building, their tendency to make links, network and share information, make them ideally suited to advance this agenda.

The aim is for a seamless web of provision where needs are recognised and assessed and interventions are formulated on a preventive basis in order to stop small, manageable difficulties developing into huge, intractable problems. Without such early interventions within an holistic multi-factoral approach, children suffering early difficulties run the risk of becoming troubled adults with all the greater social, psychological and financial consequences that this entails (Bayley, 1999). Social workers are central to the success of this project with their distinctive capacity for facilitating multi-agency co-operation.

CHANGING PATTERNS OF SERVICE DELIVERY

The organisational patterns for service delivery across all public services are now moving to multi-professional, multi-disciplinary and cross-departmental teams in order to reduce or eliminate such blockages. This is, in effect, what is meant by government references to cross-cutting approaches to the delivery of public services. In health and social care, this translates into multi-agency working and there are signs of new interprofessional teams being created. Ovretveit (1996) argues that it is important to be able to distinguish the type of multi-disciplinary team so that:

- practitioners understand their role;
- managers can make changes to improve service quality;
- planners can decide which type is most suited to the needs of a client population;
- researchers can contribute to knowledge about which type is most effective.

Apart from increasing the knowledge and skills base of individual practitioners who came with different levels of prior training and staff development, the delivery mode of child protection training would not be profession-specific and thus unlike much conventional training. The additional benefit of such a system-wide training programme would be closer integration within teams and across the local service.

An important way of describing joint practitioner teams refers to the extent to which the team manages its resources as a collective and permanent presence or as separate professional services. Table 7.1 illustrates the advantages and disadvantages. One of the vexed questions about effectiveness in the organisation of interprofessional care is how to mitigate against the impact of the structural inhibitors thwarting attempts to cut across professional boundaries. These can be exemplified by the variety of geographical boundaries covered by health, social services and education authorities, combined with different pay scales and terms of employment (Young and Haynes, 1993; Leathard, 1994). In services the Education, Health and Social Work structural hierarchies have traditionally militated against collaboration, preserved their separate professional role identities, and inhibited interprofessional working (Fagin, 1992; Rawson, 1994; Department for Education and Employment, 1998).

This has thwarted repeated attempts to achieve the much-vaunted seamless service for children and families in difficulties as recommended in the Children Act (DH, 1989a). This problem can be overcome at the planning stage by providing each local service with a specific geographical catchment area which enables creative innovative thinking to flourish within and between agencies. Another way of describing joint practitioner teams refers to *how the team is led and how its members are managed*. Team management is a potentially controversial subject where the challenge for multi-disciplinary teams is to establish a structure that allows an appropriate autonomy for practitioners from different professions but also permits the team manager to control the use of staff time (Onyet et al., 1994). The professional background of such a manager will invariably cause concerns about favouritism or a bias towards those from a similar background. Old rivalries and jealousies could also quickly surface and threaten team harmony and collaborative working.

The job of manager therefore calls for highly developed diplomatic skills both internally and externally in relation to other agencies. Generally, there needs to be information cascade within the safeguarding system and outside it that addresses the broader children and families' services framework. It is vital that we ensure more fluid communication between agencies in order to make certain as far as is possible that the right service is supporting the right families at the right time. Within a focused strategy, it is a crucial management task to liaise with other services providers in our efforts to achieve the following:

- To streamline the referral processes between each service.
- To exchange referrals and share in consultation.
- To avoid families or referrers feeling passed around the system.
- To maintain service accountability.
- To monitor the service eligibility criteria.

The multi-disciplinary nature of services offering intensive input, advice, information, parental guidance, and direct work with children in their own homes, or in preferred contexts such as schools, is indicative of a non-stigmatising acceptable service. The issue of roles and boundaries between different professionals has long been debated in the literature on health and social care and there is evidence that change is now happening (Munley et al., 1982; NISW, 1982).

OVERCOMING THE HURDLES TO IMPLEMENTATION

Despite understanding the challenges to multi-disciplinary working and having a better organisational framework there are still various hurdles to overcome in order to implement the Working Together principles. While there is some evidence of the positive benefits of skills mixing and sharing knowledge, thus leading to a blurring of former professional identities, there is other evidence that paradoxically suggests the encouragement of generic interprofessional working actually *reinforces* the boundaries between professions (Brown et al., 2000). It is possible that as staff continue to train together, develop generic working and eventually harmonise their status and pay differentials, there may be some resistance to relinquishing former roles and perhaps even be a *strengthening* of the boundaries between professions. The challenge for the managers in this will be to preserve the distinctive individual professional expertise base but not at the expense of service coherence. The challenge for practitioners meanwhile will be to maintain a sense of loyalty to an identity while at the same time enabling that identity to change. Table 7.2 over the page provides an illustration of the areas for consideration when planning the depth and extent of multi-disciplinary care for a child.

Services targeted at areas of social disadvantage where high levels of truancy, school exclusion, child protection registrations, juvenile crime, unemployment, and emerging child mental health problems can be identified support the social exclusion agenda of the government. However, it is necessary to ensure the representative nature of the workforce in terms of gender, ethnic diversity and disability. The literature on race and gender emphasises the significance of balance and proportionality with regard to the demographic nature of the area being served. Yet all the evidence suggests that in children and families' welfare services there are unrepresentative and

Table 7.1

Advantages	Disadvantages
Collective sharing responsibility	Time consuming consultation
More efficient use of staff (enabling development of specialists)	Increase in admin and communication cost
Effective service provision (overall service planning)	Conflicting and different leadership styles, values and language
Satisfying working environment (more relevant and supportive services)	Reduced independences and autonomy of practitioners
Better risk management, auditing of services and research	Difficult for professionals to make individual decisions
Ease of access for children and families	Inequalities in status
Development of new ideas, roles and ways of working	Minimises the importance of professional differences
Opportunity for shared supervision	Risk of professional collusion
Enhancement of professional skills	Separate educational backgrounds
Avoidance of isolation for practitioners	Blurring roles
Efficient sharing of education and resources	
Promotes professional openness	

Table 7.2   Scale of collaboration, co-operation and co-ordination

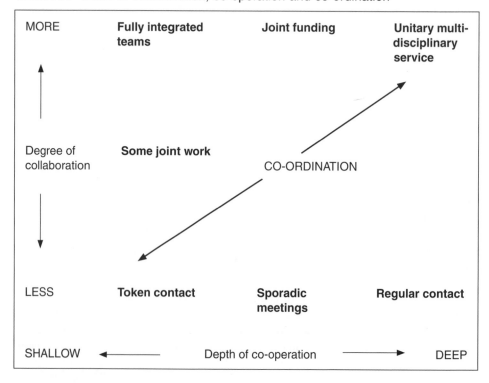

disproportionate numbers of female, white, middle-class professional staff (Dominelli, 1998; Cote, 1997; Bhugra ,1999; Bhugra and Bahl, 1999).

The practical results of efforts to encourage interprofessional working aiming to improve the quality, delivery and co-ordination of all services for children and young people need to be rigorously evaluated (DH, 1998; Tucker et al., 1999; Rodney, 2000).

THE EXPERIENCE OF INTERPROFESSIONAL WORKING

If new services can ensure the availability of time which will permit a reflective, considered atmosphere this could optimise our professional judgement. This would contrast with previous work experiences that could be characterised by reactive, unplanned and overburdened workloads that allowed very little time for considered judgements. This welcome capacity to reflect, however, might present certain dilemmas in cases where, for example, some staff feel they may not in the short term, be addressing the underlying causes of some children's problems, particularly where some longer-term input could prove valuable.

Staff are under pressure to reduce waiting lists and respond quickly to emerging problems with early interventions of a short-term nature. The concern here is that this may result either in early re-referrals or may indeed create an eventual need for help from specialist services if that short-term input is inadequate or the situation deteriorates. On the other hand, having too much time to think about every detail of a child's circumstances can emphasise the complexity and multiple explanations available, thereby leading to caseload drift and ineffective decision making.

One evident strength of the new team cultures is the potential for co-counselling and training support systems for these kinds of concerns. Teams can learn to utilise the best aspects of skills mixing by using each other as resources of expertise and specialist knowledge, to the advantage of service users, and by tackling the challenges in incorporating new ideas and different ways of approaching child and family difficulties. A consultation and training role (now in place in many children and families' teams offering support and advice to other professionals) can also contribute to more interprofessional understanding, particularly in the health and education sectors where old contacts and relationships could be employed to positive effect.

The activity that follows focuses on the challenges in interprofessional child protection work and provides you with a chance to reflect on and discover some positive ways forward.

- If you are working in a multi-disciplinary team, or know someone who is, think about the advantages and disadvantages you personally feel exist.
- Now discuss in supervision your thoughts and list the practical differences you could introduce to reduce the disadvantages.

ACTIVITY

Commentary

Establishing new teams, in an existing professional network of statutory and voluntary providers within established agencies and a dynamic context of shrinking resources, austerity measures and multiple initiatives, is not an easy task. There are opportunities for collaboration between these providers and new teams but there are also challenges to face in fitting in without duplicating or undermining existing good work. Changes in the wider system in areas such as school health provision and fluctuations in the voluntary sector emphasise the importance of collaborative meetings to enhance opportunities for maintaining and improving the Working Together principles and integrated provision rather than causing confusion. Multi-disciplinary teams require skilled management and supervision and constant monitoring using a systems perspective to note their alliances, interactions and communication patterns.

However, there is some potential here for confusion about specific services because of the variety of voluntary and statutory agencies working in the broad area of family support and especially in disadvantaged locations (Hetherington and Baistow, 2001). Church, voluntary and charitable groups have existed in these locations for many years and created their own distinctive role within the diverse range of formal and informal provision of welfare services. There is in these circumstances the prospect of a duplication of efforts or, at worse, mixed messages being given to families from the different agencies. The interprofessional nature of new teams carries the potential for enabling a better understanding of how the overall picture of support services fits together.

It is possible that as new teams continue to train together and develop generic working there may be some resistance to relinquishing former roles and even a strengthening of the boundaries between professions. The challenge for service managers will be to preserve the distinctive individual professional expertise base but not at the expense of service coherence. When attempting to engage children and families already suffering under the pressure of racism and discrimination it is crucial that children, families and carers will have the maximum choice when engaging with services aiming to meet their needs (Bhui and Olajide, 1999). In addition, new teams would benefit from some formal service user involvement, especially if with children and young people this could be done separately away from parents or carers, at the clinical audit, monitoring, review, and strategic planning levels of the service (Treseder, 1997; Barnes and Warren, 1999; Alderson, 2000). Conventional uni-professional services have tended to miss this opportunity for empowering service users.

REVOLUTION OR EVOLUTION?

We have seen that a child protection system will be influenced and formulated by the conflicting definitions of and perspectives on child abuse. This system will also be influenced by the shape of the existing professional network and by the roles which agencies take or are given within the process. The crucial dilemma, around which the system is built, is the child's right not to be abused and the parent's right not to be interfered with by agents of the state. Twenty years ago we heard a familiar lament: concerns about the child-care agents of the state doing too much and too coercively, and about them doing too little and too ineffectually, resulted in a call for legislation and policy that would attempt to proceed in two directions simultaneously, both looking towards better protection of the child and better protection of the parent (Fox Harding, 1991).

This is the key debate for all child protection systems in the post-Munro period: how well will they be able to hold these mutually antagonistic demands at the forefront of their work? And how well will they be able to intervene to prevent serious abuse and to act in a non-interventionist way towards those families where there is no threat of serious abuse? Can a balance be struck between these two poles of behaviour, or is constant conflict between the two inevitable? In the child protection system, inter-agency work is compulsory. Unfortunately, doing inter-agency work well, and striving for good inter-agency practice, is not. Do we need a revolution in safeguarding practice or must we rely on an evolutionary process? Poor practice is shown by a grudging communication with, and the lack of inclusion of, other agencies. It is also shown by the resistance behind the conviction that *'my agency or practitioner group knows best, and we have nothing to gain from the input of other agencies or practitioners'*.

The journey towards good practice begins with an acknowledgement that all agencies and practitioner groups have something to offer in child protection work and is followed by striving to let others participate in the fullest possible way in the process, thereby combating the urge to think and work in unilateral ways (Murphy, 2004).

The responsibility for achieving good practice is a shared one. It does not rest with one agency or one particular practitioner group. Neither does it rest solely with individual practitioners or their managers: although the latter have an important role to play, they share this crucial responsibility with local child-care systems as well as local and national political systems.

The level of achievement of good practice will vary over time, place, and even between cases. It is vital that we constantly strive to improve our practice at all levels, remembering that a positive inter-agency interaction is re-created with each new interaction and each new case that comes into the system. Inter-agency collaboration requires constant attention, re-motivation and energy (Murphy, 2000). Positive inter-agency and multi-disciplinary practice is not easy to achieve. In some ways the unilateral, single-agency path is easier to organise and control. However, good child protection work is itself not easy to accomplish but it becomes more attainable when set within the context of positive, systems-based, inter-agency practice.

8

SOCIAL INCLUSION AND CULTURAL AWARENESS

INTRODUCTION

This chapter considers the implications for employing a socially inclusive and culturally aware model of practice as an inherent feature of systems thinking. The optimum methods and models of practice to achieve this central policy aim and measures of effectiveness against the dimensions of culture, class, ethnicity, religion, sexuality, disability, poverty, age, and homelessness are taken into account. Discussing the sociology and social construction of childhood is important in helping social workers understand the complexities at play in safeguarding children and young people in an ethnically rich and culturally diverse society which is evolving constantly. The role of anti-racist and anti-discriminatory practice in this area of practice should not be understated as the current economic austerity fosters resentment and anger among those affected by unemployment, poverty and social exclusion.

The increasing visibility of overtly racist political organisations and the respectability provided by their election to the European Parliament act as a warning of the threats posed to immigrant or established minority groups. The needs of asylum seekers and refugee children, the importance of cultural identity and the common trans-cultural characteristics of health and psycho-social problems are all part of a systems-informed practice. The role played by spirituality and religion and inter-generational family tensions within different ethnic minority communities should not be underestimated here. This poses real dilemmas for social workers seeking to place children's welfare uppermost while also acknowledging the cultural dislocation and confusion experienced by many parents. Thus an understanding of the way oppression and discrimination impacts on working practices to hinder systems practice is crucial.

A CULTURALLY INCLUSIVE THEORETICAL MODEL

Using an integrated systems model means understanding that changes in any aspect of the family system can affect other parts of the system. Attachment insecurity in one member is likely to have ripple effects through the whole system as we saw in Chapter 6. These dynamics mean that changes which occur in one part of the system, (e.g., within the parent/child relationship) can alter some aspect of the association between secure attachment and couple relationship quality.

A growing body of research is finding concordance between a mother's adult attachment and their attachment relationship with their child. It has been widely assumed that the quality of the parent/child relationship is the linking mechanism, that adults who are securely attached themselves tend to provide a secure base for their children (Byng-Hall, 1998). It has also been suggested that the relationship between a child's parents plays a central role in the generational transmission of working models of attachment. That relationship quality may play a causal role in affecting parenting style and children's adaptation. In other words, the family system plays a part as well as the dyadic parent/child relationship.

By extrapolating from recent research findings some authors have concluded that the transmission of attachment relationships from grandparents to parents to children is not simply a matter of parenting. When a person learns early on that they are worthy of love, and that adults will be responsive and available in times of need, they are more likely to establish satisfying relationships with other partners and to have the inclination and ability to work towards solving relationship problems and regulating emotions so that they do not escalate out of control (Mikulincer et al., 2002).

This leads to a place for culturally aware practice in working with children and adolescents on their difficulties, not only for problems which are clearly involving the whole family but also for occasions when problems arise in dyadic relationships. For example, a young person may be in conflict with family cultural values, perhaps because of their developmental stage, and also in dispute with the same gender parent. This also raises the question of how to help adults move on and restructure their adult attachment where this is part of the problem.

The following experiential activity aims to help you increase your sensitivity and awareness of differences that may be taken for granted or are being denied and provides a chance to reflect more deeply on these.

- Consider the above ideas in the context of your own children or those of a close friend/relative.
- Reflect on their circumstances, their position on the child development/attachment continuum, and any specific cultural issues you feel are having an impact.

ACTIVITY

Commentary

There have been enormous steps in the last five years in looking at the interactions between attachment and systems theory. The contribution of these two theories to understanding the dilemmas faced by individuals throughout the lifecycle has been well established. That attachment style can develop and may change throughout a child or young person's life, in the context of their experiences in relationships, enhances the understanding of family systems and thereby offers a valuable tool to help construct a culturally aware practice. Peer pressure and external systems play a large part in influencing the self-identity of every young person, therefore their position along the child development/attachment continuum is a vital part of the systems perspective.

Overall there is wide support in the research findings for practitioners who are working with individuals or families to pay close attention to the attachment styles and relationships (dyadic) within each family as well as working with the entire family system. The duality of the approach enables a more detailed understanding of family dynamics. Utilising the concepts embodied in the systems model also supports the practice of combining family, group, and individual therapies as appropriate. While there is still a long way to go here it is clear that thinking about the family system alone, or about the complexities of attachment relationships alone, will prove to be limiting (Walker and Akister, 2004).

However this is easy to say and hard to do. How we should work with attachments remains unclear. Systems theory offers clear ways of working with a family or child and can include work that is focused on the dyadic relationships which may alter attachments. Social workers need to consider a place for individual, couple and whole family interventions and their potential impact on the attachment relationships in order to enhance cultural competence. Furthermore, there is increasing evidence that the specificity in the associations of mental health problems and cultural factors indicates that the relationship between ethnicity and perception of mental health problems in children and adolescents is complex and cannot be understood in isolation from other factors or a more culturally relevant understanding of conceptual models.

MENTAL HEALTH AND CULTURE

Thus cultural variations will affect the prevalence rates, similarities and differences in children's and young people's mental health. The use of *ICD 10* and *DSMIV* medical classifications offers a limiting paradigm with which to understand many problems. Not all children with symptoms of mental health problems will show a marked impairment, while conversely some children will experience a significant psycho-social impairment without reaching the clinical threshold for diagnosis (Silberg, 2001). In a child protection context the symptoms of abuse are often disguised, acted out, or misunderstood. The way forward is to continually question and critically examine the assumptions we make about the assessment and intervention methodology to ensure we keep pace with the constantly changing cultural environment of children and young people. Victoria Climbié was considered by her carers to be possessed by demons, which was consistent with the belief system and advice from the African evangelical church they attended. Beating her was held to be an appropriate method for removing these demons which were responsible for her 'naughty behaviour'. Yet a social worker's assessment would probably have interpreted her behaviour as grief or separation anxiety as a result of being away from her natural parents.

The importance of social workers developing a culturally aware practice for working with children and young people cannot be overstated. If we are to truly reach them therapeutically and create the sort of relationship within which they can begin to understand themselves better and recover from abusive experiences, then we need to work hard at knowing them fully. This means adapting and developing our methods and models of practice to fit each child and not the other way round. This means resisting offering a *monotherapeutic* experience to every child or young person regardless of their unique characteristics (Walker, 2005). In so doing we can engage with them and enable their needs to permeate our working practices more comprehensively. This necessitates our ensuring that we do not make generalisable assumptions about a child or young person's home life, customs or beliefs from a cursory question or by relying solely on information about their religion, ethnic origin or family background (Parekh, 2000; Hartley, 2003; Kehily and Swann, 2003).

Children and young people are developing psychologically in an external world in which information and the power it has to influence and shape their beliefs and feelings have never been greater. The control and manipulation of that information is being concentrated in a few hands which are themselves closely identified with a narrow ideological doctrine that legitimates certain forms of behaviour, attitude and culture. Developed countries in the West that are led by America dominate the production, marketing and distribution of products, representing brand names and iconic images aimed at maximising profits in the global marketplace (Hall, 1993). Children and young people are viewed as consumers and in this context the nature of their indigenous culture is seen as another part of their identity that can be moulded in order to maintain cultural conformity. Their desperate need to fit in, be included and be the same as other children is exploited relentlessly by corporations propagating certain values that reinforce the consumerist culture of the early twenty-first century.

Children and young people face considerable challenges in maintaining their cultural integrity in the face of institutional racism, homophobia, economic activity, or migration patterns. The consequences of these may lead to significant emotional and psychological problems being expressed: for example, by high rates of school exclusion among African-Caribbean children (Okitikpi, 1999); by the self-harm, suicide and para-suicide of gay and lesbian young people (Trotter, 2000); and by unemployment among Bangladeshi youth (Jones, 1996). The cultural assets of minority children regularly go unrecognised, denied or devalued within the wider community (Newman, 2002). It is crucial therefore that the support offered by social workers includes opportunities to celebrate their heritage and creates links with other members of their cultural or social group. Children from migrant cultures are especially vulnerable to feelings of inferiority, resulting in their frustration, anxiety and poor school attainment (Spencer, 1996). In the USA the promotion of resilience in black communities is an important strategy aimed at developing cultural confidence and enhancing their problem-solving capacities (Reynolds, 1998).

DEFINING CULTURE

The following practical activity will illustrate how a word or term that appears throughout the interprofessional literature can mean different things to different people and will thus make this more explicit.

ACTIVITY

- Quickly jot down all the associations you have with the word culture.
- Get a colleague at work to do the same and compare notes to see any differences and similarities, then discuss these together.

Commentary

Culture is a word that appears in our everyday discourse, so much so that as with much common parlance it ceases to require any great effort on our part at understanding what it means. We all seem to know what we are talking about when we mention culture. Yet the variety of definitions and interpretations of the word allow it an elasticity that is more of a hindrance to clarity than a help. The increasing need to improve our direct work with children and young people requires us to examine their changing cultural environment for evidence of how we might harness new ways of understanding both them and their troubles. At a general level culture is associated with high art, refinement, superior taste, etc., or a popular culture that is associated with the masses, low taste, the tabloid media, and TV soap operas.

We can also acknowledge that there is a 'therapy culture', namely something associated with western methods of responding to individual human psychological difficulties. Depending on the context this can be used as a term of criticism, implying that society's problems are caused by the culture of therapy which posits people as victims and weak-willed (Masson, 1988; Furedi, 2003), or it can be used in a benign sense as illustrative of how advanced societies are becoming in attending to the stresses and pressures of modern life. What is certain is that those of us seeking to help troubled children and adolescents need to develop our understanding of how cultural influences can affect, maintain, and ultimately provide solutions for, the psychological difficulties of young people.

Culture in the anthropological sense has come to mean the way of life followed by a people. This concept developed as the history of western expansionism and colonialism encountered manifestations of difference around the world. These encounters prompted a reaction at several levels of consciousness: politically there was a need to justify the appropriation of native land and resources and economically the imperial explorers required raw materials to service industrialisation; but psychologically there was a fear of difference that had to be rationalised. Hence the early attempts at racial categorisation and efforts to construct order from diversity and the chaos in human lifeways. Culture can also be defined in opposition to nature as the product and achievement of human beings representing a rising above of our natural instincts. In this sense human nature is typically understood as the opposite of culture. Culture can also mean the difference between humans and animals, namely the capacity to use language and complex communication to symbolise that which is not present (Jenkins, 2002).

Thus the bearers of a culture are understood to be a collectivity of individuals such as a society or community. However, the cultural patterns that shape the behaviour of children and young people in groups should not be confused with the structure of institutions or social systems, even though there is a link between these. We can think of culture in one sense as the organisation of experience shared by members of a community, including their standards for perceiving, predicting, judging and acting. This means that culture includes all socially standardised ways of seeing and thinking about the world; of understanding relationships among people, things and events; of establishing preferences and purposes; of carrying out actions and pursuing goals (Valentine, 1976; Haralambos, 1988; Jenkins, 2002). As the history of the past three centuries demonstrates the impact of western imperialism has reproduced its economic and political structures worldwide, resulting in the development of industrial societies in former agrarian countries that have disrupted cultural patterns.

Inequalities in the distribution of wealth among these newly developing countries have created expectations and increasing demands for fairer trade relationships. Globalisation combined with instant international communications has brought the consequences of these unequal relationships and the needs of poor nations to our attention more than ever before. Thus developed nations are being confronted with a variety of cultures with a common experience of exploitation and a need to reconcile conflicting feelings, guilt, confusion and responses. There is still a requirement for systematic knowledge about groups or categories of humanity who are more mobile and are attracted to western lifestyles of wealth, materialism and welfare. In the early part of this new millenium the recent history of ethnic conflicts, population changes and poverty has prompted the emigration of refugee and asylum seekers towards the West.

The more privileged and comfortable strata of western societies, as well as new urban communities in former agricultural economies, are today facing the reality of desperately poor people who feel more and more marginalised and neglected. Resentment is a feature of the reaction of wealthier nations to inflows of dependent people and the realisation among refugees that they are not universally welcome. There is a need therefore to render knowledge about difference and cultural diversity coherent in order to inform public attitudes and social policy, as well as enhance therapeutic practice. One way of doing this is to attribute a culture or subculture to a broad variety of social categories. Hence we encounter relatively meaningless terms such as the culture of poverty, youth culture, pop culture, black culture, or drug culture. There is even a refugee culture that apparently explains the motivation of families from troubled or impoverished regions to take incredible risks to seek refuge and safety.

CONCEPTUALISING CULTURE

Cultural relevance can initially be understood in the context of a desire to improve our practice in order to meet the needs of the growing multi-cultural and ethnically diverse society developing around us. It assumes that historical and orthodox assumptions about human growth and behaviour have served their purpose in meeting the needs of children and young people in particular circumstances at particular points in time. In the early stages of the twenty-first century changes are now required to address and respond to the psychological and emotional problems of a modern generation of families and offspring who cannot be easily fitted into existing theoretical paradigms. There is increasing evidence for the need to refine and develop our methods and models of assessment and intervention in order that they will prove more relevant and accessible to children and young people from a much wider range of backgrounds than was the case in the not too distant past (Madge, 2001).

This is not to say that children and young people in the majority ethnic communities do not require improved methods of help and support. They are being socialised and exposed to quite a different society from that of former generations. The pace of life, enhanced stressors, individualism and consumerism have all been blamed for producing heightened states of arousal and stimulation. Evidence has begun to emerge of genetic changes, the development of new illnesses, and of course a range of new risk factors to people's mental health: especially the availability of cheap psychoactive drugs and greater access to alcohol. Parents report increased stress in economically austere times which can become manifest in child abuse. Depictions of family life, for example in children's literature, have also changed dramatically in the past forty years, from misleading idyllic paternalistic havens of safety and security to the grim reality of poverty, child abuse, divorce, mentally ill parents and personal and institutional racism (Tucker and Gamble, 2001).

Ethnicity requires some clarification as another term that can be used in a variety of contexts but without much thought as to its meaning. Its use alongside the term culture causes confusion, especially when the two become almost synonymous. This is because there is no easy definition, but we at least need to know the complexities of the use of the term ethnicity because it perhaps reflects something deeper and more ambivalent about the way we internally manage difference and otherness. Part of the problem here lies in mixing up birthplace with ethnic identity. A white person born in Africa and a black person born in Britain can be defined by their ethnic grouping and place of birth. Further confusion has historically prevailed due to the way the official census data have been collated. In the UK since 1951 the methods of data collection have altered from just recording the country of birth, to including the birthplace of parents, to 1981 when there was no question on ethnicity. In 1991 a question on ethnicity offered a range of categories and in 2001 there were further changes to account for citizens with dual or mixed heritage.

The term race is now generally accepted to be redundant as a meaningful scientific category, however *the idea of race* as a general descriptor of assumed national, cultural or physical difference persists in society (Amin et al., 1997). The concept is embraced at the policy level with legislation such as the Race Relations Act in the UK and institutions such as the Commission for Racial Equality. Legislation (such as the 1989 Children Act, the 2004 Children Act and the Children's National Service Framework which contextualises work with children and young people) expects practitioners to take account of a child's religious persuasion, racial origin and cultural and linguistic background, without adequate guidance as to what is meant by 'race' or 'culture'. The issue becomes even more complex when we consider census data that show the increase in numbers of children from dual and mixed heritage backgrounds and consider the particularly complex set of problems they can encounter.

ETHNICITY AND CULTURE

The linkage between race, ethnic identity and inequality has been repeatedly established in terms of their effect on wealth, status and power. These socio-economic and other environmental variables are recognised as risk factors for the development of children and young people. The data show that black and other ethnic minority young people and adults charged with anti-social behaviour are more likely to receive punitive or custodial disposals in the criminal justice system rather than community options geared towards a better understanding of their causality. High levels of psychological problems are reported from male and female black populations within young offender institutions. Socially constructed notions of racial difference thus remain a potent basis for identity, namely our sense of sameness and difference (Bilton et al., 2002). This has led to frequent criticisms of discriminatory and stereotyping attitudes within the legal system.

Earlier scientific work in the nineteenth and twentieth centuries had attempted to conceptualise race and classify people in different countries according to their supposedly inherent superiority or inferiority. Similar comparisons were made on the basis of gender and class which permitted the tolerance of inequalities based on innate biological differences. A eugenics movement was inspired by such findings whose aim was to improve the genetic stock of the human race by eradicating those people with less than perfect genetic dispositions. In the latter part of the last century advances in genetic research were able to dismiss these earlier notions of racial hierarchies and classifications and the supposed link between biology and behaviour (Kohn, 1995).

However, some vestiges of these outdated concepts still survive at the popular level as people try to understand where they fit into an ever-shrinking world where much more is known about other countries, customs and culture. Cheap air travel, faster communication and the creation of refugees and asylum seekers from troubled areas are bringing images, experiences and feelings to our collective consciousness. Skin colour, language and religion are still interpreted as signifiers of more profound differences in abilities and outlook, as well as being used to justify discriminatory practices or outright racism. For some people the notion of white superiority is barely below the surface, especially in the context of a colonial history and latter immigration. Table 8.1 provides an example of the incredible cultural diversity in the United Kingdom that belies populist notions of an Anglo Saxon monoculture. This is a clear example of an economically successful country that has benefited from immigration while perpetuating xenophobia and a racist hysteria that are reflected in the popular media. It is therefore vital that we understand the specific manifestations of cultural differences in every country rather than try to prescribe a universal explanatory theory. We need therefore to find an explanation for inequalities that can attend to the social construction as well as the individual internal construction of difference and the link with culturally aware systems practice.

Table 8.1   People born outside Great Britain and resident here, by countries of birth,1991

Countries of birth	No. resident in Britain	% of Britain's population
Northern Ireland	245,000	0.45
Irish Republic	592,000	1.08
Germany	216,000	0.39
Italy	91,000	0.17
France	53,000	0.10
Other EC	133,900	0.24
Scandinavia & EFTA	58,300	0.11
E.Europe & former USSR	142,900	0.26
Cyprus	78,000	0.14
Rest of Near & Middle East	58,300	0.11
Aust, NZ & Canada	177,400	0.32

Countries of birth	No. resident in Britain	% of Britain's population
New Commonwealth	1,688,400	3.08
Jamaica	142,000	0.26
Rest of Caribbean	122,600	0.22
India	409,000	0.75
Pakistan	234,000	0.43
Bangladesh	105,000	0.19
Rest of South Asia	39,500	0.07
South East Asia	150,400	0.27
East Africa	220,600	0.40
West & Southern Africa	110,700	0.20
Rest of the World	566,200	1.03
Asia	231,000	0.42
North Africa	44,600	0.08
South Africa	68,000	0.12
Rest of Africa	34,300	0.06
USA	143,000	0.26
Rest of Americas	42,000	0.08
Total born outside GB	**3,991,000**	**7.27**

Source: Owen, D. 1995

SOCIALLY AND CULTURALLY INCLUSIVE PRACTICE

Dilemmas in the trends towards cultural relevance have been highlighted by references to the practice of forced/arranged marriages and dowry, the genital mutilation of children, and the harsh physical punishments condoned by some societies (Midgley, 2001). These practices can be used to counter the argument for respecting ethnic and cultural diversity and support the notion of universal values as the basis for competent practice. Ethnic rivalries and the pride in national identity on which these are based also sit uneasily with culturally competent aspirations of international collaboration and mutual understanding. As we noted earlier, the definition of significant harm is subject to interpretation and the quality of usually physical evidence while psychological harm or impact is not easily measured or articulated. The legal system in England and Wales is adversarial in nature, seeks to prove guilt or innocence, and has been acknowledged as culturally insensitive. The Climbié case is a reminder that too much of a focus on ethnic customs and cultural sensitivity or misunderstanding anti-discriminatory practice can produce fatal consequences.

However, rather than seek answers to these difficult issues in an introspective way, this emphasises the need for social workers to reach out to the international community with service users in order to continue to debate, discuss and strive for ways to discover solutions. In the area of child protection we need to understand the impact such practices and the beliefs on which they are based are having on those adults promoting them and the children and young people experiencing them.

Cultural competence has also been defined as developing skills in assessing the cultural climate of an organisation and being able to practise in a strategic manner within it. It has also been broadened to include any context in which workers practise in order to permit effective direct work at many levels (Baldwin, 2000; Fook, 2012). Whether at the strategic organisational level or the direct interpersonal level, we can actively resist those pressures to conformity and routinised practice that in often discreet and inconspicuous ways can undermine efforts to practise in culturally relevent ways. The requirements of social justice demand vigilance and creativity in order to contribute towards an emancipatory practice that can liberate both workers and service users from prescribed practice orthodoxies. Such practice is the antithesis of stereotyped, one-dimensional thinking: it is instead consistent with systems theory and characterised by (Leonard, 1997):

- a commitment to standing alongside oppressed and impoverished populations;
- the importance of dialogic relations between workers and service users;
- an orientation towards the transformation of processes and structures that perpetuate domination and exploitation.

These characteristics are in harmony with culturally inclusive practice. They do not imply that practitioners should reject statutory practice for the voluntary sector, child care for community work, or systems theories for advocacy. These simplistic oppositional devices do not help us manage the complexities and dilemmas inherent when seeking different practice orientations (Healy, 2002). The possibilities for creative practice within organisational constraints are there. They may be limited and subject to time pressures, but in the personal relationship with service users and particularly with children and adolescents with mental health problems the rewards are unquantifiable for both workers and clients. Even introducing a small change in practice can have a much larger disproportionate and beneficial impact.

There is growing interest in the development of multi-disciplinary and interprofessional working in order to maximise the effectiveness of interventions to meet the diverse needs of multi-cultural societies and service users (Magrab et al. 1997; Oberheumer, 1998; Tucker et al., 1999). The characteristics of such work apply in a framework that is familiar to health and social care staff working therapeutically. This begins with assessment and then proceeds through decision making, planning, monitoring, evaluation, and finally to closure. It has been argued that this common framework offers the optimum model for encouraging reflective practice to be at the core of contemporary work (Taylor and White, 2000; Walker, 2003a). Reflective practice offers the opportunity to shift beyond functional analysis to making active links between the value base, the policy-making process, and the variety of interventions conducted.

The following activity aims to enable you to apply abstract theory to real practice situations where different professionals are expected to work more effectively together.

- Consider the opposite material in the context of a child protection case you are involved with.
- What are the key ideas that you feel you can put into practice which could make a difference in your work?

Commentary

Combining reflective practice with socially and culturally inclusive practice, we have the opportunity to make a major contribution towards responding to the social policy aspiration of inclusion and anti-oppressive practice. In so doing we can facilitate closer co-operation between professionals coming into contact with vulnerable families on a shared agenda of challenging institutional and personal discrimination (Eber et al., 1996; VanDenBerg and Grealish, 1996; Sutton, 1999). Drawing together the elements of practice that can contribute towards a model of culturally relevant care means it is possible to define cultural competence as a set of knowledge-based and interpersonal skills that will allow individuals to understand, appreciate and work with families from cultures other than their own. Five components have been identified (Kim, 1995) as comprising culturally competent care:

- An awareness and acceptance of cultural differences.
- A capacity for cultural self-awareness.
- An understanding of the dynamics of difference.
- Developing a basic knowledge of a family's culture.
- Adapting practice skills to fit the cultural context of the child and family.

These are consistent with other work which critiqued the historical development of cross-cultural services and offered a model of service organisation and development designed to meet the needs of black and ethnic minority families (Dominelli, 1998; Bhugra, 1999; Bhugra and Bahl, 1999). Culture has been defined as the sets of shared cultural perspectives, meanings and adaptive behaviours derived from the simultaneous membership of and participation in a multiplicity of contexts such as geographical, religion, ethnicity, language, race, nationality and ideology. It has also been described as the knowledge, values, perceptions and practices that are shared among the members of a given society and passed on from one generation to the next (Leighton, 1981). Four specific theories have been identified in modern practice for example that attempt to harmonise systems theory with cultural competence (Falicov, 1995):

- *Ethnic focused*: this stresses that families differ but assumes that the diversity is primarily due to ethnicity. It focuses on the commonality of thoughts, behaviours, feelings, customs and rituals that are perceived as belonging to a particular ethnic group.

(Cont'd)

- *Universalist*: this asserts that families are more alike than they are different. Hence, universalist norms are thought to apply to all families.
- *Particularist*: this holds that all families are more different than they are alike. No generalisations are possible as each family is unique.
- *Multidimensional*: this goes beyond the one-dimensional definition of culture as ethnicity and aims at a more comprehensive and complex definition of culture that embraces other contextual variables.

A theoretical framework for multi-cultural social work suggests that an overarching theory needs to be employed that will permit different theoretical models to be applied and integrated. The synthesis between systems theory and social work practice offers a more comprehensive way of achieving this. In this way, both clients' and workers' identities can be embedded in multiple levels of life experiences with the aim of enabling a greater account to be taken of each client's experience in relation to their context. The power differentials between workers and families are recognised as playing an important role in the working relationship. Clients are helped by developing a greater awareness of themselves in relation to their different contexts, thereby resulting in practice that will be contextual in orientation and will, for example, draw upon traditional healing practices (Sue et al., 1996).

Ethnocentric, and particularly eurocentric, explanations of emotional and psychosocial development are not inclusive enough to understand the development of diverse ethnic minority groups. Failing to understand the cultural background of families can lead to unhelpful assessments, non-compliance, poor use of services and alienating the individual or family from the welfare system. By using an anti-discriminatory, empowerment model of practice, social workers are ideally placed to work with other professionals in multi-disciplinary contexts that will enable the whole team to maintain a focus on culturally inclusive practice. For example, the increased demand for help from parents and children who were themselves suffering from the effects of abuse and subsequent mental health problems prompted policy initiatives to invest in and reconfigure child and adolescent mental health service provision in more acceptable and accessible ways by the previous government.

The aim is to make these more accessible and acceptable to all cultures by improving multi-agency working (Davis et al., 1997; House of Commons, 1997; Mental Health Foundation, 1999). However, in order to be effective all staff need to address the different belief systems and explanatory thinking behind psychological symptoms. Skills and values are required to articulate these concepts in such teams. Challenging crude stereotypes, questioning implicit racism, and simply ensuring that other staff stop and think about their assumptions can help and combining these actions with a respectful consideration of indigenous healing practices within diverse populations can also optimise helping strategies. The traditional methods and models of therapeutic practice have failed to take full account of cultural factors but the contemporary literature is attempting to catch up. The following areas can offer valuable guidance on enhancing your communication skills (Whiting, 1999):

- Families may have different styles of communicating fear, grief, anxiety, concern and disagreement.
- Emphasis should be placed on listening, with a goal of understanding a family's perspective.
- Care should be taken to explain the agency culture to the family.
- Steps should be taken to recognise and resolve conflicts which may occur between the cultural preferences, understandings and practices recommended by professionals.
- Communication can be enhanced if you demonstrate sensitivity towards the family's cultural values.
- Appreciating the family's cultural understanding of the problem will help build a trusting relationship.

Case Example

A family of Iraqi asylum seekers fled the country before the American and British invasion in 2003. The father, Ishmael, had worked in a civil service position in a government agency connected to the petroleum industry. He had been accused of passing information to the UN regarding breaches of the sanctions imposed on the use of oil revenues. Ishmael claims he was tortured and had death threats made against his wife and three children.

The children are all under ten years of age and his wife Misra is a nurse. Some of the children speak very little English. The family have been dispersed to a market town in a northern county where there are very few Iraqis or any families from Middle Eastern countries. The local housing department has referred the family to your office following reports of racist attacks on the run-down council estate where they have been housed in emergency accommodation.

A teacher has called your team three times in the past fortnight expressing concern about one of the children who is wetting and soiling in class, provoking bullying and humiliating behaviour from other children.

Commentary

Using a systems perspective your first task will be to make a map of all the people, agencies and services connected to this family. You will find it helpful to then make contact with as many as you can within a realistic timescale in order to start to plan your response. This information-gathering exercise will enable you to begin to evaluate the various

(Cont'd)

agendas and the perceptions of other staff working with or concerned about the family. Your priority here must be to establish meaningful contact with the family and gain some factual evidence of the racist incidents for a possible criminal prosecution against the perpetrators, as well as offering them a caring, sympathetic relationship. Bear in mind that the family are likely to be highly suspicious of your motives and will require a lot of genuine evidence that they should trust you. Their naturally defensive behaviour may come across as hostile/uncommunicative and you will need to deal with this in a non-confrontational manner.

A translator/interpreter should accompany you, having been fully briefed beforehand about your task and the different roles each of you must hold, as well as to assess their suitability for this particular task. Do not assume that every interpreter will be the same and try to evaluate their beliefs/attitudes and whether there may be ethnic or religious differences between them and the family. For a variety of reasons they might be inappropriate for this task, despite having the right language skills. A strict translation of words and terms will be unhelpful and therefore some time will need to be spent on interpretating the interpretation. From the very beginning you will be able to better engage with the family by:

- enabling everyone to have their say;
- circular questioning to assist with the expression of feelings;
- reinforcing the integrity of the family system;
- noting patterns of communication and structure.

Having established a helping relationship, a systems perspective will enable you to locate the family system within a wider system of agencies, resources and a local environment that is generally hostile. Your networking skills can also mobilise the statutory agencies to provide what is required to attend to the immediate areas of concern and clarify roles and responsibilities. A case conference or network meeting can put this on a formal basis with an action checklist for future reference in order to monitor the plan. One option may be to plan some family sessions together with a colleague from another agency such as Health or Education. This could combine assessment and intervention work to ascertain the medium-term needs whilst using therapeutic skills to help the family establish their equilibrium. What is key here is enabling the family to re-establish their particular coping mechanisms and ways of dealing with stress, rather than trying to impose an artificial solution on them. Maintaining a systems-wide perspective can help you evaluate the factors and elements which will then build sufficiently to form a contemporary picture of their context. Working with them as a family and demonstrating simple things like reliability and consistency will provide them with an emotional anchor, namely a secure enough base to allow them to begin to manage themselves in due course.

CULTURAL EVOLUTION AND SYSTEMS CHANGE

What the above tells us is that the subjects of culture, race and ethnicity are evolving all the time as society changes and develops according to demographic changes, advances in social science research and the personal internal psychic changes happening as a result of external modifications to the environment and vice versa. We can observe that previous assumptions about superiority, normality and behaviour among different peoples have been discarded. Thus we need to hold in mind a provisional understanding of what is at present acceptable as terms and descriptions to describe the diversity of populations. These may not be suitable in the changing landscapes of the future (Alibhai-Brown, 1999).

Restricted conceptualisations of culture as a set body of information (i.e., something to be learned in order to better understand a child or young person) offers a static model for engaging with all troubled children. It is more useful to think of culture as a process for generating frameworks of perception, a value system and a set of perspectives. Knowledge about culture is not something external that may be found, memorised and then utilised. Cultural competence is therefore best understood as engaging in the process of transaction where difference will be encountered and where we will try to evolve our meaning-making skills (Tseng, 2002).

Holliday takes up this notion by trying to distinguish between large culture and small culture: he emphasises the need to move beyond the orthodox definition of culture as related to ethnicity, national and international characteristics. Small culture is also distinct from sub-culture which is normally taken to mean something within and subservient to large culture. Small culture in Holliday's meaning is a way of understanding many cultures in all types of social grouping which may or may not have significant ethnic, national or international qualities. Thus the apparent patterns and characteristics of cultures on closer inspection will reveal the variations and variability within and between cultures in reciprocal patterns of influence.

A prescribed, normative and superficial notion of large cultural differences leads to an exaggeration of those differences, resulting in the psychological concept of 'other' reduced to a simplistic, easily digestible, or exotic or degrading stereotype (Holliday, 1999). An example from ethnographic research in Southall, West London, revealed that people there had a sophisticated understanding of culture and community. When asked what was meant by culture it became clear that a person could speak and act as a member of a Muslim community in one context; in another, could take sides against other Muslims as a member of the Pakistani community; and in a third count themselves as part of the Punjabi community that excluded other Muslims but included Hindus, Sikhs, and even Christians (Baumann, 1996). Thus a more enlightened concept of culture accepts it is a dynamic, ongoing group process which operates in changing circumstances to enable group members to make sense of, and operate meaningfully within, those circumstances. For counsellors and psychotherapists it offers a way of illuminating the full inter-cultural complexity of our world.

CELEBRATING DIVERSITY AND DIFFERENCE

Culture defines accepted ways of behaving for members of a particular society. But such definitions will vary from society to society, leading to misunderstandings and a failure to engage therapeutically in a helping relationship. Klineberg (1971) offered an example of just such a misunderstanding. Amongst the Sioux Indians of South Dakota it is regarded as incorrect to answer a question in the presence of others who do not know the answer: such behaviour would be regarded as boastful and arrogant as well as an attempt to shame others. In addition to this the Sioux regard it as wrong to answer a question unless they are absolutely sure of the correct answer. A white American teacher in a classroom of Sioux children who is unaware of their culture might easily interpret this behaviour as a reflection of their ignorance or hostility. In a therapeutic context we can imagine our reaction to exploratory questions which resulted in such a silent response, with consequent interpretations of resistance and further attention being paid to that area. An understanding of the role of certainty and respect on the other hand could open up creative possibilities for engagement.

Culture is not static: it is an organic, living entity with an external and internal presence. Any attempt to define it or individuals is bound to be provisional because people, and more especially children and young people, will be developing rapidly at many levels of physicality and consciousness. They will do so in an equally fast-changing and bewildering societal context that will set the scene for our understanding of culture. It is possible, however, to select some common characteristics that can help us think about the concept of culture in a more useful way that will allow us to focus our safeguarding efforts to the best advantage of children and young people (Jenkins, 2002):

- Culture is definitely human: it is the characteristic way that humans do things, rooted in our capacity for complex communication and reflexive relationships.
- Culture carries within it implications of controlled development and change: it is the medium within which human individuals grow and become competent.
- Culture is also a matter of differentiating human collectivities, and their characteristic patterns of behaviour, from one another.

It is vital that we understand the different ways in which child and adolescent development is conceptualised by diverse communities. In western industrialised countries there is a more clearly defined division between childhood and adolescence as compared with developing countries. The change is less pronounced and shorter in countries where there is less tradition of further and higher education and a greater sharing of domestic or agricultural labour between adults and younger family members. There is an assumption in western industrialised countries that adolescence has been stretched so that it covers a much greater time-span than in previous generations and this is cited as a cause of much problematic behaviour and psychological problems in contemporary young people. There is also evidence of the earlier onset of puberty in the more affluent societies and delays in the onset of menarche have been reported in girls who are exceptionally physically active (Beckett, 2003). On the other hand, children from non-western countries or whose parents were raised there will have expectations and experiences based on a very different time-span. Parents may have been married at the age of 12 or 13 years old and perhaps could have served as soldiers in civil wars or been responsible for the care of several younger siblings.

GLOBALISATION AND IDENTITY

The term globalisation has begun to feature in the literature, reflecting profound shifts in the economic and social patterns of relationships between the richer industrialised countries and the poorer developing ones. It involves a closer international economic integration prompted by the needs of capitalism, but also has demographic, social, cultural and psychological dimensions (Midgley, 2001; Pieterse, 2004). Consistent with the link between the social context of child protection problems, it is therefore crucial to consider the global context in terms of the challenges for building culturally relevant practice.

Critics of globalisation would argue that its impact is to maintain unequal power relationships between the richer and poorer countries so that patterns of wealth and consumer consumption in Europe and North America can be sustained. This involves an exploitation of labour as well as other resources in poorer countries, thereby preventing these from achieving a diverse and equitable economic and social structure within which health and social welfare programmes can develop. The consequences of globalisation are being noticed in the way traditional social care systems are taking on the characteristics of business ethics and commercialism (Dominelli, 1999; Mishra, 1999). One of the side effects of this process has been the standardisation and conformity required of consumer consumption patterns in order to maximise profits. The consequence of this has been the steady and inexorable erosion of traditional markers of indigenous cultural identity combined with an elevation of global branding.

The paradox of globalisation is that as new varieties of cultural expression are encountered and celebrated there is an underlying impulse on the part of powerful western nations to impose a sameness on the developing nations. Thus, at a supra-systems level, there has been a parallel process occurring, namely an individual rejection of difference by powerful countries that have the technology as well as the military capacity to influence the majority of powerless countries. This must both steer and reinforce the latent fear of the other inside individuals who then feel they have permission to reject black and ethnic minority families. This contradiction is further illuminated by government policies against racism and at the same time their resorting to draconian measures to control the immigration of refugees and asylum seekers (Walker, 2005).

This globalisation of culture produces deeply contradictory states for individuals and groups that then produce consequences for the development of an integrated sense of self. Hence we may observe the way young black people are regarded as predisposed to violence and disorder, resulting in persecutory oppression and aggressive reactions that are interpreted by police as evidence of anti-social predisposition. At the same time, however, black athleticism and success in international sport produces a celebratory image that masks denigratory undertones (Briggs, 2002). Young white people can be seen and heard imitating the black youth culture in terms of their dress and accent, while African-Caribbean youngsters, for example, may learn the patois of their grandparents and celebrate Rastafarianism by wearing dreadlocks which some white people would regard as a hostile anti-establishment stance. Similarly, young Asian women can be torn between accepting the aspirations of their white peers for sexual independence and socialisation and abiding by the expectations of some Asian parents as regards social restrictions and arranged marriages.

This critique of the latest phase of capitalist development echoes earlier concerns about the impact on economic growth and subsequent erosion of traditional government policies of full employment and social welfare (Corrigan and Leonard, 1978; Bailey and Brake, 1980). A failure to fully develop social welfare services, or to have them subjected to the gyrations of speculative global financial markets, invariably corrodes the quality and the depth of preventive or child protection services that have been designed to reach children and families in personal and culturally appropriate ways. This means that services are pared down to the minimum, oriented towards crisis intervention, and designed in the narrowest terms to conform with inflexible eligibility criteria that will limit access. These features are inconsistent with culturally relevant systems practice that aims to spread accessibility, improve acceptability, and enrich our creative potential to respond to a diverse society where multiple systems within systems will function and interact.

9

TOWARDS AN INTEGRATED APPRAISAL AND EVALUATION

INTRODUCTION

In an interim report Munro (2011a) suggested that too often questions will be asked about whether certain rules and procedures have been met but not about whether these have actually helped children. Everyone in the profession will be familiar with specific meetings and paperwork that do not make a shred of difference to children being any safer.

Whilst *some* regulation is obviously needed here, we have to reduce this to a smaller and more manageable size. Professionals should be spending more of their time with children: asking them how they feel and whether they understand why a social worker is involved with their family, as well as finding out what they want to happen. Imposing timescales on form-filling puts pressure on professionals which can distract them from making decent quality judgements. We now have more knowledge about the kind of parenting that really harms children. Assessments should be skilled enough to distinguish between those families who are most in need and parents who are struggling and just in need of a bit of help, and possibly not from social workers (Munro, 2011a).

The title for this chapter was deliberately chosen to challenge the plethora of books, guidance, legislation and research that use the terms assessment and intervention. If we examine these terms they offer the prospect of reinforcing the inspectorial and oppressive nature of safeguarding practices and the new trend towards a more child protection/surveillance culture which can hamper attempts to work closer with the child and family as observed by Munro. If we think about the language of social work more closely then we can reflect on how appropriate this is (or vice versa) and so instead of assessment and intervention let us see what difference using the terms appraisal and support makes. Munro challenges the orthodox assumptions about different methods of social work practice that need to be re-examined and refined in order to continue to ensure that the profession is using the most relevant and effective ways of working in contemporary child and family safeguarding practice.

Recent evidence has provided suggestions for improving effectiveness and in particular good reflective support and supervision for social workers has been seen as vital for the difficult process of analysing and synthesising the wide-ranging information about a child's circumstances (Platt, 2011). Perhaps the most important factor to consider in all this is how the very vocabulary and language of social work guidance and legislation can set the context for distancing and separating us from our clients. Consider the general definition of assessment and its origins as listed below.

ASSESSMENT

The term comes from the Latin word *assessum*, which is the past participle of *assidere*. It means to determine, estimate or judge the value of; to evaluate or assess the situation:

- To give or charge with (as with penalties in sports).
- To impose or subject to (taxation and legal).
- To determine the value of.

This language seems to equate assessment to something that is imposed, done to, or based, as well as the financial worth of an object/commodity. It seems to imply something that is non-inclusive as well as alienating and a rather unpleasant experience that carries with it undertones of threat or penalty. Do service users feel that is what is happening to them when social workers *undertake an assessment*? Is this the vocabulary of partnership and empowerment?

The following activity aims to develop your skills in empathy and service users' perceptions in the context of an interprofessional assessment.

ACTIVITY

- Set aside some time at work or home and think about the last assessment that was done on you (perhaps for income tax, a medical problem, a state benefit or occupational health).
- How did this experience feel at the time and how did it affect you while you were waiting for the outcome?

Now put yourself in the shoes of a parent/carer/child/family with whom you are engaging in the assessment process. You may very well feel that this is a partnership and you really want it to be so, but then probably so did the tax inspector, doctor or civil servant assessing you, *but did it actually feel like that to you?*

APPRAISAL

Now consider the definition of that other similar word, appraisal, one that is often used synonymously with assessment in various social work documents or procedures. It comes from the late middle English apprize, which means price or value (in English, precious), and from which we also get appreciate:

- To set a value; to estimate the worth of, particularly by persons appointed for the purpose, as in to appraise goods and chattels.
- To estimate; to conjecture.
- To praise; to commend.

What do you notice about the differences between the two words? Which one would you prefer to use when collecting information or engaging with a family to try to understand their situation? Which word would you prefer to appear on official documentation that you received in your own home about your own personal circumstances? The notion of conjecture has echoes of hypothesising which we discussed earlier, while the idea of estimate suggests uncertainty or probability: once again these are words that seem to be more tentative, explorative and possibly even engaging. Look again at bullet point three above: there is indeed something here that has progressive connotations of success, something that perhaps resonates with the old Winnicott notion of 'good enough parenting' or the systems theory of positive feedback.

FEMINIST-INFORMED PRACTICE

One way that children's services can tilt the balance away from repressive child protection procedures and illustrate the pragmatic use of feminist-informed systems theory is in the example of family group conferences. Introduced some years ago, and borrowing from New Zealand Maori traditional practices, these have challenged the orthodoxy in British social services planning which places primacy on professional social workers' power, values and perceptions. The key idea in these conferences is that family meetings will be convened where there are concerns about the welfare of a child or children. The family in these circumstances will be widely defined and extended family members will be encouraged to participate. Their task will be to create their own plan for the child of concern by assuming responsibility in deciding how to meet the needs of that child (Morris and Tunnard, 1996).

Thus social workers' roles change dramatically, from an inspectorial/adversarial role largely prescribed by procedures and a restricted definition of their task, to one that is more consistent with the skills and knowledge demanded by family therapy. In the context of family group conferences social workers can emphasise the communication, negotiation, mediation and facilitation skills that are better informed by a systems approach which seeks to focus on problem solving and highlight the strengths within a family system. Clearly a therapeutic stance is required here, one that means social workers have to embrace the concept of partnership practice and resist the seductive simplicity of deciding what is best for children and their families.

At the heart of the family group conference is a re-definition of social work practice with children and families. It throws into sharp focus a tangible example of the elusive and often ill-defined notion of empowering practice. It represents a challenge to social work that is driven by a defensive culture and to social workers comforted by the ability to retreat into procedural safety when faced with complexity, uncertainty, and the normal swings and roundabouts of family life. On the other hand, this approach fits with social workers using a family therapy approach to their work. The FGC model proposes limits to the intrusion of the professional planning model: it suggests that the model should form the frame within which family decision making should take place and that that decision making should be carried out in whichever way proves appropriate for individual families (Morris and Tunnard, 1996).

Feminist critics refer to domestic violence and the abuse of children by men as examples of the way many families are organised by a male abuse of power, as something which is not sufficiently incorporated into systems theory. The hidden nature of the abuse, together with the impossible dilemmas faced by women attempting to protect themselves and their children, mean that it is likely to be a factor affecting the interactions between family members. Social workers have equally been criticised for doubly oppressing women who, whilst attempting to manage their dilemmas and contradictory feelings, can also find themselves accused of failing to protect their children. Various studies have over the years confirmed the under-reporting of this crime: in Britain, for example, it has been suggested that domestic violence occurs in 30–50 per cent of male-female relationships (Kelly, 1996; Walker, 2001b).

Critics argue that family therapy therefore colludes with a male abuse of power because in seeking, for example, to foster parental control over difficult children the method is actually reinforcing patriarchal authority. Statutory child-care workers are themselves in a bind as they have a primary duty to prioritise the safety of children whilst recognising the risks posed to women who are frightened to report domestic violence and face having their children removed. Both the child protection system and the criminal justice system reflect public policies that implicitly collude with actual and threatened violence against women and children and deter both parties from testifying and providing evidence against male perpetrators. Paradoxically, they also underplay the serious issue of female violence against male partners or lesbian partners.

Recent research has highlighted the serious physical, psychological and emotional consequences for children who witness or are unwittingly involved in domestic violence. In 90 per cent of recorded incidents children will have been in the next room and in 30 per cent they will have tried to intervene to protect their mother from assault (Hester et al., 2000). Students of systems theory thus face having to make sense of concepts of interactivity and circular process, whilst simultaneously recognising the inequality and structural privileges provided to men. A thorough understanding of this crucial variable in contemporary relationship dynamics is thus required for family support staff who are seeking to incorporate family therapy into their work with families where domestic violence is likely to be a major, yet also unacknowledged, factor.

Fortunately there is a growing body of literature that offers reliable evidence that we may employ when seeking to intervene in a thoughtful, ethical and empowering way on behalf of the victims as well *as the perpetrators* of domestic violence (Hague, 2000; Home Office, 2000; Vetere and Cooper, 2001; Walker, 2001d). Apart from direct work with families where there is a suspicion but no open acknowledgement of domestic violence, systems theory can be put into practice within an inter-agency context. Well coordinated multi-agency collaboration has the potential to improve services to women and children experiencing domestic violence and to maximise their continual safety and wellbeing (Hester et al., 2000; Rivett and Rees, 2004). Using a feminist framework permits us to gain an understanding of the various inter-agency relationships, rivalries and power positions that may be played out in attempts at partnership practice.

EVALUATING SOCIAL WORK: THE PEOPLE'S PERSPECTIVE

The language of social work appears to be further complicated when the profession expends huge energy on how to describe the people we are trying to help. Are they service users, clients, or consumers? The concept of the social work consumer is not new and is one of several attempts to find a language that suggests both rights and people as the recipients of a service. Integrated practice suggests something which closes the gap between service users, social workers and other agencies, yet it still seems to be an elusive outcome to evaluate and achieve. The consumer perspective has been a feature in the evaluation of social work for many years: Mayer and Timms's classic survey of clients showed how social work clients' views on methods and purpose differed from those of their social workers'. They referred to this as a clash of perspective while much subsequent research found similar disparities, suggesting that social work could be more effective in achieving its goals when the views of clients and workers were congruent on what the goals were and how these could be achieved (Rees and Wallace, 1982; Cheetham et al., 1992; Pawson and Tilley, 1997).

However, when contemplating the power positions that various people in the safeguarding system possess it seems axiomatic that parents/carers have precious little. It has often been found that clients will judge effectiveness using different criteria from those of social workers: for example, they will value practical help more than social workers who will value insight and behavioural change more. Making an evaluation should take such factors into account, not only when considering the effectiveness of outputs but also in prioritising goals, such as when we must ask 'Whose goals and outcomes are more important?' But despite the current high status ostensibly being given to consumers' views these are no more 'objective' or 'valid' than practitioners' and caution is required in interpreting these for several reasons:

- Previous knowledge of services may colour consumer opinions i.e., unsuccessful encounters with social workers beforehand may lead to less than enthusiastic accounts of current interventions or indeed over enthusiastic accounts of minimal successes.
- Levels of expectation will influence consumer feedback i.e., those with very low expectations will be more impressed by any success than those with high expectations.
- A lack of information on alternatives means consumers will have no basis on which to judge.
- Anxieties over confidentiality and the results of expressing any negative opinion may lead consumers to give more favourable assessments of services than might otherwise be justified.

CONSUMERS AS PRODUCERS OF WELFARE

An evaluation should take into account not only the welfare produced by the formal organisation but also that produced by consumers, carers and other external providers. Thus in assessing the effectiveness of an output, such as intensive home care in avoiding looked-after proceedings, the outcomes for carer wellbeing should be included. In addition, the inputs they make (such as the practical costs of heating and accommodation) should be taken into account. The emotional or psychological costs of struggling with poverty, inadequate housing, or mental illness are equally important here. If these costs to carers become too great, and they then become clients as well as the child at risk, the effectiveness of the intensive home care may be more doubtful because if carers cannot cope the situation can rapidly deteriorate. In such circumstances greater efficiency and effectiveness might well be achieved by changing the goal or having several options available according to the changing circumstances in the family and professional system.

HOW TO EVALUATE

Many social workers will tend to avoid evaluations or will interpret these in such a way that they come to mean brief, retrospective reviews of various pieces of work or initiatives. You may also hold the view that your agency has to collect so much performance-related information for the government that anything that appears to detract from work with service users and your primary responsibilities has to be avoided. However, accountable practice demands that the public services need to justify what they do and must therefore find useful ways of demonstrating this.

An action evaluation model, developed in Bradford (Fawcett, 2000), has been based on a partnership between the university, the social services department and the health trust: this has been aimed at demystifying the evaluation process and providing staff with the tools and support they need to conduct evaluations. Action evaluations take place in the workplace and focus on areas that are viewed as important by those who are involved with the findings and feeding these into the services being studied. The main characteristics of these are as follows:

- *Outline the current situation*: collect the baseline information and establish the service's overall aims and objectives: this can include quantitative data (such as numbers of people using a service) and qualitative data (such as the details of service users' experiences).
- *Specify the available resources, the overall aim and any objectives:* any project or initiative is likely to have a number of objectives, but it is important to be specific about these and what the broad overall purpose of the activity is.
- *Link the goals to specific objectives*: identifying the desired outcomes or goals will enable staff to work backwards through any intermediary stages in the process: this helps to provide progress indicators and show how goals can be achieved.
- *Detail why the agreed objectives and goals were decided upon*: no evaluation will go strictly according to plan, therefore it will be necessary to record how these goals were established: a record must be kept of the reasoning behind the aims and any deviations clearly stated and made transparent. This information needs to be easily retrievable so it can be used to explain why any goals have been changed.
- *Monitor and review the activity*: information from all stakeholders can be collated here, including recommendations for changing or improving the service. Activity related to goals can be appraised, and evidence of progress summarised. It is important to document how and why progress was made and what obstacles were encountered as these data can be used as feedback for service purchasers and planners, thereby reflecting an inclusive, bottom-up approach to evaluation.

An integrated systems methodology for evaluating child protection practice and improving organisational learning has been offered by Munro and Hubbard (2011). This seeks to reinforce the application of systems theory to ensure that management, staff, clients and other stakeholders are able to assess the factors that influence social work practice and outcomes: the aim of doing so is to make certain that *organisational cultural factors are recognised as influencing the effectiveness of decision making*: once an organisational system changes from being a top-down, linear management hierarchy, where blame and scapegoating are the norm, there will be a chance to improve the patterns of interaction with families and other professionals, remove constraints on practice, help with prioritisation, and improve the consistency of care. This approach requires senior managers to take feedback from staff and clients more seriously and to recognise the causal complexity that causes problems for social workers. The method of evaluation emphasises the need to develop a learning culture within child protection services, where reviews and critical reports are not the end-point where mistakes are made but the starting-point for genuine changes to occur.

The following activity has been designed to develop your skills in research and maintain your continuous professional development which is a mandatory requirement for registration in any professional context.

ACTIVITY

- Search the intranet for some social work material such as a journal research paper on the evaluation of a new project.
- See if you can work out the methodology employed and whether or not the results have had any influence on the working practices in your agency.

THE SOCIAL WORK DILEMMA

In a climate of public sector financial constraints that impose strict guidelines on the use of resources and require demonstrable outcomes for practice, social workers are invariably being pulled in a great many directions. This makes the task of achieving a more integrated safeguarding practice more difficult. On the one hand there will be the familiar overtures to work systematically in a focused manner within the budget limits, but on the other there will be highly vulnerable and dependent clients who we are told should have needs-led services. This implies that no conflict exists between the resource limitations and service user needs when clearly the opposite is true. Experienced staff will be well aware that in some cases long-term support will be the only option for some of the most damaged and disadvantaged clients, yet service managers will impose artificial limits to the length of time spent on these cases (Walker and Beckett, 2011).

As workers we all know that a case closed prematurely will likely re-appear in due course and probably be much harder to work: indeed this is particularly the case when clients have experienced losses, neglect and a lack of care in the past and these aspects are then reproduced in their relationship with a social worker. Finding a way out of this dilemma is one of the modern challenges to professional ethical practice. This task is made all the harder because there is no reliable and robust evidence base to call upon in order to justify a particular plan of intervention. Social workers seeking evidence-based practice using therapeutic skills and techniques will soon find the literature on evaluation in this field rather less than helpful (Walker and Beckett, 2011).

There is, for example, an historical legacy of reluctance among psychotherapists to employ quantitative empirical methods to investigate the effectiveness of their practice. This is partly because therapists have tended to prefer demonstrating results using case study descriptions to support their particular theoretical model.

It is also because they have not been trained in these methodologies and are more comfortable with qualitative research that emphasises the more intangible elements of the subtle processes at work during the therapeutic experience (Target, 1998; Cowie, 1999). If we are trying to implement therapeutic work with service users this makes it harder to justify our approach. Questioning the reliability and validity of the research methodology will have a bearing on the status of the therapeutic effectiveness.

Reliability is chiefly about whether the same person was assessed on a different day or location, or by another researcher, the result would be similar or different. Validity refers to whether the research is telling us what we think it is: in other words, whether what service users say about how they are is accurate. These concepts of reliability and validity matter because of the tendency in quantitative research to interpret and generalise from findings, thereby influencing the choice of treatment or intervention. Research is also used to justify the investment in social work organisation and methods, with the result that practitioners can be left feeling buffeted about by the subsequent changes imposed on their practice as well as cynical about the underlying rationale.

Integrated practice is hampered and constrained by a variety of professional standards, training, values and knowledge bases. In addition the stereotypes surrounding nurses, doctors, police officers and social workers are hard to shake off, particularly when cardboard cut-out characterisations appear in the mainstream media, soap operas and films. News reporting, especially in tabloid newspapers, will reinforce these one-dimensional stereotypes, and sometimes this will happen in subtle ways which can then influence perceptions between professionals and the public.

It is not hard to understand that social work practitioners trained to take more account of the social and environmental context of service users' lives can also use this to take account of the financial pressures influencing their practice. These pressures are not based on rational, evidence-based research methods about effective, integrated interventions but on resource constraints. This is at the heart of our dilemma in contemporary social work, namely how to deliver effective services within artificial limits to practice. But rather than descend into brutal cynicism or negative/defensive practice we can learn to use the principles of evaluation and effectiveness to our own and our clients' advantage. There are ways of using the available research evidence base and combining it with participatory partnership practice to ensure that the arguments for better quality resources and cost effectiveness are articulated.

The old adage about prevention being better than cure has a weight and enduring simplicity that can resonate in the minds of service managers or budget controllers. It is almost impossible to prove that a specific intervention undoubtedly prevented something else from happening, but governments and social policy experts have still generated expensive intervention programmes on this basis. For example, the multi-million pound SureStart programme that was launched early in this century was based on the untested assumption that such a vast programme would prevent anti-social, educational and health problems in the future with a generation of disadvantaged children. It is therefore part of the received wisdom that an investment of this nature will prove helpful.

REFLECTIVE AND REFLEXIVE PRACTICE

Reflective practice seems likely to re-emerge and be more emphasised in social work education and training contexts as the impact of the Munro reforms begins to take hold. Contemporary social work literature contains references to reflective practice as well as reflexive practice and it would be unsurprising if practitioners were confused by these terms. They are close together in spelling, sound and meaning, but are actually very different: they remain important for practice because they are closely linked to the concept of evaluation and how to move away from the dilemmas described above. Reflective practice was first considered as early as the 1930s as an active, persistent and careful consideration of any belief or supposed form of knowledge in light of the grounds that supported it and the further conclusions to which it tended (Walker and Beckett, 2011). This definition was applied to the context of professional practice by later writers who argued that reflective practice consisted of reflection *in* action, or thinking while doing, and reflection *on* action, which occurs after an incident takes place. Reflective practice therefore encompasses the need for a useful outcome to the reflective process that will lead to a change in practice.

Previous research by Buckley (2000) highlighted the need for social work education and training to focus on the ideological, cultural and organisational influences that shaped practitioner perspectives and determined case careers, particularly in the area of child protection. Evidence confirmed the dissonance between the 'official' child protection discourse and the complexities and dilemmas of everyday practice. It also highlighted practitioners' apparent lack of awareness of the dynamics that determined the way in which decisions and assessments would be reached (again echoing Munro's conclusions). The need to encourage and facilitate social workers' use of systems theory as a means of addressing these complex areas is central to the Munro changes which emphasise having sufficient time to work with families, to think about what is going on, and then in high quality supervision to discuss their impressions, facts, feelings and intuitions.

Reflection in assessment and intervention practice is crucial because of our need to make sense of a lot of information, whether this is written, verbal, or emotional, and including the impact of our own working practices on service users and other people connected to them. Reflective practice is the antithesis of the standardised routine practice prescribed by increasingly bureaucratic organisations. It is essential that we maintain a critical, independent stance that enables us to respond pro-actively to diverse situations and meet the professional standards of practice because of (Smale et al., 2000):

- the often complex conflicts of interest involved in the nature of social problems;
- the unique mix of the skills, resources, experience, strengths, weaknesses and gaps involved, particularly where some people's behaviour is defined as 'the problem';
- the need to understand and unravel the complexities of relationships that perpetuate social problems through self-defeating strategies and mutually defeating interactions: the need for maintenance of the marginal position of the worker;

- the frequent necessity for an exchange model of relationship to achieve effective and lasting changes;
- the risk that procedures, guidelines, and the worker's own behaviour and that of their organisation can contribute to and perpetuate the problems that that worker is intending to resolve;
- a need to identify and respond to the unintended and unforeseen consequences of social interventions.

Reflexive practice is derived from the term reflexivity which gained currency in contemporary debates about the need to conduct research that did not depend on notions of universality and objectivity in social research. Reflexivity is recommended as a critical practice for social research and the social work practice that flows from it (Alvesson and Sköldberg, 2000; Pels, 2000). Critical practice is regarded as a challenge to the orthodoxy and contested notions of realism. These debates are connected to a broader discussion of the merits of postmodernism that try to consider the best ways of finding out the effects and impacts that social work practices have in new ways that challenge the classic models of quantitative research (May, 2002; Walker, 2001c). In this context reflexive practice means that we can embrace evaluation from a sceptical position about reality and certainty, whilst also working hard to ensure the process of evaluation is culturally competent and conscious of the power relationships between service users and social workers.

Reflexivity suggests that we interrogate previously taken-for-granted assumptions: it contends that knowledge does not have fixed stable meanings but that it is made rather than revealed thanks to research efforts (Taylor and White, 2000). Empowering social work practice can be described and defined as we have tried to do here, but actually explaining how it may be applied in practice requires reflexivity. Reflective practice assumes that we can all become more skilled at applying child developmental theories to our practice for example, whereas reflexivity takes this further and questions *whether or not this is possible*.

These debates may seem obscure or irrelevant to our everyday practice, but they will find expression in practical ways that can then have a large impact on the type of social work we do. The increasing emphasis in strategic planning, government guidance and occupational standards rests, as we have noted elsewhere in this book, on risk assessment, risk analysis and risk management. These can be considered as a reaction to the postmodern project of deconstructing orthodox theories and rejecting expert discourses with uncertainty and multiple explanations for social phenomena. It is possible to suggest that the resulting anxiety and lack of guidance would naturally produce attempts by organisations and individuals to exert control and authority (Parton, 1999; Dean, 1997). Anxiety can flourish where there is an intellectual vacuum or no eligibility criteria for our service, procedure manuals, mission statements or assessment matrixes that will signpost our interventions.

Without these anchors of stability in the turmoil of clients' sometimes chaotic, disorganised and painful lives, we may feel more overwhelmed or driven by the meandering, directionless process of a service user's family process. However, if we are sceptical about risk assessment and understand the limitations of contemporary evaluation practice, how can we begin to scrutinise our practice in ways that will satisfy intellectual as well as ethical considerations? An empowering and emancipatory social work practice that liberates both client and worker from their mutually helpless positions combined with inner self-knowledge is a powerful prospect. This offers a practical and achievable solution to the dilemmas described above whilst preserving the heart of the value base for social work practice.

The activity below aims to enhance your reflective skills and develop your capability to problem solve as well as think creatively across professional boundaries.

ACTIVITY

- Spend a few minutes reflecting on what you have read so far in this chapter.
- Now jot down some notes to begin to construct an integrated model of practice that embraces systems theory with the value base of social work.

Commentary

An integrated evaluative model of social work prioritises the task of understanding the experience of the service user whilst also preserving the importance of explanatory power in the context of a plurality of social interpretations that embraces a range of explanations. Within this model discriminatory processes can be exposed and resisted while participatory and partnership approaches are given legitimacy. It also reminds us of the crucial importance of supervision and the capacity to gain some insight into our own feelings and reactions to clients' distressing circumstances: not the supervision of administrative management, but the much more valuable supervision based on the systems context of social work practitioners that links the inner world with the outer. Its characteristics are that it:

- offers a both/and rather than either/or position;
- conserves what is useful and practical;
- tolerates inconsistency and the messiness of lived experience;
- bears uncertainty and challenges complacency;
- accepts that change is continuous while research is static.

BUILDING AN INTEGRATED PRACTICE

Nevertheless, social workers have to assess needs, evaluate risks and allocate resources in a way that is equitable as far as possible for a wide range of children and families in various situations. Challenging oppression in relation to key issues such as poverty and the social marginalisation that underpins interactions in social welfare requires an holistic approach to social change that tackles oppression at the personal, institutional and cultural levels (Dominelli, 2002). Government social policy has had a debilitating impact on state welfare services and in the process a new role has been devised for statutory social work, not so much as a provider of services or even as a therapeutic intervention, rather as a front-line service focused on the management of exclusion and the rationing of scarce resources (Jones, 1997). An empowering social work practice rooted in systems theory principles rejects this prescription.

The following activity focuses on a potential real-life situation where your ability to work under pressure in an interprofessional way will be critical.

- Felicity, aged 8, discloses to you that her uncle who babysits while her parents go out comes into her bed and touches her in a way that makes her feel uncomfortable.
- How would you ensure that she is given the opportunity to tell her story in a safe way, and how would you proceed following this event?

ACTIVITY

Commentary

Calder (2008) recommends an approach which is supportive of the child and offers them security. This includes listening without asking questions, controlling our emotions, and not becoming anxious (or at least not showing this). In addition we can also reassure the child that it's appropriate to tell their story but not promise to keep the information confidential. If the child appears to be in immediate danger the reporting should occur straight away. Children and young people are often frightened to disclose events because of the threats made by a sexual abuser. It may take an incident or a sudden awareness due to knowledge gained about sex from school or peers that will lead to the realisation that abuse is occurring. Teachers will be the key professionals most in contact with and sensitive to sudden changes in a child. Better awareness, training and more frequent contact from workers on a consultative basis will open up the possibilities for them to share concerns or worries and discuss their dilemmas around false alarms or breaching confidentiality, or perhaps facing very angry parents/carers. Maintaining a systems approach using the enhanced Working Together guidance offers better opportunities to detect such changes and create an atmosphere of professional trust and reassurance.

Social workers must counteract oppression, mobilise users' rights, and promote choice, yet also act within the organisational and legal structures which users experience as oppressive (Braye and Preston-Shoot, 1997). Finding their way through this dilemma and reaching compromises, or discovering the potential for creative thinking and practice, are the challenges and opportunities open to social workers who are committed to a socially inclusive practice. This means treating people as a whole and as being in an interaction with their environment, of respecting but not colluding with their understanding and interpretation of their experience, and seeing clients at the centre of what workers are doing (Payne, 1997).

The unique psychosocial perspective of social work offers a vast reservoir of knowledge and skills that we may bring to bear on the problems of socially excluded children and families. A depressed, black, lone parent for example could be seen in deficit pathological terms, with poor early attachment requiring a 'parental' figure to explore repressed or ambivalent feelings. A whole person approach, however, would perceive this person as a survivor with resilience and positive characteristics, despite a racist infrastructure, within which they can be linked with others in similar circumstances in order to learn collective ways of supporting and changing their circumstances.

Social workers using systems-based practice are ideally placed to work with other professionals in multi-disciplinary contexts to enable the team to maintain a focus on better practice. There is evidence that inter-agency training models improve the coordination of efforts between different professionals, especially in the important area of primary care and early intervention (Firth et al., 1999; Walker, 2001b; Sebuliba and Vostanis, 2001). Social work has traditionally valued its distinctive role in human welfare provision, spanning the gap between the psychological and social interpretations of human growth and development.

Social workers' skills in facilitating service user empowerment, particularly with children and families, are indicated in any vision of the future shape of service provision (Walker, 2001c). Systems ideas and practical skills are both required to enable families and young people to support each other and raise a collective awareness of shared issues. Investigations of indigenous healing practices and beliefs can provide a rich source of information that we may utilise in the helping process. Advocacy skills, in which young people are encouraged to be supported and represented by advocates of their choice, would also contribute to influencing current service provision (Ramon, 1999).

The notion that social workers should respect diversity, build on an ethnic group's strengths and provide for individual and social change is not new (Pentini-Aluffi and Lorenz, 1996). Reviews of social work practice highlight the need for more rigorous evaluations of what works with each client, the individual circumstances this happens in, and the methods involved (Thompson, 1995; Cheetham, 1997; Shaw et al., 2004). Traditional quantitative and qualitative methodologies select narrow, easily discernable outcomes as measures of impact. These negate the wider influence of interventions felt in the community or the minute personal narrative insights and feelings which are less quantifiable. By translating research findings into practice in the context of community welfare services, social work can contribute to a more holistic response that will meet the needs of every child and family that requires it.

The following activity aims to stretch your imagination and think creatively about improving working relationships with other professional staff.

- Think about the local systems of support for children and families in your area.
- Now consider which individuals within those systems you feel are easier to work with and which ones are more difficult.
- Discuss this in supervision or with a colleague if preferable. What are your explanations/ hypotheses for these differences?

10

CONCLUSION

This book contains a number of resources, ideas, exercises and points of reflection based on evidence and the wisdom derived from a vast number of sources, my own experiences, colleagues, students and children and families, not unlike many similar texts beforehand. The starting-point and stimulus for writing it was the Munro report, the preceding debates over Peter Connelly's killing, and the emerging evidence from social workers and researchers led by Professor Munro in Hackney, that it was possible even under the most challenging conditions, to re-imagine a social work practice with children and families that most social workers would aspire to implement. But it is worth acknowledging that Hackney had begun to transform social work practice well before the current government took over and the financial crisis shocked the body politic and led to the subsequent economic austerity measures.

This book has been published in the early stages of a period of economic inertia where public sector services and jobs are shrinking and thus the consequences for the extra demands this will generate on social workers and other professionals involved in the welfare system and particularly in safeguarding and child protection. While what is known as the 'Hackney model' is being developed in other local authorities, the cuts to the welfare system and a political ideology that sees a bigger role for volunteers and private companies are set to create a very different model of how health and social care has been organised and delivered to date. The evidence in this text supports the notion that with careful planning it is possible to establish interprofessional teams that will include social workers who will in turn be able to integrate with and mobilise primary health care staff, teachers, police officers and those in the independent and voluntary agencies within the social environments of children and families (and be influenced and possibly managed by social workers) (Falloon and Fadden, 1995; Jowitt and O'Loughlin, 2005; Ruch, 2009).

Any model of social work practice in this area has to be able to find its place within the existing and constantly changing mosaic of professional and voluntary provision located in communities and informal networks. The book has illustrated how it is possible to create a system of multi-disciplinary expertise and resources that are both accessible and acceptable to service users and can work together. Internationally, there have been successful attempts to identify common interprofessional training needs to enable staff to work better in integrated service delivery systems (DH/DfEE,1996; Magrab et al., 1997; Department for Education and Employment, 1998).

The range of professions potentially undertaking work with children and families to prevent abuse or protect children brings different skills, training, experience and knowledge to the task. There are however some basic attributes which all members of a multi-disciplinary service or team should possess. These are consistent with a systems model of social work practice, but they may not be reflected in other professional training and education or indeed familiar to volunteers:

- Empathetic interviewing and counselling skills.
- A working knowledge of child development and the context of abuse.
- An up-to-date working knowledge of child and family problems.
- An understanding of the impact of major life events on children's lives.
- An awareness of how a professional's own life experiences will inform the ways in which they will approach others.

It has been acknowledged throughout that other professionals do not experience the same level of supervision or the same type of supervision that permits reflective practice. The tradition in social work of such supervision is constantly brought under pressure by managerialist prescriptions for brief, task-centred working practices, risk assessments and the prioritisation of caseloads. However, supervision that enables workers to understand and learn from the interactive processes experienced during work is a valuable tool to encourage them to reflect on child and family practice that can be emotionally draining. Some may find the experience unsettling while others will draw immense comfort from it. Both will benefit and have their practice enhanced as a result.

In multi-disciplinary and interprofessional contexts a culture of such enlightened supervision for all staff can create a rich climate for professional growth and improve the quality of service to young people at risk of harm. The evidence outlined in previous chapters suggests there is an appetite here to incorporate this social work model of supervision into the new multi-disciplinary family support teams and a genuine desire on the part of politicians and employers to improve the safeguarding of vulnerable children and young people.

The book has also demonstrated how social workers can bring a distinctive contribution to interprofessional and multi-disciplinary work. Effective multi-disciplinary team working or inter-agency working requires the notion of power to be addressed and shared more equally between staff. It also requires that that power be shared by adopting more participative practices with clients and the community being served. Social workers' skills in advocacy and empowerment combined with a psychosocial approach are therefore crucial in making this happen. Workers also bring with them a concept of oppression and how discriminatory social contexts can blight the lives of children and families. This wider social and political perspective can raise awareness among other staff and inform and enrich other professionals' intervention practice.

Yet it has been emphasised throughout that it is crucial not to lose sight or sound of the child in all this and to remember that for a child to voice their fear of abuse takes great courage: while most professionals will appear to take into account the problems a child has, welfare decisions will often be made *for* the child rather than *with* the child. As a team professionals will need to put the child's rights first when making decisions and it is only when this occurs that child-care professionals can believe protection policies do indeed protect children and their rights. Great strides have been made in this regard, but with the knowledge gained about gaps in services leaving children at risk child-care professionals must continuously monitor procedures and their policy of inter-agency working to ensure that decisions are made in children's best interests (Walker and Thurston, 2006).

If the future of social work with children and families is to be fashioned in the context of the Munro recommendations, where multi-disciplinary teams are brought together to foster collaborative work and draw upon the best practice of all professionals, then social work has a rare opportunity. Over forty years ago Seebohm put forward a progressive view of the shape of personal social services that sought to reconstruct the history of fragmented provision in child welfare (HMSO, 1968). The latest policy guidance from the Social Work Reform Board has mapped out the direction of social work provision and the form it will be structured in which both echo Seebohm. It aims to foster interprofessional work, avoid duplications of effort, cut down on time-consuming paperwork, and be child centred.

A systems-informed approach offers a chance to deliver an holistic service to every family by social workers using and combining the optimum mixture of theory and practice resources in the most accessible and acceptable way to better protect children from harm. The impact will be hard to measure as a change of this magnitude takes time and evaluating its effectiveness will be problematic.

It is suggested that an old Buddhist saying is 'If you sow thistle seeds, you cannot expect apple trees to grow' (Butcher, 2012). This captures a fundamental point relating to the limits of possibility in a period of economic retrenchment and ideological shifts in policy, discussed in this book.

BIBLIOGRAPHY

Abrahams, N., Casey, K. and Daro, D. (1992) 'Teachers' knowledge, attitudes and beliefs about child abuse and its prevention', *Child Abuse and Neglect*, 16 (2): 229–38.

Adams, A., Erath, P. and Shardlow, S. (2000) *Fundamentals of Social Work in Selected European Countries*. Lyme Regis: Russell House.

Ainsworth, M., Blehar, M., Waters, E. and Wall, S. (1978) *Patterns of Attachment: A Psychological Study of the Strange Situation*. New York: Erlbaum.

Alderson, P. (2000) *Young Children's Rights*. London: Save the Children/Jessica Kingsley.

Alderson, P. (1994) *Young Children's Rights: Exploring Beliefs, Principles and Practice*. London: Jessica Kingsley.

Alibhai-Brown, Y. (1999) *True Colours: Public Attitudes to Multiculturalism and the Role of the Government*. London: IPPR.

Allan, M., Bhavnani, R. and French, K. (1992) *Promoting Women*. London: Social Services Inspectorate/HMSO.

Alvesson, M. and Sköldberg, K. (2000) *Reflexive Methodology: New Vistas for Qualitative Research*. London: Sage.

Amin K., Drew, D., Fosam, B., Gillborn, D. and Demack, S. (1997) *Black and Ethnic Minority Young People and Educational Disadvantage*. London: Runnymede Trust.

Audit Commission (1994) *Seen But Not Heard*. London: HMSO.

Audit Commission (2002) *Recruitment and Retention: A Public Service Workforce for the Twenty-first Century*. London: Audit Commission.

Bailey, R. and Brake, M. (1975) *Radical Social Work*. London: Edward Arnold.

Bailey, R. and Brake, M. (1980) *Radical Social Work and Practice*. London: Edward Arnold.

Baker, K. and Coe, L. (1993) 'Growing up with a chronic condition: transition to young adulthood for the individual with cystic fibrosis', *Holistic Nurse Practice*, 8 (1): 8–15.

Bakan, J. (2011) 'The Kids Are Not All Right', *The New York Times*. Available at: www.nytimes.com/2011/08/22/opinion/corporate-interests-threaten-childrens-welfare.htm, accessed 14 May 2012

Baldwin, M. (2000) *Care Management and Community Care*. Aldershot: Ashgate.

Baldwin, N. (ed.) (2000) *Protecting Children, Promoting Their Rights*. London: Whiting & Birch.

Bannister, A. and Huntington, A. (2002) *Communicating With Children and Adolescents: Action For Change*. London: Jessica Kingsley.

Baradon, T., Sinason, V. and Yabsley, S. (1999) 'Assessment of parents and young children: a child psychotherapy point of view', *Child Care Health and Development*, 25 (1): 37–53.

Barford, R. (1993) *Children's View of Child Protection Social Work: Social Work Monographs*. Norwich: University of East Anglia.

Barker, P. (1998) *Basic Family Therapy*. London: Blackwells Science.

Barlow, J. (1998) 'Parent training programmes and behaviour problems: findings from a systematic review', in A. Buchanan and B. Hudson (eds), *Parenting, Schooling, and Children's Behaviour: Interdisciplinary Approaches*. Alton: Ashgate.

Barnes, M. and Warren, L. (1999) *Paths to Empowerment*. Bristol: Policy Press.

Barton, A. (2002) *Managing Fragmentation*. Aldershot: Ashgate.

BASW (2012) *BASW Response to the DfES Green Paper: Every Child Matters*. Birmingham: BASW.

Bateson, G. (1973) *Steps to an Ecology of Mind*. St. Albans: Paladin.

Baumann, G. (1996) *Contesting Culture*. Cambridge: Cambridge University Press.

Bayley, R. (1999) *Transforming Children's Lives: The Importance of Early Intervention*. London: Family Policy Studies Centre.

Beckett, C. (2003) *Child Protection: An Introduction*. London: Sage.

Bee, H. (1992) *The Developing Child*, 6th edn. New York: HarperCollins.

Bee, H. (1994) *Lifespan Development*. New York: HarperCollins.

Belsky, J. (1980) 'Child maltreatment: an ecological approach', *American Psychologist*, 35: 320–35.

Bentovim, A. (2002) 'Working with abusing families in child abuse: defining understanding and intervening', in K. Wilson A. James and (eds), *The Child Protection Handbook*. London: Balliére Tindall. Chapter 24.

Bentovim, A. and Bingley Milier, L. (2002) *The Family Assessment*. London: DH /Pavilion.

Berg, I.K. (1991) *Family Preservation: A Brief Therapy Workbook*. London: BT Press.

Berg, I.K. and Jaya, A. (1993) 'Different and same: family therapy with Asian-American families', *Journal of Family and Marital Therapy*, 19 (1): 31–9.

Berg, I.K. and Kelly, S. (2000) *Building Solutions in Child Protective Services*. New York: Norton.

Berridge, D. (1997) *Foster Care: A Research Review*. London: HMSO.

Bhugra, D. (1999) *Mental Health of Ethnic Minorities*. London: Gaskell.

Bhugra, D. and Bahl, V. (1999) *Ethnicity: An Agenda for Mental Health*. London: Gaskell.

Bhui, K. and Olajide, D. (eds) (1999) *Mental Health Service Provision for a Multi-cultural Society*. London: Saunders.

Bifulco, P. and Moran, K. (1998) *Wednesday's Child: Research into Women's Experiences of Neglect and Abuse in Childhood and Adult Depression*. London: Routledge.

Bilton, T., Bonnet, K., Jones, P., Lawson, T., Skinner, D., Stanworth, M. and Webster, A. (2002) *Introductory Sociology*. Basingstoke: Palgrave Macmillan.

Bingley-Miller, L., Fisher, T. and Sinclair, I. (1993) 'Decisions to register children as at risk of abuse', *Social Work and Social Science Review*, 4 (2): 101–18.

Blom-Cooper, L. (1987) *A Child in Mind: Protection of Children in a Responsible Society: The Report of the Commission of Inquiry into the Circumstances Surrounding the Death of Kimberley Carlile*. London: Borough of Greenwich.

Blyth, E. and Cooper, H. (1999) Chapter 8 *Children, Child Abuse and Child Protection: Placing Children Centrally*. Chichester: Wiley.

Bourne, D. (1993) 'Over-chastisement, child non-compliance and parenting skills: a behavioural intervention by a family centre social worker', *British Journal of Social Work*, 23 (5): 481–500.

Bowlby, J. (1969) *Attachment and Loss*. Vol 1. London: Hogarth.

Bradshaw, J. (1972) 'The concept of human need', *New Society*, 30 (3): 72.

Brandon, M., Belderson, P., Warren, C. and Howe, D. (2008) *Analysing Child Deaths and Serious Injury through Abuse and Neglect: What Can We Learn? A Biennial Analysis of Serious Case Reviews*. Nottingham: DCSF.

Braye, S. and Preston-Shoot, M. (1997) *Practising Social Work Law*, 2nd edn. London: Palgrave Macmillan.

Brearley, P.C., with Hall, M.R.P., Jeffreys, P.M., Jennings, R., and Pritchards, S. (1982) *Managing Risk and Uncertainty in Social Work: A Literature Review*. London: Routledge and Kegan Paul.

Briggs, S. (2002) *Working with Adolescents: A Contemporary Psychodynamic Approach*, Basingstoke, Palgrave Macmillan.

Brome, V. (1978) *Jung: Man and Myth*. Basingstoke: Macmillan.

Brown, B., Crawford, P. and Darongkamas, J. (2000) 'Blurred roles and permeable boundaries: the experience of multidisciplinary working in community mental health', *Health and Social Care in the Community*, 8 (6): 425–35.

Brown, J.H. and Christensen, D.N. (1999) *Family Therapy Theory and Practice*, 2nd edn. London: International Thompson.

Browne, K. (2002) 'Child abuse: defining, understanding and intervening', in K. Wilson and A. James (eds), *The Child Protection Handbook*. London: Balliére Tindall.

Buchanan, A. (2002) 'Family support', in D. McNeish, T. Newman and H. Roberts (eds), *What Works For Children? Effective Services for Children and Families*. Buckingham: Open University Press.

Buckley, H. (2000) 'Child protection: an unreflective practice', *Social Work Education*, 19 (3): 253–63.

Buckley, H. (2003) *Child Protection: Beyond the Rhetoric*. London: Jessica Kingsley.

Burnham, J. (1984). *Family Therapy*. London: Tavistock Publications.

Butcher, D. (2012) Seven Wonders of the Buddhist World', *Radio Times*. Available at: www.radiotimes.com/episode/k5nkq/seven-wonders-of-the-buddhist-world, accessed 14 May 2012

Butler, I. and Roberts, G. (1997) *Social Work with Children and Families: Getting into Practice*. London: Jessica Kingsley.

Butler-Sloss, E., Lord Justice (1988) *Report of the Inquiry into Child Abuse in Cleveland 1987*, Cmnd 412. London: HMSO.

Byng-Hall, J. (1998) *Rewriting Family Scripts: Improvisation and Systems Change*. New York: Guilford Press.

Calder, M. (2003) 'The Assessment Framework: a critique and reformulation', in M. Calder and S. Hackett (eds), *Assessment in Childcare*. Lyme Regis: Russell House.

Calder, M. (ed.) (2008) *Contemporary Risk Assessment in Safeguarding Children*. Lyme Regis: Russell House.

Calder, M. and Hackett, S. (2003) *Assessment in Childcare*. Lyme Regis: Russell House.

Calder, M. and Horwath, J. (eds) (1999) *Working for Children on the Child Protection Register*. Aldershot: Arena.

Campbell, B. (1988) *Unofficial Secrets*. London: Virago.

Campbell, D. and Draper, R. (eds) (1985) *Applications of Systemic Family Therapy*. London: Grune & Stratton.

Cannan, C., Berry, L. and Lyons, K. (1992) *Social Work and Europe*. London: Macmillan/ BASW.

Carr, A. (2000) *What Works with Children and Adolescents?* London: Routledge.

Carter, B. and McGoldrick, M. (1999) *The Expanded Life Cycle: Individual, Family & Social Perspectives*, 3rd edn. Boston: Allyn & Bacon.

Casey, A. (1988) 'A partnership with child and family', *Senior Nurse*, 8 (4): 8–9.

Casey, A. (1993) 'Development and use of the partnership model of nursing care', in G. Glasper and A. Tucker (eds), *Advances In Child Health Nursing*. London: Scutari.

Cawson, P., Wattam, C., Brooker, S. and Kelly, G. (2000) *Child Maltreatment in the United Kingdom: A Study on the Prevalence of Child Abuse and Neglect*. London: NSPCC.

Chalmers, I. (1994) 'Assembling the evidence', in Alderson, P. et al. (eds), *What Works? Effective Social Interventions in Child Welfare*. Barkingside: Barnardo's.

Charles, M. and Hendry, E. (2000) *Training Together to Safeguard Children.* London: NSPCC.

Charles, M. with Stevenson, O. (1991) *Multidisciplinary is Different: Sharing Perspectives.* Nottingham: University of Nottingham.

Cheetham, J. (1997) *Evaluating Social Work Effectiveness.* Milton Keynes: OU Press.

Cheetham, J., Fuller, R., McIvor, G. and Petch, A. (1992) *Evaluating Social Work Effectiveness.* Buckingham: Open University Press.

Children's Society (2002) *Thrown Away.* London: The Children's Society.

Christiansen, E. and James, G. (eds) (2000) *Research with Children, Perspectives and Practices.* London: Falmer.

Christopherson, J. (1989) 'European child-abuse management systems, in comparison of child and parent training interventions', *Journal of Consulting and Clinical Psychology*, 65 (1): 93–109.

Cleaver, H., Unell, I. and Aldgate, J. (1999) *Children's Needs: Parenting Capacity.* London: DH.

Clifford, D. (1998) *Social Assessment Theory and Practice.* Aldershot: Aldgate.

Coleman, M., Ganong, L. and Cable, S. (1997) 'Beliefs about women's intergenerational family obligations to provide support before and after divorce and remarriage', *Journal of Marriage and the Family*, 59 (1): 165–76.

Collins, C. (1998) *Our Children at Risk: Children and Youth Issues.* London: YMCA.

Corby, B. (1987) *Working With Child Abuse.* Milton Keynes: Open University Press.

Corby, B. (2000) *Child Abuse: Towards A Knowledge Base,* 2nd edn. Buckingham: Open University Press.

Corrigan, P. and Leonard, P. (1978) *Social Work Practice under Capitalism: A Marxist Approach.* London: Macmillan.

Cote, G L. (1997) 'Socio-economic attainment, regional disparities, and internal migration', *European Sociological Review*, 13 (1): 55–77.

Cowie, H. (1999) 'Counselling psychology in the UK: the interface between practice and research', *The European Journal of Psychotherapy, Counselling and Health*, 2 (1): 69–80.

Crawford, M. and Kessel, A. (1999) 'Not listening to patients: the use and misuse of patient satisfaction studies', *International Journal of Social Psychiatry*, 45 (1): 1–6.

Crisp, B., Anderson, M., Orme, J. and Lister, P. (2007) 'Assessment Frameworks: a critical reflection', *British Journal of Social Work*, 37 (6): 1059–77.

Crisp, S. (1994) *Counting on Families: Social Audit Report on the Provision of Family Support Services.* London: Exploring Parenthood.

Crittenden, P. (1997) 'Patterns of attachment and sexual behaviour: risk of dysfunction versus opportunity for creating integration', in L. Atkinson and K. Zucker (eds), *Attachment and Psychopathology.* New York: Guilford Press.

CSCI (2004) *Factsheet: Children's Views and Report on Keeping Children Safe from Harm.* London: Commission for Social Care Inspection.

Dale, P. (2004) 'Like a fish in a bowl: parents' perceptions of child protection services', *Child Abuse Review*, 13: 137–57.

Dale, P., Davies, M., Morrison, T. and Waters, J. (1986) *Dangerous Families.* London: Routledge.

Dallos, R. and Draper, R. (2000) *An Introduction to Family Therapy.* Buckingham: Open University Press.

Davis, A., Ellis, K. and Rummery, B. (1997) *Access to Assessment: Perspectives of Practitioners, Disabled People, and Carers.* Bristol: Policy Press.

Davis, J., Rendell, P. and Sims, D. (1999) 'The joint practitioner – a new concept in professional training', *Journal of Interprofessional Care*, 13 (4): 395–404.

Dean, M. (1997) 'Sociology after society', in D. Owen (ed.), *Sociology After Postmodernism*. London: Sage.

Debell, D. and Everett, G. (1997) *In a Class Apart: A Study of School Nursing*. Norwich: East Norfolk Health Authority.

Debell, D. and Walker, S. (2002) *Norfolk Family Support Teams Final Evaluation Report*. Chelmsford: APU Centre for Research in Health and Social Care.

DeMause, L. (1998) 'The history of child abuse', *Journal of Psychohistory*, 25 (3): 622–43.

Dennehy, A., Smith, L. and Harker, P. (1997) *Not to be Ignored: Young People, Poverty and Health*. London: Child Poverty Action Group.

Department for Education and Employment (1998) *Towards an Interdisciplinary Framework for Developing Work with Children and Young People*. Childhood Studies Discipline Network. Conference presentation, Cambridge, Robinson College.

Department for Work and Pensions (2003) *Annual Report*. London: HMSO.

DES (1988) *Child Protection in Schools*. London: Department of Education and Science, Circular 4/88.

De Shazer, S. (1982) *Patterns of Brief Family Therapy: An Ecosystemic Approach*. New York: The Guilford Press.

DfE (2011) *Revised Working Together Guidance*. London: HMSO.

DfES (2002) *Don't Suffer in Silence: An Anti-bullying Pack for Schools*. London: HMSO.

DfES (2003a) *Keeping Children Safe*. London: HMSO.

DfES (2003b) *The Children Act Report 2002*. Nottingham: HMSO.

DfES (2003a) *Children in Need*. London: HMSO.

DfES (2003b) *Every Child Matters*. London: HMSO.

DfES (2004a) *Refocusing Children's Services Towards Prevention: Lessons from the Literature*. Research report 510. London: HMSO.

DfES (2004b) *The Children Act*. Nottingham: HMSO.

DfES (2005a) *Common Core of Skills & Knowledge for the Children's Workforce*. London: HMSO.

DfES (2005b) *Common Assessment Framework*. London: HMSO.

DfES (2006) *Working Together to Safeguard Children: A Guide to Inter-agency Working to Safeguard and Promote the Welfare of Children*. London: HMSO.

DfES (2010) *Children Looked After in England and Wales*. London: DfES.

DH (1988) *Protecting Children: A Guide for Social Workers Undertaking a Comprehensive Assessment*. London: HMSO.

DH (1989a) *Children Act*. London: HMSO.

DH (1989b) *The Children Act 1989: An Introductory Guide for the NHS*. London: HMSO.

DH (1991a) *Child Abuse: A Study of Inquiry Reports 1980–1989*. London: HMSO.

DH (1991b) *Family Placements, the Children Act 1989, Guidance and Regulations*, 3. London: HMSO.

DH (1991c) *Working Together under the Children Act 1989*. London: HMSO.

DH (1995) *Child Protection: Messages from Research*. London: HMSO.

DH (1996) *National Commission of Inquiry into Child Protection*. London: HMSO.

DH (1997) *General Household Survey*. London: HMSO.

DH (1998) *Disability and Discrimination Act*. London: HMSO

DH (1999a) *Working Together to Safeguard Children*. London: HMSO.

DH (1999b) Lac circular (99) 33. *Quality Protects Programme: Transforming Children's Services 2000–01*. London: HMSO.

DH (1999c) *Executive Summary, Convention on the Rights of the Child: Second Report to the UN Committee on the Rights of the Child by the United Kingdom*. London: HMSO.

DH (1999d) *Framework for the Assessment of Children in Need and Their Families*. London: HMSO.

DH (1999e) *The Protection of Children Act*. London: HMSO.

DH (2000a) *Framework for the Assessment of Children in Need and their Families*. London: HMSO.

DH (2000b) *Quality Protects: Disabled Children, Numbers and Categories*. London: HMSO.

DH (2001a) *National Plan for Safeguarding Children from Commercial Sexual Exploitation*. London: HMSO.

DH (2001b) *Children (Leaving Care) Act*. London: HMSO.

DH (2002) *Child in Need Survey*. London: HMSO.

DH (2003a) *Children Looked After by Local Authorities*. London: HMSO.

DH (2003b) *Guidelines for the Appointment of General Practitioners with Special Interests in the Delivery of Clinical Services: Child Protection*. London: HMSO.

DH (2003c) *The Victoria Climbié Inquiry*. London: HMSO.

DH (2003d) *Green Paper: Every Child Matters*. London: DH.

DH (2003e) *What to do if You Are Worried a Child is Being Abused*. London: HMSO.

DH (2004) *National Service Framework for Children, Families, and Midwifery Services*. London: HMSO.

DH (2010a) *Prioritising Need in the Context of Putting People First, a Whole System Approach to Eligibilty for Social Care*. London: TSO.

DH (2010b) *Working Together*. London: HMSO.

DH (2011a) *Health and Social Care Bill*. London: HMSO.

DH (2011b) *Capabilities Framework*. London: HMSO.

DH/DfEE (1996) *Children's Service Planning: Guidance for Inter-Agency Working*. London: HMSO.

DH/SSI (2002) *Safeguarding Children: A Joint Chief Inspectors Report on Arrangements to Safeguard Children*. London: DH.

DHSS (1974a) *Report of the Committee of Inquiry into the Care and Supervision Provided in Relation to Maria Colwell*. London: HMSO.

DHSS (1974b) *Non-accidental Injury To Children*, LASSL (74), (13). London: DHSS.

DHSS (1983) *Child Abuse: A Study of Inquiry Reports 1973–1981*. London: HMSO.

DHSS (1986) *Child Abuse – Working Together: A Draft Guide to Arrangements for Interagency Cooperation for the Protection of Children*. London: HMSO.

DHSS (1988) *Working Together*. London: HMSO.

Dimigen, G., Del Priore, C., Butler, S., Evans, S., Ferguson, L. and Swan, M. (1999) 'Psychiatric disorder among children at time of entering local authority care', *British Medical Journal*, 319: 675–76.

Dingwall, R., Eekelaar, J. and Murray, T. (1995) *The Protection of Children, State Intervention and Family Life*. Aldershot: Avebury.

Dominelli, L. (2002) *Anti-oppressive Social Work Theory and Practice*. Basingstoke: Palgrave Macmillan.

Dominelli, L. (1998) 'Anti-oppressive practice in context', in R. Adams, L. Dominelli and M. Payne (eds), *Social Work: Themes, Issues and Critical Debates*. Basingstoke: Macmillan.

Dominelli, L. (ed.) (1999) *Community Approaches to Child Welfare*. Aldershot: Ashgate.

Donovan, M. (2003) 'Mind the gap: the need for a generic bridge between psychoanalytic and systemic approaches', *Journal of Family Therapy*, 25: 115–35.

Dryden, W. (1988) *Family Therapy in Britain*. Milton Keynes: Open University Press.

Dulmus, C. and Rapp-Paglicci, L. (2000) 'The prevention of mental disorders in children and adolescents: future research and public-policy recommendations', *Families in Society: The Journal of Contemporary Human Services*, 81 (3): 294–303.

Durlak, J. (1998) 'Primary prevention programmes for children and adolescents are effective', *Journal of Mental Health*, 7 (5): 454–69.

Durlak, J. and Wells, A. (1997) 'Primary prevention mental health programs for children and adolescents: a meta-analytic review', *American Journal of Community Psychology*, 25 (2): 115–52.

DWP (2011) *A New Approach to Child Poverty: Tackling the Causes of Disadvantage and Transforming Families' Lives*. London: Department for Work and Pensions.

Eayrs, C. and Jones, R. (1992) 'Methodological issues and future directions in the evaluation of early intervention programmes', *Child Care, Health and Development*, 18 (1): 15–28.

Eber, L., Osuch, R. and Redditt, C. (1996) 'School-based applications of the wraparound process: early results on service provision and student outcomes', *Journal of Child and Family Studies*, 5: 83–99.

Eliason, M. (1996) 'Lesbian and gay family issues', *Journal of Family Nursing*, 2 (1): 10–29.

Elicker et al. (1992) 'Predicting peer competence and peer relationships in childhood from early parent-child relationships', in R. Parke and G. Ladd (eds), *Family-Peer Relationships*. Hillsdale, NJ: Erlbaum.

Evans, M. and Miller, C. (1993) *Partnership in Child Protection*. London: Office for Public Management/National Institute of Social Work.

Everitt, A. and Hardiker, P. (1996) *Evaluating Good Practice*. Basingstoke: Macmillan.

Fagin, C.M. (1992) 'Collaboration between nurses and physicians; no longer a choice', *Academic Medicine*, 67 (5): 295–303.

Falicov, C. (1995) 'Training to think culturally: a multidimensional comparative framework', *Family Process*, 34: 373–88.

Falloon, I. and Fadden, G. (1995) *Integrated Mental Health Care: A Comprehensive Community-based Approach*. Cambridge: Cambridge University Press.

Farmer, E. and Owen, M. (1995) *Child Protection Practice: Private Risks and Public Remedies*. London: HMSO.

Favlov, J. (1996) *Study of Working Together "Part 8" Reports: Fatal Child Abuse and Parental Psychiatric Disorder*, DH – ACPC Series, Report No. 1. London: HMSO.

Fawcett, B. (2000) 'Look, listen and learn', *Community Care*, July. Sutton: Reed.

Fawcett, B., Featherstone, B. and Goddard, J. (2004) *Contemporary Child Care Policy and Practice*. Basingstoke: Palgrave Macmillan.

Ferguson, H. (2008) 'Liquid social work: welfare interventions as mobile practices', *British Journal of Social Work*, 38 (3): 561–79.

Ferguson, H. and O'Reilly, M. (2001) *Keeping Children Safe: Child Abuse, Child Protection and the Promotion of Welfare*. Dublin: Framar.

Fielding, N. and Conroy, S. (1994) 'Against the grain: co-operation in child sexual abuse investigations', in, M. Stephens and S. Becker (eds), *Police Force Police Service: Care And Control In Britain*. Basingstoke: Macmillan.

Fineman, S. (1985) *Social Work Stress and Intervention*. Aldershot: Gower.

Firth, M., Dyer, M. and Wilkes, J. (1999) 'Reducing the distance: mental health social work in general practice', *Journal of Interprofessional Care*, 13 (4): 335–44.

Fook, J. (2012) *Social Work: Critical Theory and Practice*, 2nd edn. London: Sage.

Forder, A. (1976) 'Social work and system theory', *British Journal of Social Work*, 6 (1): 23–42.

Forrester, D. (2000) 'Parental substance abuse and child protection in a British sample', *Child Abuse Review*, 9 (4): 235–46.

Fox-Harding, L. (1991) *Perspectives in Child Care Policy*. London: Longman.

Freeman, I., Morrison, A., Lockhart, F. and Swanson, M. (1996) 'Consulting service users: the views of young people', in M. Hill and J. Aldgate (eds), *Child Welfare Services: Developments in Law, Policy, Practice and Research*. London: Jessica Kingsley. pp. 88–97.

Freeman, M. (1984) *State, Law and the Family*. London: Tavistock.

Freud. S. (1973) *Three Essays on the Theory of Sexuality*. Standard edition. Vol. 6. London: Hogarth Press.

FRG (1986) *FRG's Response to the DHSS Consultation Paper: Child Abuse – Working Together*. London: Family Rights Group.

Friedlander, M.L. (2001) 'Family therapy research: science into practice, practice into science', in M.P. Nichols and R.C. Schwartz (eds), *Family Therapy: Concepts and Methods*, 5th edn. Boston: Alleyn & Bacon.

Fulcher, J. and Scott, M. (1999) *Sociology*. Oxford: Oxford University Press.

Fuller, R. (1991) 'Evaluating social work effectiveness: a pragmatic approach', in T. Furniss (ed.), *The Multi-professional Handbook of Child Sexual Abuse*. London: Routledge.

Furedi, F. (2003) *Therapy Culture*. London: Routledge.

Gadsby Waters, J. (1992) *The Supervision of Child Protection Work*. Aldershot: Avebury.

Gardner, R. (1998) *Family Support: Practitioners Guide*. Birmingham: Venture.

Garmezy, N., Masten, A.S. and Tellegren, A. (1984) 'The study of stress and competence in children: a building block for developmental psychotherapy', *Child Development*, 5: 97–111.

Garratt, D., Roche, J. and Tucker, S. (eds) (1997) *Changing Experiences Of Youth*. London: Sage/Open University Press.

George, C. (1996) 'A representational perspective of child abuse and prevention: internal working models of attachment and caregiving', *Child Abuse and Neglect*, 20 (5): 411–24

Ghate, D. and Daniels, A. (1997) *Talking About My Generation*. London: NSPCC.

Gibbons, J. and Wilding, J. (1995) *Needs, Risks and Family Support Plans: Social Services Departments Responses to Neglected Children*. Norwich: University of East Anglia.

Giller, H., Gormley, C. and Williams, P. (1992) *The Effectiveness of Child Protection Procedures*. Nantwich: Social Information Systems.

Gillingham, P. (2011) 'Decision-making tools and the development of expertise in child protection practitioners: are we "just breeding workers who are good at ticking boxes"?', *Child & Family Social Work*, 10: 1365–2206.

Glisson, C. and Hemmelgarn, A. (1998) 'The effects of organisational climate and inter-organisational coordination on the quality and outcomes of children's service systems', *Child Abuse and Neglect*, 22 (5): 401–21.

GMC (1993) *Confidentiality and Child Abuse*. London: General Medical Council, July, No. 3.

Goldenberg, I. and Goldenberg, H. (2004) *Family Therapy – An Overview*. Pacific Grove, CA: Thomson Learning.

Goldner, V. (1991) 'Sex, power and gender: a feminist analysis of the politics of passion', *Journal of Feminist Family Therapy*, 3: 63–83.

Goldstein, H. (1973) *Social Work Practice: A Unitary Approach*. South Carolina: University of South Carolina.

Gordon, G. and Grant, R. (1997) *How we Feel: An Insight into the Emotional World of Teenagers*. London: Jessica Kingsley.

Gordon, L. (1989) *Heroes of Their Own Lives*. London: Virago.

Gorell Barnes, G. (1998) *Family Therapy in Changing Times*. Basingstoke: Macmillan.

Gouldner, A. (1954) *Patterns of Industrial Bureaucracy*. New York: Free.

Gray, J. (2004) 'The interface between the child welfare and criminal justice systems in England', *Child Abuse Review*, 13: 312–23.

Gregg, S. (1995) *Preventing Anti-social Behaviour in At-risk Students*. London: OERI.

Griffin, C.(1993) *Representations of Youth: The Study of Youth and Adolescence in Britain and America*. Cambridge: Polity Press.

Gross, D., Fogg, L. and Tucker, S. (1995) 'The efficacy of parent training for promoting positive parent-toddler relationships', *Research in Nursing and Health*, 18: 489–99.

Hague, G. (2000) *Reducing Domestic Violence, What Works?* PRCU Briefing Note. London: HMSO.

Hague, G. and Malos, E. (1993) *Domestic Violence: Action for Change*. Cheltenham: New Clarion Press.

Haley, J. (1976) *Problem Solving Therapy*. San Francisco, CA: Josey-Bass.

Hall, S. (1993) 'Culture, community, nation', *Cultural Studies*, 7 (3): 16–29.

Hallett, C. (1995) *Interagency Coordination in Child Protection*. London: HMSO.

Hallett, C. and Birchall, E. (1992) *Coordination and Child Protection: A Review of the Literature*. London: HMSO.

Haralambos, M. (1988) *Sociology: Theses and Perspectives*. London: Unwin Hyman.

Haralambos, M. and Holborn, M. (1991) *Sociology: Themes and Perspectives*, 3rd edn. London: Collins Educational.

Harbin, F. and Murphy, M. (eds) (2000) *Substance Misuse and Childcare*. Lyme Regis: Russell House.

Hardiker, P. (1995) *The Social Policy Contexts of Services to Prevent Unstable Family Life*. York: Joseph Rowntree Foundation.

Hardiker, P., Exton, K. and Barker, M. (1991) 'The social policy contexts of prevention in child care', *British Journal Of Social Work*, 21: 341–59.

Hare-Mustin, R. (1991) 'Sex, lies and headaches: the problem is power', *Journal of Feminist Family Therapy*, 3: 39–61.

Harrison, R., Mann, G., Murphy, M., Taylor, A. and Thompson, N. (2003) *Partnership Made Painless*. Lyme Regis: Russell House.

Hartley, J. (2003) *A Short History of Cultural Studies*. London: Sage.

Healy, K. (2002) *Social Work Practices: Contemporary Perspectives on Change*. London: Sage.

Heisenberg, W. (1930) *Physikalische Prinzipien der Quantentheorie*. Leipzig: Hirzel. (English translation, *The Physical Principles of Quantum Theory*. Chicago: University of Chicago Press.)

Hellinckx, W., Colton, M. and Williams, M. (1997) *International Perspectives on Family Support*. Aldershot: Ashgate.

Helm, D. (2010) *Making Sense of Child and Family Assessment: How to Interpret Children's Needs*. London: Jessica Kingsley.

Helman, C. (2001) *Culture, Health and Illness*, 4th edn. London: Arnold.

Hendrick, H. (ed.) (2005) *Child Welfare and Social Policy: An Essential Reader*. Bristol: Policy Press.

Hennessey, E. (1999) 'Children as service evaluators', *Child Psychology and Psychiatry Review*, 4 (4): 153–61.

Hern, M., Miller, M., Sommers, M.J. and Dyehouse, J. (1998) 'Sensitive topics and adolescents: making research about risk taking behaviours happen', *Issues in Comprehensive Pediatric Nursing*, 21: 173–86.

Hester, M., Pearson, C. and Harwin, N. (2000) *Making an Impact: Children and Domestic Violence*. London: Jessica Kingsley.

Hetherington, R. and Baistow, K. (2001) 'Supporting families with a mentally ill parent: European perspectives on interagency cooperation', *Child Abuse Review*, 10: 351–65.

Hill, M. (1999) *Effective Ways of Working with Children and their Families*. London: Jessica Kingsley.

Hill, M., Laybourn, A. and Borland, M. (1996) 'Engaging with primary-age children about their emotions and well-being: methodological considerations', *Children and Society*, 10: 129–44.

HMSO (1968) *Local Authority and Allied personal Social Services*. Cmnd 3703. London: HMSO.

Hoffman, L. (1981) *Foundations of Family Therapy*. New York: Basic Books.

Hollander, H. (2002) 'Psychodramas with "at risk" youth: a means of active engagement', in A. Bannister and A. Huntington (eds), *Communicating With Children and Adolescents: Action For Change*. London: Jessica Kingsley.

Holliday, A. (1999) 'Small cultures', *Applied Linguistics*, 20 (2): 23–64.

Holt, C. (1998) 'Working with fathers of children in need', in R. Bayley (ed.), *Transforming Children's Lives: The Importance of Early Intervention*. London: Family Policy Studies Centre.

Holterman, S. (1995) *All our Futures: The Impact of Public Expenditure and Fiscal Policies on Britain's Children and Young People*. Barkingside: Barnardo's.

Home Office (1988) *The Investigation of Child Sexual Abuse*, Circular 52/1988. London: Home Office.

Home Office (2000) *Living Without Fear: Multi-agency Guidance for Addressing Domestic Violence*. London: HMSO.

Home Office (2004) *The Bichard Report*. London: HMSO.

Home Office (2008) *Crime in England & Wales*. London: HMSO.

Home Office (2010) *Social Trends*. London: HMSO.

Home Office/DH (2001) *Achieving Best Evidence in Criminal Proceedings*. London: HMSO.

House of Commons (1997) *Child and Adolescent Mental Health Services*. London: HMSO.

House of Commons, Health Committee (2009) *Health Inequalities Report*. London: HMSO.

House of Lords (1986) *Gillick v West Norfolk and Wisbech Area Health Authority*, 1 AC 112.

Howarth, J. (2002) 'Maintaining a focus on the child?', *Child Abuse Review*, 11: 195–213.

Howe, D. (1986) *Social Workers and their Practice in Welfare Bureaucracies*. Aldershot: Gower.

Howe, D. (1989) *The Consumer's View of Family Therapy*. London: Gower.

Howe, D., Brandon, M., Hinings, D. and Schofield, G. (1999) *Attachment Theory, Child Maltreatment and Family Support*. Basingstoke: Macmillan.

Hugman, R. (1991) *Power in Caring Professions*. London: Macmillan.

Iwaniec, D. (1995) *The Emotionally Abused and Neglected Child: Identification, Assessment and Intervention*. Chichester: Wiley.

Jack, G. (2004) 'Child protection at the community level', *Child Abuse Review*, 13: 368–83.

Jack, R. and Walker, S. (2000) *Social Work Assessment and Intervention*. Cambridge: Anglia Polytechnic University.

Jenkins, R. (2002) *Foundations of Sociology*. Basingstoke: Palgrave Macmillan.

Jin. W. (2011) *Poverty and Inequality*. London: Institute of Fiscal Studies.

Jones, T. (1996) *Britain's Ethnic Minorities: An Analysis of the Labour Force Survey*. London: Policy Studies Institute.

Jones, L. and O'Loughlin, T. (2002) 'Developing a child concern model to embrace the framework', in M. Calder and S. Hackett (eds), *The Child Care Assessment Manual*. Lyme Regis: Russell House.

Jowitt, M. and O'Loughlin, S. (2005) *Social Work with Children and Families*. Exeter: Learning Matters.

Jung, C.G. (1972) *Synchronicity: An Acausal Connecting Principle*. New York: Princeton University Press.

Kay, J. (1999) *A Practical Guide: Protecting Children*. London: College of Health/Cassell.

Kay, J. (2003) *Protecting Children: A Practical Guide*. London: Continuum.

Kearney, P., Levin, E. and Rosen, G. (2000) *Alcohol, Drug and Mental Health Problems: Working with Families*. London: National Institute of Social Work.

Kehily, J. and Swann, J. (2003) *Children's Cultural Worlds*. London: Wiley/OUP.

Kelly, L. (1996) 'When woman protection is the best kind of child protection: children, domestic violence and child abuse', *Administration*, 44 (2): 118–35.

Kelson, M. (1995) *Consumer Involvement Initiatives in Clinical Audits and Outcomes*. London: College of Health.

Kempe, C.H., Silverman, F.N., Steele, B.F., Droegmueller, W. and Silver, H. (1962) 'The battered child syndrome', *Journal of the American Medical Association*, 181: 1.

Kemps, C. (1997) 'Approaches to working with ethnicity and cultural issues', in K. Dwivedi (ed.), *Enhancing Parenting Skills*. London: Wiley. pp. 59–77.

Kiddle, C. (1999) *Traveller Children: A Voice for Themselves*. London: Jessica Kingsley.

Kim, W.J. (1995) 'A training guideline of cultural competence for child and adolescent psychiatric residencies', *Child Psychiatry and Human Development*, 26 (2): 125–36.

Klineberg, O. (1971) 'Race and IQ', *Courier*, 24: 10.

Kohn, M. (1995) *The Race Gallery*. London: Jonathan Cape.

Koprowska, J. (2005) *Communication and Interpersonal Skills in Social Work*. Exeter: Learning Matters.

Kotch, J.B., Chalmers, D.J., Fanslow, J.L., Marshall, S. and Langley, J.D. (1993) 'Morbidity and death due to child abuse in New Zealand', *Child Abuse and Neglect*, 17 (2): 233–47.

Kurtz, Z. (1996) *Treating Children Well: A Guide to Using the Evidence Base in Commissioning and Managing Services for the Mental Health of Children and Young People*. London. Mental Health Foundation.

Kyngas, E. (1998) 'Adolescents' perception of physicians, nurses, parents and friends', *Journal Of Advanced Nursing*, 27: 760.

Laing, R.D. (1969) 'Interventions in social situations'. Philadelphia Association. Cited in *Context*, 60: 2–7, April 2002. Warrington: Association for Family Therapy and Systemic Practice.

Laming, H. (2003) *The Inquiry into the Death of Victoria Climbié*. London: HMSO.

Lansdowne, G. (1995) *Taking Part: Children's Participation in Decision-making*. London: IPPR.

Larner, G. (2000) 'Towards a common ground in psychoanalysis and family therapy: on knowing not to know', *Journal of Family Therapy*, 22: 61–82.

Lask, B. (1979) 'Family therapy outcome research', *Journal of Family Therapy*, 1 (4): 87–91.

Laufer, M. (ed.) (1985) *The Suicidal Adolescent*. London: Karnac.

Leathard, A. (1994) *Going Inter-professional*. London: Routledge.

Leighton, A.H. (1981) 'Culture and psychiatry', *Canadian Journal of Psychiatry*, 26 (8): 522–9.

Leonard, P. (1975) 'Towards a paradigm for radical practice', in R. Bailey and M. Brake (eds), *Radical Social Work*. London: Arnold.

Leonard, P. (1997) *Postmodern Welfare: Reconstructing an Emancipatory Project*. London: Sage.

Lindon, J. (2003) *Child Protection*, 2nd edn. London: Hodder and Stoughton.

Little, M. and Mount, K. (1999) *Prevention and Early Intervention with Children in Need*. Aldershot: Ashgate.

Lloyd, E. (ed.) (1999) *Parenting Matters: What Works in Parenting Education?* London: Barnardo's.

Lyon, C. and de Cruz, R. (1993) *Child Abuse*, 2nd edn. Bristol: Jordan.

MacDonald, G. (2002) 'Child protection', in D. McNeish, T. Newman and H. Roberts (eds), *What Works For Children? Effective Services for Children and Families*. Buckingham: Open University Press.

MacDonald, G. and Roberts, H. (1995) *What Works in the Early Years? Effective Interventions for Children and their Families*. Barkingside: Barnardo's.

Madanes, C. (1981) *Strategic Family Therapy*. San Francisco, CA: Jossey-Bass.

Madge, N. (2001) *Understanding Difference: The Meaning of Ethnicity for Young Lives*. London: National Children's Bureau.

Magrab, P., Evans, P. and Hurrell P. (1997) 'Integrated services for children and youth at risk: an international study of multidisciplinary training', *Journal of Interprofessional Care*, 11 (1): 99–108.

Martin, R. (2010) *Social Work Assessment*. Exeter: Learning Matters.

Masson, J. (1988) *Against Therapy*. London: Collins.

May, T. (ed) (2002) *Qualitative Research in Action*. London: Sage.

Mayseless, O. (1996) 'Attachment patterns and their outcomes', *Human Development*, 36: 206–23.

McGlone, F., Park, A. and Smith, K. (1998) *Families and Kinship*. London: Family Policy Studies Centre.

McGoldrick, M., Pearce, J. and Giordano, J. (eds) (1982) *Ethnicity and Family Therapy*. New York: Guilford Press.

McLeod, A. (2008) *Listening to Children: A Practitioner's Guide*. London: Jessica Kingsley.

McNeish, D. and Newman, T. (2002) 'Involving children and young people in decision making', in D. McNeish, T. Newman and H. Roberts (eds), *What Works For Children?* Buckingham: Open University Press.

Mental Health Foundation (1999) *The Big Picture: Promoting Children's and Young People's Mental Health*. London: Mental Health Foundation.

Messent, P. (1992) 'Working with Bangladeshi families in the East End of London', *Journal of Family Therapy*, 14 (3): 287–305.

Micklewright, J. and Stewart, K. (2000) *Well-being of Children in the European Union: New Economy*. London: Institute for Public Policy Research.

Middleton, L. (1997) *The Art of Assessment*. Birmingham: Venture.

Midgley, J. (2001) 'Issues in international social work: resolving critical debates in the profession', *Journal of Social Work*, 1 (1): 21–35.

Mikulincer, M., Florian, V., Cowan, P.A. and Cowan, C.P. (2002) 'Attachment security in couple relationships: a systemic model and its implications for family dynamics', *Family Process*, 43 (3): 405–34.

Miller, G. and Prinz, R. (1990) 'Enhancement of social learning family interventions for childhood conduct disorders', *Psychological Bulletin*, 108: 291–307.

Milner, J. and O'Byrne, P. (2009) *Assessment in Social Work*, 3rd edn. London: Macmillan.

Ministry of Justice (2011) *Re-offending of Juveniles: 2009 Cohort Statistics*. London: Ministry of Justice

Minuchin. S. (1974) *Families and Family Therapy*. London: Tavistock Publications.

Minuchin. S. (1984) *Family Kaleidoscope*. London: Harvard University Press.

Mishra, R. (1999) *Globalization and the Welfare State*. Northampton MA: Edward Elgar.

Modood, T. and Berthoud, R. (1997) *Ethnic Minorities in Britain*. London: Policy Studies Institute.

Moore, J. (1992) *The ABC of Child Protection*. Aldershot: Ashgate.

Morris, J. (2000) *Having Someone Who Cares? Barriers to Change in the Public Care of Children*. London: National Children's Bureau Enterprises Limited.

Morris, K. and Tunnard (1996) *Family Group Conferences: Messages from UK Practice and Research*. London: Family Rights Group.

Morrissey, J., Johnsen, M. and Calloway, M. (1997) 'Evaluating performance and change in mental health systems serving children and youth: an interorganizational network approach', *The Journal of Mental Health Administration*, 24 (1): 4–22.

Morrison, T. (1993) *Supervision in Social Care*. London: Longman.

Morrison, T. (1997) 'Emotionally competent child protection organisations: fallacy, fiction or necessity?', in J. Bates, R. Pugh and N. Thompson (eds), *Protecting Children: Challenges and Change*. Aldershot: Arena.

Morrow, V. (1998) *Understanding Families: Children's Perspectives*. London: National Children's Bureau.

Moules, T. and Ramsay, J. (1998) *The Textbook of Children's Nursing*. Cheltenham: Stanley Thornes.

Mrazek, P.J., Lynch, M.A. and Bentovim, A. (1983) 'Sexual abuse of children in the United Kingdom', *Child Abuse and Neglect*, 7: 147–53.

Muncie, J., Wetherall, M., Dallos, R. and Cochrane, A. (eds) (1997) *Understanding the Family*. London: Sage.

Munley, A., Powers, C.S. and Williamson, J.B. (1982) 'Humanising nursing home environments: the relevance of hospice principles', *International Journal of Ageing and Human Development*, 15: 263–84.

Munro, E. (2005) 'Improving practice: child protection as a systems problem', *Children and Youth Services Review*, 27: 375–91.

Munro, E. (2008) *Effective Child Protection*, 2nd edn. London: Sage.

Munro, E. (2011a) *The Munro Review of Child Protection – Interim Report: The Child's Journey*. London: DfE

Munro, E. (2011b) *The Munro Review of Child Protection – A Child-Centred System: Final Report*. London: DfE.

Munro, E. and Calder, M. (2005) 'Where has child protection gone?', *The Political Quarterly*, 76 (3).

Munro, E. and Hubbard, A. (2011) 'A systems approach to organisational change in children's social care', *British Journal of Social Work*, 41: 726–43.

Murphy, M. (1996a) *The Child Protection Unit*. Aldershot: Avebury.

Murphy, M. (1996b) *Child Protection Specialist Units*. Aldershot: Avebury.

Murphy, M. (1997) 'Staff care in a multidisciplinary context', in J. Bates (ed.), *Protecting Children: Challenges and Change*. Aldershot: Arena.

Murphy, M. (2000) 'The interagency trainer', in M. Charles and E. Hendry (eds), *Training Together to Safeguard Children*. London: NSPCC.

Murphy, M. (2003) 'Keeping going', in R. Harrison, G. Mann, M. Murphy, A. Taylor and N. Thompson (eds), *Partnership Made Painless*. Lyme Regis: Russell House.

Murphy, M. (2004) *Developing Collaborative Relationships in Interagency Child Protection Work*. Lyme Regis: Russell House.

Murphy, M. and Oulds, G. (2000) 'Establishing and developing co-operative links between substance misuse and child protection systems', in F. Harbin and M. Murphy (eds), *Substance Misuse and Childcare*. Lyme Regis: Russell House.

Murray, A. (1997) 'The effects of infants' behaviour on maternal mental health', *Health Visitor*, 66 (2).

NCB (2005) *Social Inclusion*. London: National Children's Bureau.

NCH (1979) *Who Cares?* London: National Children's Homes.

NCH Action for Children (2010) *Fact File*. London: NCH.

Newman, T. (2002) *Promoting Resilience: A Review of Effective Strategies for Child Care Services* Barkingside: Barnardo's.

NFPI (2010) *Delivery of Parenting Skills Programmes*. London: National Family and Parenting Institute.

NISW (1982) *Social Workers: Their Role and Tasks*. London: National Institute of Social Work/Bedford Square Press.

Norman, A. and Brown, C. (1992) 'Foreword', in C. Cloke and J. Naish (eds), *Key Issues in Child Protection for Health Visitors and Nurses*. London: NSPCC/ Longman.

NSPCC (1996) *Childhood Matters: The Report of The National Commission of Inquiry into the Prevention of Child Abuse, Vol. 1*. London: HMSO.

NSPCC (2000) *Child Maltreatment in the United Kingdom*. London: NSPCC.

NSPCC (2010) *Ten Pitfalls and How to Avoid Them: What Research Tells Us*. London: NSPCC.

Oberheumer, P. (1998) 'A European perspective on early years training', in L. Abbott and G. Pugh (eds), *Training to Work in the Early Years: Developing the Climbing Frame*. Buckingham: Open University Press.

O'Hagan, K. (1989) *Working With Child Sexual Abuse*. Milton Keynes: Open University Press.

O'Hagan, K. (1993) *Emotional and Psychological Abuse of Children*. Buckingham: Open University Press.

O'Loughlin, M. and O'Loughlin, S. (2008) *Social Work with Children and Families*, 2nd edn. Exeter: Learning Matters.

Office of Population, Censuses and Surveys (OPCS) (2002) *The British Census 2001*. London: HMSO.

Ofsted (2008) *Learning Lessons, Taking Action: Ofsted's Evaluations of Serious Case Reviews, April 2007–March 2008*. London: DCSF.

Okitikpi ,T. (1999) 'Educational needs of black children in care', in R. Barn (ed.), *Working With Black Children and Adolescents in Need*. London: BAAF.

Okitikpi, T. and Aymer, C. (eds) (2008) *The Art of Social Work Practice*. Lyme Regis: Russell House.

Onyet, S., Heppleston, T. and Bushnell, N. (1994) *A National Survey of Community Mental Health Teams: Team Structure*. London: Sainsbury Centre for Mental Health.

Oullette, P., Lazear, K. and Chambers, K. (1999) 'Action leadership: the development of an approach to leadership enhancement for grassroots community leaders in children's mental health', *The Journal of Behavioural Health Services and Research*, 26 (2): 171–85.

Ovretveit, J. (1996) 'Five ways to describe a multidisciplinary team', *Journal of Interprofessional Care*, 10 (2): 163–71.

Owen, D. (1995) *1991 Census Statistical Papers 1–9. Centre for Research in Ethnic Relations*, London: Commission for Racial Equality.

Oxford English Dictionary (2010) Electronic version. Oxford: Clarendon.

Papatheophilou, A. (1990) 'Child protection in Greece', in A. Sale and M. Davies (eds), *Child Protection Policies and Practice in Europe*. London: NSPCC.

Parekh, B. (2000) *Rethinking Multiculturalism: Cultural Diversity and Political Theory*. Basingstoke: Palgrave.

Parkinson, J. (1992) 'Supervision *vs* control', in C. Cloke and J. Naish (eds), *Key Issues in Child Protection for Health Visitors and Nurses*. London: NSPCC/ Longman.

Parsloe, P. (ed) (1999) *Risk Assessment in Social Care and Social Work*. London: Jessica Kingsley.

Parton, N. (1985) *The Politics of Child Abuse*. Basingstoke: Macmillan.

Parton, N. (1991) *Governing the Family*. Basingstoke: Macmillan.

Parton, N. (1999) 'Reconfiguring child welfare practices: risk, advanced liberalism and the government of freedom', in A.S. Chambon, A. Irving and L. Epstein (eds), *Reading Foucault for Social Work*. Chichester: Columbia Press.

Parton, N. (2002) *Discovery and Inclusion: Submission to the Victoria Climbié Inquiry, Phase 2, Seminar 1*. London: HMSO.

Parton, N. (2011) 'Child protection and safeguarding in England: changing and competing conceptions of risk and their implications for social work', *British Journal of Social Work*, 41 (5): 854–75.

Pawson, R. and Tilley, N. (1997) *Realistic Evaluation*. London: Sage.

Payne, M. (1997) *Modern Social Work Theroy*. London: Macmillan.

Payne, M. (2005) *Modern Social Work Theory*, 3rd edn. Basingstoke: Palgrave Macmillan.

Peace, G. (1991) *Inter-professional Collaboration: Professional and Personal Perspectives, Part 2*. Manchester: Boys' and Girls' Welfare Society.

Pearce, J. (2000) 'Front-line workers faced pressures of isolation, lack of support and chaos', *Community Care*, Feb, 16–17.

Pels, D. (2000) 'Reflexivity one step up', *Theroy, Culture and Society*, 17 (3): 1–25.

Pentini-Aluffi, A. and Lorenz, W. (1996) *Anti Racist Work with Young People*. Lyme Regis: Russell House.

Perelberg, R.J. and Miller, A.C. (eds) (1990) *Gender and Power in Families*. London: Routledge.

Peters, R. and Barlow, J. (2003) 'Systematic review of screening instruments to identify child abuse during the perinatal period', *Child Abuse Review*, 12.

Pickett, J. (individual interview, 2 April 1990) in Murphy, M. (1996) *Child Protection Specialist Units*. Aldershot: Avebury.

Pickett, J. and Maton, A. (1979) 'The interagency team in an urban setting: the special unit concept', *Child Abuse and Neglect*, 3: 115–21.

Pierson, J. (2002) *Tackling Social Exclusion*. London: Routledge.

Pieterse, J.N. (2004) *Globalization and Culture*. Oxford: Rowman & Littlefield.

Pincus, A. and Minahan, A. (1974) *Social Work Practice: Model and Method*. London: Peacock.

Pitts, J. (2001) 'Korrectional kareoke: New Labour and the zombification of youth justice', *Youth Justice*, 1 (2): 3–16.

Platt, D. (2011) 'Assessments of children and families: learning and teaching the skills of analysis', *Social Work Education*, 30 (2): 157–69.

Plotnikoff, J. (1993) *The Child Witness Pack: Helping Children to Cope*. London: NSPCC/Childline.

Plummer, D.C. (2001) 'The quest for modern manhood: masculine stereotypes, peer culture and the social significance of homophobia', *Journal of Adolescence*, 24: 15–23.

Pocock, D. (1997) 'Feeling understood in family therapy', *Journal of Family Therapy*, 19: 279–98.

Polnay, J. and Blair, M. (1999) 'A model programme for busy learners', *Child Abuse Review*, 8: 284–8.

Powell, J. and Lovelock, R. (1992) *Changing Patterns of Mental Health Care*. London: Avebury.

Preli, R. and Bernard, J.M. (1993) 'Making multi-cultiralism relevant for majority culture graduate students', *Journal of Marital and Family Therapy*, 19 (1): 5–17.

Pugh, G. and Smith, C. (1996) *Learning to be a Parent*. London: Family Policy Studies Centre.

Ramon, S. (1999) 'Social work', in K. Bhui and D. Olajide (eds), *Mental Health Service Provision for a Multi-cultural Society*. London: Saunders.

Rawson, D. (1994) 'Models of interprofessional work: likely theories and possibilities', in A. Smale, G., Tuson, G. and D. Statham, (2000) *Social Work and Social Problems*. Basingstoke: Palgrave.

RCP (1991) *Physical Signs of Sexual Abuse in Children*. London: Royal College of Physicians.

Reder, P., Duncan, S. and Gray, M. (1993) *Beyond Blame: Child Abuse Tragedies Revisited*. London: Routledge.

Reder, P. and Duncan, S. (2003) 'Understanding communication in child protection networks', *Child Abuse Review*, 12: 82–100.

Reder, P. and Lucey, C. (1995) *Assessment of Parenting: Psychiatric and Psychological Contributions*. London: Routledge.

Rees, S. and Wallace, A. (1982) *Verdicts on Social Work*. London: Arnold.

Reimrs, A.S. and Treacher, A. (1995) *Introducing User-friendly Family Therapy*. London: Routledge.

Revans, L. (2002a) 'Laming probe reveals scope of communications breakdown', *Community Care*, Feb.

Revans, L. (2002b) 'Social services take on wider role as councils combine departments', *Community Care*, August.

Reynolds, A.J. (1998) 'Resilience among black urban youth: intervention effects and mechanisms of influence', *American Journal of Orthopsychiatry*, 68 (1): 84–100.

Richards, M., Payne, C. and Shepperd, A. (1990) *Staff Supervision in Child Protection Work*. London: National Institute of Social Work.

Riley, R. (1997) 'Working together: inter-professional collaboration', *Journal Of Child Health*, 1 (4): 191–4.

Rivett, M. and Rees, A. (2004) 'Dancing on a razor's edge: systemic groupwork with batterers', *Journal of Family Therapy*, 26 (2): 142–63.

Rivett, M. and Street, E. (2003) *Family Therapy in Focus*. London: Sage.

Robbins, D. (1998) 'The refocusing children's initiative: an overview of practice', in. R. Bayley (ed.), *Transforming Children's Lives: The Importance of Early Intervention*. London. Family Policy Studies Centre. pp. 86–90.

Rodney, C. (2000) 'Pathways: a model service delivery system', in: N.N. Singh, J.P. Leung and A.N. Singh, *International Perspectives on Child and Adolescent Mental Health*. London: Elsevier. pp. 421–30.

Rogers, C. (2003) *Children at Risk 2002-2003: Government Initiatives and Commentaries on Government Policy*. London: National Family and Parenting Institute.

Roth, A. and Fonagy, P. (1996) *What Works for Whom? A Critical Review of Psychotherapy Research*. London: Guilford Press.

Ruch, G. (2009) (ed.) *Post Qualifying Child Care Social Work: Developing Reflective Practice*. London: Sage.

Ruddock, M. (1998) 'Yes and but, and then again maybe', in R. Davies (ed.), *Stress in Social Work*. London: Jessica Kingsley.

Rutter, M. (1985) 'Resilience in the face of adversity', *British Journal of Psychiatry*, 147: 598–611.

Rutter, M. (1995) *Psychosocial Disturbances in Young People: Challenges for Prevention*. Cambridge: Cambridge University Press.

Rutter, M. and Smith, D. (1995) *Psychosocial Disorders in Young People: Time Trends and their Causes*. London: Wiley.

Rutter, M., Hersov, L. and Taylor, E. (1994) *Child and Adolescent Psychiatry*. Oxford: Blackwell Scientific.

Ryan, M. (1999) *The Children Act 1989: Putting it into Practice*. Aldershot: Ashgate.

Sale, A. and Davies, M. (eds) (1990) *Child Protection Policies and Practice in Europe*. London: NSPCC.

Salford Centre for Social Work Research (2004) *Education & Training for Inter-agency Working: New Standards*. Manchester: University of Salford.

Salmon, D. and Hall, C. (1999) 'Working with lesbian mothers: their healthcare experiences', *Community Practitioner,* 72 (12): 396–97.

Sandbaek, M. (1999) 'Children with problems: focusing on everyday life', *Children and Society,* 13: 106–18.

Sariola, H. and Uutela, A. (1993) 'The prevalence and context of family violence against children in Finland', *Child Abuse and Neglect,* 16 (6): 823–32.

SCIE (2003) *Assessment in Social Work: A Guide for Learning and Teaching.* London: Social Care Institute of Excellence.

SCIE (2004) SCIE Research Briefing 9: Preventing Teenage Pregnancy in Looked After Children. Available at: www.scie.org.uk/publications/briefings/briefing09

SCIE (2005) *Knowledge Review – Learning and Teaching in Social Work Education-Assessment.* London: Social Care Institute for Excellence.

Scott, D. (1997) 'Interagency conflict: an ethnographic study', *Child and Family Social Work,* 2 (2): 73–80.

Scrine, J. (1991) 'Child abuse : do social work students get enough practice experience?', *Practice,* 5 (2): 153–9.

Sebuliba, D. and Vostanis, P. (2001) 'Child and adolescent mental health training for primary care staff', *Clinical Child Psychology and Psychiatry,* 6(2): 191–204.

Seddon, D., Robinson, C. and Perry, J. (2010) 'Unified assessment: policy, implementation and practice', *British Journal of Social Work,* 40 (1): 207–25.

Segal, H. (1975) *An Introduction to the Work of Melanie Klein.* London, Hogarth Press.

Shardlow, S. and Payne, M. (1998) *Contemporary Issues in Social Work: Western Europe.* Aldershot: Arena.

Shardlow, S., Davis, C., Johnson, M., Long, T., Murphy, M. and Race, D. (2003) *Review of Education and Training for Inter-agency Working.* Manchester: University of Salford.

Sharman, W. (1997) *Children and Adolescents with Mental Health Problems.* London: Balliere-Tindall.

Shaw, H. and Coles, D. (2007) *Unlocking the Truth: Families Experiences of the Investigations of Deaths in Custody.* London: Inquest.

Shaw, I., Arksey, H. and Mullender, A. (2004) *ESRC Research, Social Work and Social Care.* London: SCIE.

Sheller, M. and Urry, J. (2003) 'Mobile transformations of "public" and "private" life', *Theory, Culture and Society,* 20 (3): 107–25.

Shepherd, S. (1991) 'Aspects of the Children Act: – a medical perspective', *Health Trends,* 23 (2): 51–3.

Silberg, J. (2001) 'Child psychiatric symptoms and psychosocial impairment: relationship and prognostic significance', *British Journal of Psychiatry,* 179: 230–35.

Simpson E. L., Lichtenstein, P. Pedersen, N., Neiderhiser, J. M., Hansson, K. and Cederblad, M. (1996) 'Conflict in close relationships: an attachment perspective', *Journal of Personality and Social Psychology,* 71 (5): 899–914.

Sinclair, R., Garnett, L. and Berridge, D. (1995) *Social Work and Assessment with Adolescents.* London: National Children's Bureau.

Skaff, L. (1988) 'Child maltreatment coordinating committees for effective service delivery', *Child Welfare,* LXVII (3): 217–30.

Skidmore, D.(1994) *The Ideology of Community Care.* London: Chapman and Hall.

Skills for Care/CWDC (2010) *Common Induction Standards.* London: Childrens Workforce Development Council.

Slack, J. (2005) 'ASBOs: lout Britain's new badge of honour', *Daily Mail,* 30 June.

Sluzki,C.E. (1979) 'Migration and family conflict', *Family Process*, 18 (4): 379–90.

Smale, G., Tuson, G. and Statham, D. (2000) *Social Work and Social Problems*. Basingstoke: Palgrave.

Smart, B. (1992) *Michel Foucault*. London: Routledge.

Smith, S. (1999) 'Primary prevention', in *Child Protection: The Role Of The Health Visitor in The Violence Against Children Study Group* (Children, Child Abuse And Child Protection, Placing The Child Centrally). Chichester: Wiley. Chapter 9.

Snell, J. (2002) 'Where does the buck stop?', *Community Care*, February.

Social Exclusion Unit (2002) *Young Runaways*. London: HMSO.

Social Services Inspectorate (1998) *Partners in Planning: Approaches to Planning Services for Children and Their Families*. London: HMSO.

Social Work Reform Board (2010) *Building a Safe and Confident Future: One Year On*. Leeds: Skills for Care.

Speak, S., Cameron, S., Woods, R. and Gilroy, R. (1995) *Young Single Mothers: Barriers to Independent Living*. London: Family Policy Studies Centre.

Speight, N. (1993) 'Non-accidental injury', in R. Meadow (ed.), *The ABC of Child Abuse*. London: System.

Spencer, J. and Flin, R. (1990) *The Evidence of Children*. London: Blackstone.

Spencer, N. (1996) 'Race and ethnicity as determinants of child health: a personal view', *Child Health and Development*, 22(5): 327–45.

Stahmann, R. (2000) 'Premarital counselling: a focus for family therapy', *Journal of Family Therapy*, 22: 104–16.

Stanton, M. and Shadish, W. (1997) 'Outcome, attrition and family-couples treatment for drug abuse: a meta-analysis and review of the controlled comparative studies', *Psychological Bulletin*, 122: 170–91.

Statham, J. (2000) *Outcomes and Effectiveness of Family Support Services: A Research Review*. London: Institute for Education, University of London.

Stein, M. and Wade, J. (2004) *Helping Care Leavers: Problems and Strategic Responses*. London: HMSO.

Stevenson, O. (ed.) (1989) *Child Abuse: Professional Practice and Public Policy*. London: Harvester Wheatsheaf.

Stevenson, O. (2000) 'The mandate for inter-agency and inter-professional work and training', in M. Charles and E. Hendry (eds), *Training Together to Safeguard Children*. London: NSPCC.

Stokes, H. and Tyler, D. (2001) 'The multi-dimensional lives of young people: young people's perspective of education, work, life and their future', *Scottish Youth Issues Journal*, 3 (Autumn).

Stone, M. (1990) *Child Protection Work: A Professional Guide*. London: Ventura.

Stuart, M. and Baines, C. (2004) *Progress on Safeguards for Children Living Away from Home: A Review of Action Since People Like Us Report*. York: JRF.

Sutton, C. (1999) *Helping Families with Troubled Children*. Chichester: Wiley.

Sylva, K. (1994) 'School influences on children's development', *Journal of Child Psychology and Psychiatry and Allied Professions*, 35 (1): 135–70.

Sue, D., Ivey, A. and Penderson, P. (1996) *A Theory of Multicultural Counselling and Therapy*. New York: Brooks/Cole Publishing.

Target, M. (1998) 'Approaches to evaluation, counselling and health', *The European Journal of Psychotherapy*, 1(1): 79–92.

Target, M. and Fonagy, P. (1996) 'The psychological treatment of child and adolescent psychiatric disorders', in A. Roth and P. Fonagy (eds), *What Works for Whom? A Critical Review of Psychotherapy Research*. New York: Guilford Press.

Taylor, B. and Devine, D. (1993) *Assessing Needs and Planning Care in Social Work.* London: Arena.

Taylor, J. and Muller, D. (1995). *Nursing Adolescents: Research and Psychological Perspectives.* Oxford: Blackwell Science.

Taylor, S. and Field, D. (1997) *Sociology of Health and Health Care*, 2nd edn. Oxford: Blackwell Science.

Taylor, C. and White, S. (2000) *Practising Reflexivity in Health and Welfare.* Buckingham: Open University Press.

Thatcher, M. (1990) *NCH George Thomas Lecture.* London: National Children's Homes.

The Violence Against Children Study Group (1999) *Children, Child Abuse And Child Protection: Placing Children Centrally.* Chichester: Wiley.

Thoburn, J., Wilding, J. and Watson, J. (1998) *Children in Need: A Review of Family Support Work in Three Local Authorities.* Norwich: University of East Anglia/DH.

Thomas, J. and Holland, S. (2010) 'Representing children's identities in core assessments', *British Journal of Social Work*, 40 (8): 2617–33.

Thomas, T. (1994) *The Police and Social Workers.* Aldershot: Gower.

Thompson, N. (2005) *Understanding Social Work.* Basingstoke: Palgrave.

Thompson, N., Murphy, M. and Stradling, S. (1994) *Dealing with Stress.* London: British Association of Social Workers/Macmillan.

Thompson, N., Murphy, M., and Stradling, S. (1998) *Meeting the Stress Challenge.* Lyme Regis: Russell House

Tite, R. (1993) 'How teachers define and respond to child abuse: the distinction between theoretical and reportable cases', *Child Abuse and Neglect*, 17: 591–603.

Toledano, A. (1996) 'Issues arising from intercultural family therapy', *Journal of Family Therapy*, 18: 289–301.

Topss (2004) *Occupational Standards for Social Work.* Leeds: Training Organisation for Personal Social Services.

Townsend, P. , Davidson, N. and Whitehead, M.(eds) (1988) *The Black Report and The Health Divide: Inequalities In Health.* London: Penguin.

Treacher, A. (1995) 'Reviewing consumer studies of therapy', in A. Treacher and S. Reimers (eds), *Introducing User-friendly Family Therapy.* London: Routledge. pp. 128–49.

Treseder, P. (1997) *Empowering Children and Young People: A Training Manual for Promoting Involvement in Decision-making.* London: Save the Children.

Trevino, F. (1999) 'Quality of health care for ethnic/racial minority populations', *Ethnicity and Health*, 4(3):153–64.

Trevithick, P. (2005) *Social Work Skills: A Practice Handbook*, 2nd edn. Maidenhead: Open University Press.

Trotter, J. (2000) 'Lesbian and gay issues in social work with young people: resilience and success through confronting, conforming and escaping', *British Journal of Social Work*, 30 (1): 115–23.

Tseng Yueh-Hung (2002) 'A lesson in culture', *ELT Journal*, 56 (1): 11–21.

Tucker, N. and Gamble, N. (eds) (2001) *Family Fictions.* London: Continuum.

Tucker, S., Strange, C., Cordeaux. C., Moules, T. and Torrance, N. (1999) 'Developing an interdisciplinary framework for the education and training of those working with children and young people'. *Journal of Interprofessional Care*, 13 (3): 261–70.

Tunstill, J. (1996) 'Family support: past present and future challenges', *Child and Family Social Work*, 1: 151–8.

United Nations (1989a) *The Conventions on the Rights of the Child.* New York: UNICEF.

United Nations (1989b) *United Nations Declaration on the Rights of the Child.* Geneva: UN.

United Nations (1998) *Human Rights Act*. Geneva: UN.

Utting, W. (1991) *Children in the Public Care: A Review of Residential Child Care*. London: HMSO.

Utting, D. (1995) *Family and Parenthood: Supporting Families, Preventing Breakdown*. York: Joseph Rountree Foundation.

Utting, W. (1993) 'Foreword', in M. Evans and C. Miller (eds), *Partnership in Child Protection*. London: Office for Public Management/National Institute of Social Work.

Utting, W. (1997) *People Like Us: The Report of the Review of Safeguards for Children Living Away from Home*. London: HMSO.

Valentine, C.A. (1976) 'Poverty and culture', in P. Worsley (ed.), *Problems of Modern Society*. London: Penguin.

VanDenBerg, J. and Grealish, M. (1996) 'Individualized services and supports through the wraparound process: philosophy and procedures', *Journal of Child and Family Studies*. 5:7–21.

Vetere, A. and Cooper, J. (2001) *Domestic Violence and Family Safety: A Systemic Approach to Working with Violence in Families*. London: Blackwell.

Visser, M.A. and Moleko, A G. (1999) 'High-risk behaviour of primary school learners', *Urban Health and Development Bulletin*, 2 (1): 69–77.

VACSG (1999) *Children, Child Abuse and Child Protection, Placing Children Centrally*. Wiley, Chichester: Violence Against Children Study Group.

Von Bertalanffy, L. (1968) *General Systems Theory:Foundation, Development, Application*. New York: Brazillier.

Vostanis, P. and Cumella, S. (1999) *Homeless Children: Problems and Needs*. London: Jessica Kingsley.

Waldvogel, J. (1997) 'The new wave of service integration', *Social Service Review,* September: 463–84.

Walker, K. (2002) 'Exploitation of children and young people through prostitution', *Journal of Child Health*, 6 (3) September.

Walker, S. (2001a) 'Consulting with children and young people', *International Journal of Children's Rights*, 12: 1–12.

Walker, S. (2001b) 'Developing child and adolescent mental health services', *Journal of Child Health Care*, 5 (2): 71–6.

Walker, S. (2001c) 'Tracing the contours of postmodern social work', *British Journal of Social Work*, 31: 29–39.

Walker, S. (2001d) 'Domestic violence: analysis of a community safety alarm system', *Child Abuse Review,* 10 (3): 170–82.

Walker, S. (2002) 'Family support and social work practice: renaissance or retrenchment?', *European Journal of Social Work*, 5 (1): 43–54.

Walker, S. (2003a) 'Interprofessional work in child and adolescent mental health services', *Emotional and Behavioural Difficulties*, 8 (3): 189–204.

Walker, S. (2003b) *Working Together for Healthy Young Minds*. Lyme Regis: Russell House.

Walker, S. (2005) *Culturally Competent Therapy: Working with Children and Young People*. Basingstoke: Palgrave Macmillan.

Walker, S. and Akister, J. (2004) *Applying Family Therapy: A Guide for Caring Professionals in the Community*. Lyme Regis: Russell House.

Walker, S. and Beckett, C. (2011) *Social Work Assessment and Intervention*, 2nd edn. Lyme Regis: Russell House.

Walker, S. and Thurston, C. (2006) *Safeguarding Children and Young People: A Guide to Integrated Practice*. Lyme Regis: Russell House.

Warner, N. (1993) *Choosing with Care*. London: HMSO.

Wattam, C. (1999) 'The prevention of child abuse', *Children & Society*, 13: 317–29.

Webb, S.A. (2001) 'Some considerations on the validity of evidence-based practice in social work', *British Journal of Social Work*, 31: 57–79.

Webster-Stratton, C. (1997) 'Treating children with early-onset conduct problems: a comparison of child and parent training interventions', *Journal of Consulting and Clinical Psychology*, 65(1): 93–109.

Werner, E. (2000) 'Protective factors and individual resilience', in *Handbook of Early Childhood Interventions*, 2nd edn. Cambridge: Cambridge University Press. Chapter 6.

White, K. and Grove, M . (2000) 'Towards an understanding of partnership', *NCVCCO Outlook*, 7. London: NCVCCO.

White, M. And Epston, D. (1990) *Narrative Means to Therapeutic Ends*. New York: W.W Norton.

White , S., Hall, C. and Peckover, S. (2009) 'The descriptive tyranny of the common assessment framework: technologies of categorization and professional practice in child welfare', *British Journal of Social Work*, 39 (7): 1197–217.

Whiting, L. (1999) 'Caring for children of differing cultures', *Journal of Child Health Care*, 3(4): 33–8.

Wilson, K. and James, A. (2002) *The Child Protection Handbook*. London: Balliére Tindall.

Wright, S. (2004) 'Child protection in the community: a community development approach', *Child Abuse Review*, 13: 384–98.

Yelloly, M. (1980) *Social Work Theory and Psychoanalysis*. New York: Von Nostrand.

Young, K. and Haynes, R. (1993) 'Assessing population needs in primary health care: the problem of GOP attachments', *Journal of Interprofessional Care*, 7(1): 15–27.

INDEX

This index is in word-by-word order. Page references in **bold** indicate tables, those in ***bold italic*** indicate figures.